CORSETS TO CAMOUFLAGE

Author's Acknowledgements

Professor Charles Thomas for all his help with research, and Nigel Steel and Terry Charman of the Imperial War Museum for their historical expertise; and Christopher Dowling who invited me to write in conjunction with the Museum's exhibition. A great number of people have been immensely kind with their time and advice, especially the staff at Sunderland City Library's local studies department, and Lindsay Fulcher, Assistant Editor of *The Lady*.

On military matters, there have been numerous comments and help, in particular from Sir Jeremy MacKenzie and Sir Rupert Smith. I'm grateful to my editor Rowena Webb and to Juliet Brightmore at Hodder & Stoughton, also to Esther Jagger, Kerry Hood and Jacqui Lewis. Louise Greenberg, for her unfailing encouragement. All those women who allowed me to record their memories, especially those in the Ack Ack, the Land Army and the Aycliffe Angels.

Note on British money in pre-decimal days
12d (pence) = 1s (shilling)
20s = £1

CORSETS TO CAMOUFLAGE

Women and War

Kate Adie

Hodder & Stoughton

Published in association with the Imperial War Museum London

For illustrations and photographs copyrights
see Photo Acknowledgements, page 246

First published in Great Britain in 2003 by Hodder and Stoughton
A division of Hodder Headline

A Hodder & Stoughton Book

1 3 5 7 9 10 8 6 4 2

A CIP catalogue record for this title is available from the British Library

ISBN 0 340 82059 4

Book design by Janette Revill

Printed and bound by Butler & Tanner

Hodder and Stoughton
A division of Hodder Headline
338 Euston Road
London NW1 3BH

Illustration on page i: Taking over from her father, the official
Bill Poster and Town Crier in Thetford, Norfolk,
pastes up the call for women in World War I.

CONTENTS

INTRODUCTION

I N OUTLINE, IN silhouette, just a glimpse – a soldier's boots, perhaps a policeman's helmet, or a glint of gold braid – all have powerful impact. And my first encounter with women in uniform is fixed in my memory as two pairs of dreadful legs, descending – nay bulging – into two clomping pairs of shoes.

In the mid-fifties it was the custom in my nice girls' school in Sunderland to expose us to the wider world through the occasional Wednesday Talk. However, instead of lectures from the Great and the Good, our militant Anglican foundation, Sunderland Church High School, produced a steady stream of the Pious or Slightly Deranged. We'd spot them heading up the main staircase, a vivid splash of long purple skirt swishing around big black boots. 'Another batty bishop from Bongoland,' we'd hiss, before composing our features for a peroration on the mischief wrought by termites upon prayer books, or the difficulties of steering the diocesan dug-out canoe through mangrove swamps.

The occasional highbrow musician was also deemed acceptable, with the memorable Florence Hooton wielding her cello like a table-tennis bat, and then announcing to a stupefied gaggle of adolescent females that she was 'about to put a very powerful instrument between my legs'. Then, one Wednesday, the staircase resounded to a particularly firm tread. Stomp stomp stomp. The headmistress's thick ankles and sensible court shoes looked positively skittish, flanked as they were by an escort of biliously coloured tree trunks.

We lifted our gaze slowly upwards. The skirts hung like cardboard, just at the length which makes your calves look fat and suggests your thighs are like a couple of marrows. Further up were jackets of unforgiving cut, boxy and mannish, restraining what were undoubtedly formidable bosoms. The bosoms swayed a fraction out of sync with the swinging arms and the marching gait. Starched collars and ties concealed what necks there might have been, as the pair pincered the headmistress between the assembly hall doors. Their expressions were impossible to read, for it appeared they wore shiny caps perched on their noses. How they saw was a mystery. They turned smartly to ascend the platform, two rhino rears in rhythmic harmony.

CORSETS TO CAMOUFLAGE

I cannot recall a single word of the lecture addressed to us. The entire impact was visual. Here were two grown-ups, people who'd achieved the enviable womanhood we yearned for, apparently dressed – well, not so much dressed as upholstered – in a manner which defied analysis. Yes, they were uniforms – but not of the familiar sagging bus conductress variety. These were bandbox-sharp with glinty buttons, spotless, with ironed-flat pockets where no balled-up old hankie would dare to lurk. We girls were being introduced to the Women's Royal Army Corps and the Women's Royal Air Force. One dark green, one blue, sort-of.

It was the legs which really fascinated. Our girlish dreams were of spiky heels and pointy toes in ice-cream colours (or perhaps scarlet if you dared to be 'fast'). Of the palest nylons with sexy black seams – perhaps the tiniest butterfly bow peeping from just above the heel. This was what lay in store after years of school uniform, with our dreams contained by regulation Indoor and Outdoor Shoes, both modelled on fishboxes, and a choice of wrinkly grey socks or hairy knee-stockings. And here were two women who'd seemingly chosen to encase their legs in some kind of ancient lisle, vaguely reminiscent of something seen in the dusty windows of surgical appliance suppliers. And who had acquired footwear suitable for marching on Moscow.

Our teenage imaginations trembled. And there and then, I decided that uniforms were not for me.

Nor did I come from a military family. World War II was over when I was born, and the easy familiarity with khaki and blue had disappeared instantly in peacetime. Admittedly, my home town in north-east England was a fruitful recruiting ground for the Durham Light Infantry, and the occasional warship was heaved into the mouth of the River Wear by over-enthusiastic tugs, pranging the inner piers. But we had no barracks or local air station, only strange fields where concrete squares marked the floors of a wartime army camp, and unpleasantly ponging concrete 'pillboxes' lurking below the coastal cliffs, still ready to defend our shores.

Except for the plentiful bomb-sites on which we children played, Sunderland having been pasted regularly by the Germans, I assumed that this ship-building town and its people had been only peripherally involved in the two world wars. The men had 'gone off to have a crack at Jerry'; the women had stayed to 'keep the home fires burning.' I had little inkling of the extent to which an ordinary industrial town had found itself inexorably drawn into war, a place where daily life changed fundamentally twice in the twentieth century, as far distant events affected life, work, and the north-east skies overhead. I never guessed at the extraordinary extent to which everyone had been 'in the wars' – especially the women. Maids who became munitions workers, schoolgirls on fire-watch, housewives who joined voluntary units, and all those who joined the services. Military history is a male preserve, dominated by the image of the male warrior. Nevertheless, the unprecedented progress of women towards equality during the twentieth century is brought into sharp relief by war, although that progress often went unnoticed, and unsung, behind the striking deeds of valour on the battlefield.

I'm reminded of an exchange between my first Newcastle landlady and her neighbour, when I was a student in the sixties:

'Your husband was away four years, wasn't he?'

'Aye, he was, North Africa with Monty, and he never stopped about the sand and the flies . . .'

'What can you say. . . .'

'Well, I could've said about the air-raid sirens, the black-out, the bombs, the rationing . . . but I didn't.'

'Ever talk about your job in the RAF?'

'He wasn't interested in welding.'

I regarded my landlady with curiosity: a very short, wiry Geordie widow, who was always asking me to sort out 'men's work' around the house – wonky electric plugs, the ancient Hoover and so on.

Welding?

So, years ago, in the aftermath of World War II, I'd had intimations of a different life for women in wartime, but no sense of its significance, and certainly no interest in uniforms and all that they conveyed.

And as a child, there was already a certain amount of prejudice residing in my soul. I'd been a Brownie, and had discovered that In The Pack no element of individuality was entertained. All Brownies wore turd-coloured bag-like shifts, with a leather belt and a custard yellow tie. Fatter Brownies looked like hamsters feeding permanently on a banana. The outfit was surmounted by a chocolate-coloured knitted Thing, which slid off your head the moment you had to do some Brownie ritual, usually involving imaginary toadstools. If you were diligent your sleeve was peppered with weird symbols, proclaiming your status as a girl well versed in raffia-craft or whatever. The good aspect of the uniform was that it blended into the dust and dirt which was swirled up by Brownie Games in dingy church halls and left-over wartime prefab huts. In other words, it worked, but did nothing for you. Still, in the days before preteen fashion-aware culture took hold, none of us minded much.

For a start, everyone wore school uniform, which was clearly designed by someone who disliked children, especially girls. Decades on, the subject of the Horrible School Hat still provokes wrath and despair among my contemporaries. Ditto the School Divided Skirt ('no girl shall wear a skirt which is more than two inches from the floor when kneeling'). Then there was the School Winter Coat, a creation which had a life of its own. So hairy and stiff that, when new, it stood by itself without visible support. You didn't exactly wear it, you engaged with it, and once you were lined up in the daily crocodile, two by two, you were described by onlookers as The Russian Army off to the Front. But there was always joy to be derived from the fact that other schools clearly employed professional tailoring sadists to produce even more ludicrous and demeaning styles. And then there was the one good aspect: absolutely no decisions to be made in the morning. No agonising in and out of the wardrobe. Just climb into the same old stuff and all will be right with the world.

So at a very early age, I'd sampled the impact of uniforms: their power to deliver an instantaneous message, their ability to reduce the individual to a unit, simultaneously marking you out and blending you in.

As my teens approached, the Girl Guides made overtures. Whatever the excitements of more badges and a bit of damp camping, I was becoming aware that evenings spent in a blue bag-like sack, plus beret, were not exactly seductive-sounding. And so it was that the arrival of the WRAC and WRAF, stomp stomp stomp, sealed my views on uniforms and aroused my curiosity.

Members of the World War I Women's Land Army consider getting themselves up as girls for their act at a local Red Cross concert. 'But have we the clothes for it?' they wonder. From Punch, *1917*

CHAPTER ONE

MAIDS IN ARMOUR

EVEN IN MY obscure world of Scandinavian Studies at university, war and battles intruded. Monday mornings were spent in seminars trying to figure out just how many ways a Viking could vanquish his enemy, all involving an axe, a tree and an unfortunate amount of exposed intestine. Down through history came the names of warriors, carved elegantly in runic letters on to huge standing stones. Language commemorated frenzied fighting by those wearing bear-shirts – going berserk. Songs celebrated heroic deeds, centuries after they happened. Men of valour bestrode history – but only a few women could be glimpsed through the fog of war.

Student parties in the 1960s were crowded, unglamorous affairs in Newcastle. Nevertheless one night I headed for the bathroom of a particularly grubby flat in the student-infested suburb of Jesmond only to find Queen Elizabeth I perched on the edge of the bath, a bottle of Newcastle Brown Ale in her hand.

Opposite: Joan of Arc, *painting by Peter Paul Rubens, c. 1620*

Dame Flora Robson *was* the Virgin Queen, everyone's Tudor icon, etched into cinema history in *Fire Over England*, one of those sweeping historical romps which gripped audiences in the grey days of war. A vision of velvet and pearls, starched ruff above a polished steel breastplate as she addressed her troops at Tilbury, ready to take on the dastardly Spanish. The white horse pawed the ground, the soldiers' armour glittered, the pennants on the lances fluttered and the words rang out: 'I know I have the body of a weak and feeble woman, but I have the heart and stomach of a king, and a king of England too; and think foul scorn that Parma or Spain, or any prince of Europe, should dare to invade the borders of my realm.' Cue much cheering from the front stalls.

The vision in the bathroom was wearing a dowdy brown dress rather than slashed brocade and silk. Dame Flora was a warm, down-to-earth woman, born in South Shields, who happened to be visiting the small theatre in Jesmond that bore her name, and she'd unexpectedly answered the university Dramatic Society's party invitation. A practical, observant actress, she regaled us with stories of the behind-the-scenes lunacies of film-making, especially the dratted horse at Tilbury which had had a mind of its own and very active bowels. Wearing a breastplate over a dress boned and stuffed like a Christmas turkey had been no picnic either, and the horse had been in total agreement, going into a huge sulk at the umpteenth take and sagging un-regally, ears back.

On screen, though, it was romantic perfection, evoking the ultimate warrior-queen, an inspiration at the head of her troops; a figure that has ridden through history in and out of the mist of battle, giving ride to legend and not a little sexual *frisson*. Boadicea and Joan of Arc, Japanese empresses and Celtic queens, assorted Germanic women and Roman gladiatrixes, Saxon leaders and, of course, Amazons: there is a long and rather fuzzy list of names which confirms the potency of the image, but is rather short on detail. The list grows longer as a feminist view of history digs for concealed heroines, the victims of male prejudice, air-brushed out of official history. However, the subservient position which has been the lot of women in most societies for centuries underlines the significance of attitudes held by all, not just men. Where women lacked legal status, had no political power, were deemed lesser creatures by the official religion, and belonged to the huge majority tied to hearth and home through children and lack of money, the creature who broke out and flourished a sword in the ultimate masculine world of war was truly exceptional; even, the twentieth century, with well-documented world wars, gives ample evidence of the automatic relegation of women's contributions to the realm of side-show and supporting cast. Medals and recognition follow traditional rules – and there is

still an uncomfortable feeling about including auxiliary and civilian efforts on war memorials.

Distinguishing historical truth from exciting myth is made all the harder by the fact that the battlefield is the source of many an inflated story, and both victory and defeat produce tales to excuse the excesses of all sides. Sheer necessity must have dictated circumstances in which a number of aristocratic women led men to war: their rank and position marked them out as automatic leaders, frequently in default of a suitable male. Hierarchy gave them power, and the advantages of education lent them authority. Religion added the dimension of inspiration – especially when virginity was added to the menu of leadership virtues: to have foresworn the usual role of womanhood could be seen as adding strength and confirming that 'no ordinary woman' was taking up the sword. Joan of Arc was variously described by commentators as 'above sex', thus entering a state which qualified her for a military role. And the concept of the Virgin Queen was a powerful image which set Elizabeth I apart and aloof from the usual dependency on male power.

At the level of ordinary soldier, the presence of fighting women can usually be detected by laws forbidding their inclusion in armies. From pre-Roman Celtic gatherings to the English Civil War come mutterings against those who would relinquish the domestic role and join the fight.

What history usually fails to record or recall is the non-heroic side of war: those who cooked, cleaned, supplied, did the washing, tended the wounded and comforted the warriors. Baggage-trains and camp-followers, battlefield scavengers, wives and tarts. An army is a hungry and demanding beast, its commander forever being quoted about its appetite. Marching on its stomach, Napoleon is thought to have said; going on its belly like a serpent, according to Frederick the Great of Prussia. Never mind invasion and battles, an army needs food and drink in order to stay together and be prepared. In the colourful account of the adventures of 'Mother Ross' at the end of the seventeenth century, somewhat embellished by the author Daniel Defoe, the daily task of foraging undertaken by the advance party of camp-followers in Flanders is minutely described:

> I put the carcass of the sheep [which she had just found and killed] on my mare, the fowls I hung about my neck; drove my sheep before me, and so marched to the place designed for the camp, called Havre . . . I pitched my tent near a deserted public house, allotted for Colonel Hamilton's quarters; turned my sheep out to grass and hung up my mutton on a tree to cool: I then went to the Colonel's quarters, over which as soon as it was appointed a guard was set; but by a bribe, I struck him so blind, that he could not see me and my husband's comrades, who lent a friendly hand, carry off a large

Kit Ross in the uniform of the Scots Regiment of White Horses

quantity of faggots, hay and straw for my mare, and my own bed; fill all my empty flasks with beer, and roll off a whole barrel to my tent . . . I made four crowns a-piece of my sheep, besides the fat, which I sold to a woman who made mould candles for the men, and made a good penny of my fowls and pigeons.

Mother Ross, or Kit Davies or Christian Welch or Mrs Christian Ross or Mrs Jones – she had four husbands – was celebrated by Defoe in his account of her life as a soldier 'who in several campaigns under King William and the late Duke of Marlborough, in the quality of a Foot Soldier and Dragoon gave many signal Proofs of an unparallell'd Courage and personal Bravery'. Born in Dublin, she inherited a pub from her aunt, married her servant Richard Welch and bore him three children. One night he disappeared, and a year later a letter arrived from Holland explaining that he'd been press-ganged into the army after being carried aboard a ship dead drunk. Twenty-six years old, she set off to find him: 'I cut off my hair and dressed me in suit of my husband's having had the precaution to quilt the waistcoat to preserve my breasts from hurt which were not large enough to betray my sex and putting on the wig and hat I had prepared I went out an bought me a silver hilted sword and some Holland shirts.' That a mere change of dress should deceive all and sundry was not so incredible at a time when skirt and breeches were never considered interchangeable between the sexes: you wore a man's clothes – you were assumed to be a man.

Kit joined an infantry regiment and over the years took part in numerous battles: 'We spared nothing, killing, burning, or otherwise destroying whatever we could not carry off. The bells of the churches we broke to pieces, that we might bring them away with us. I filled two bed-ticks, after having thrown out the feathers, with bell-metal, men's and women's clothes, some velvets and about a hundred Dutch caps, which I had plundered from a shop; all of which I sold by the lump to a Jew, who followed the army to purchase our pillage, for four pistoles.' After fighting at Blenheim she finally discovered her husband, but continued to serve at his side until she was seriously wounded at the battle of Ramillies in 1705. At that point, common to many who lived a life in disguise, the game was up when her injuries needed attention. The surgeons informed the commanding officer of the Scots Regiment of White Horses that the 'pretty dragoon' was a woman.

Unfazed, the CO supervised a second wedding in front of the military, insisting that she resume marital relations with her husband – until then she'd avoided sex for fear that pregnancy would reveal her deceit. Out of uniform, Kit took up full-time occupation as a sutler, providing the army with food and drink and indulging in a great deal of profitable foraging. She was granted a privileged place ahead of the army, rather than with the followers to the rear, though it was still a risky business as she bargained or plundered her way between her own troops and the enemy, loading her mare with beef, butter and bacon: 'Which I had scarcely done when I heard the signal gun, an alarm given the foragers, that the whole body of the enemy was coming upon us; and that their seeming to march to the left, was only to cover the filing of their infantry into the woods. The terror with which the foragers were struck at the news is hardly credible! The fields were strewn with corn, hay and utensils, which they had not the courage to take along with them.'

A cantinière in regimental jacket during the Crimean War, 1854-6

Until the end of Marlborough's campaigns, in 1712, several children and husbands decorated her life. She was an ambiguous figure, both harassed by randy soldiers and respected by the Duke himself, who said he would as soon take her advice as that of any brigadier in the army. Celebrated in story and ballad, she received a shilling a day pension for life from Queen Anne, ending her days as an out-pensioner at the Royal Hospital in Chelsea.

Other women were alongside Kit Ross on her travels, and her ilk were common on the battlefield until well into the nineteenth century. Sutleresses, sometimes known as *vivandières* and *cantinières*, came to acquire semi-official recognition, and often wore the jackets of the regiments they accompanied. Wives were not uncommon, for campaigns could last for years, and families often had no choice but to follow the flag. Also the army needed seamstresses, cooks and billet organisers, and someone to nurse the wounded. And then there were the women who made a reasonable living from prostitution, who often had a vague claim to be 'nurses'. Not unexpectedly, the character of the camp-following was regarded by many outsiders as something of a rabble of tarts, profiteers and corpse-thieves. But they were necessary, and anyway, the armies they supported were hardly of high moral character and models of propriety.

So why join this motley band as a soldier? The reasons given have always tended to be based on the standard theme of 'following a soldier', and indeed there are many well-documented cases where the search for a husband, or the desire to follow a fiancé or lover, was clearly the over-riding motive. Women who were on their own were in a vulnerable position in society and had little social status.

In 1743, during the War of Austrian Succession, George II became the last British king to command his army personally in battle, at Dettingen. He was probably

A Union camp in the American Civil War, Washington DC, 1862

unaware that one of his dragoons was Mary Ralphson, known as Trooper Mary. Her husband Ralph was in the 3rd Dragoons, and she had accompanied him from Scotland on the campaign only to find herself amid the fighting, whereupon she 'equipped herself in the uniform and accoutrements of a Dragoon who fell wounded by her side, mounted his charger and regained the battle line'. Having had a taste of fighting, she was seen on the field at both Fontenoy and Culloden. Somewhere in the fray at Fontenoy was Phoebe Hassel (or Hessel), who was slashed in the arm by a bayonet and who, according to popular stories, had been serving in the 5th Regiment of Foot ever since her father had enlisted her as a fife player.

Sheer survival could also bring women shoulder to shoulder with men in battle. Much celebrated in Holland was Kenau Haaselaer, a widow who led a tenth of the fighting force, thought to number three hundred women, against the Spanish at the siege of Haarlem in 1572: 'women who fought with manly passion both inside and outside the walls'. In the mid-seventeenth century the English Civil War saw a number of noblewomen leading the defence of their castles and manors, while their humbler sisters were spotted among the Scots soldiers marching on Newcastle: 'women who stood with blue caps among the men'. They cannot have been the only ones, for King Charles I was moved to issue a proclamation which banned women in armies from wearing men's clothing.

Memoirs, popular ballads, stage plays and novels all commemorated female soldiers, and military reports often carried confirmation that the dead on the battlefield included a number of women. Not such a number as to warrant significance, not so few as to be rare birds.

Joining up as an act of female rebellion seems much less common – if at all acknowledged. What is common to many of the women who were discovered to have disguised themselves as sailors and soldiers is their discovery of the 'freedom' which wearing breeches gave them. Those who told their stories after their spell of service all emphasise the extraordinary moment when they were free of their skirts. It was not only freedom of movement that was gained, but the freedom to act very differently. And not just in the social context – joining the men in public places, drinking, perhaps smoking and swearing – but in the sense of being expected to take decisions and act independently without reference to another male, and being accorded respect just for being a man.

Modern terminology would suggest 'empowerment', but it was the mere taste of not being the dependent, subservient sex that often gave these women a reason to continue with their venture into a hard and rigidly masculine world. Clothing delineated one's sex in an inflexible manner, right into the twentieth century. Just the suggestion of 'maids in breeches' was so upsetting that the phrase was only permissible when applied to the stage. Long hair, frilly headwear, petticoats and then corsets – in the general population there was never any doubt about gender as defined by clothes. Even the poorest women had flannel petticoats and a shawl, and were definably woman-shaped. So stepping out of these garments was a revolutionary act, either of defiance or of experiment. Cutting one's hair was another.

Women-as-soldiers also got paid – irregularly at times, and sometimes only with the spoils of war, but the potential for earning more than a pittance as an unskilled single woman was enticing. And then there was the status of being 'a man'. Women with no education discovered that there was a different way of seeing the world – and being seen by it. The main penalty was isolation, and the inability to share both physical space and thoughts and feelings without revealing too much. Relationships? In the public's eyes, the complication of sexual involvement was usually thought to be confined to falling in love with a male soldier. Sexual complications and notions of homosexuality were not part of the perceived situation, and gender confusion or uncertainty were not contemporary preoccupations. 'Cross-dressing' had not been invented as a social issue to be studied, and the psychological aspects of desiring to wear male attire and to take up a wholly masculine line of work were yet to be discovered. These women were seen not as 'deviant', but as 'different'.

Nevertheless, throughout the seventeenth and eighteenth centuries there was public fascination with the women who were revealed as having fought alongside men: they were popular, and they were seen as 'adventuresses'; and although they represented a threat to the conventional order of things, they were on the whole cheered on for having had the audacity to act 'the man'. Those who went to sea were thought particularly dashing, for concealment there, in the confines of a ship, was even harder. Lady pirates such as Anne Bonney and Mary Read were absorbed into folklore in their own lifetimes. Many other women, such as Mary Ann Talbot, were reported as serving on naval ships of the line, their sex only revealed when captured or injured. Mary Ann retired on a pension of £20 a year granted for 'wounds received in action'.

Hannah Snell too was awarded a pension, having served briefly in the army, deserted, then headed for Portsmouth and enlisted in Colonel Fraser's Regiment of Marines. She led a colourful life, enhanced by an equally colourful biography entitled *The Female Soldier; or the Surprising Life and Adventures of Hannah Snell*. There was much that was surprising therein, including a description of being wounded at the siege of Pondicherry in India (six shots in the right leg, seven in the left, and another in the groin). Hannah maintained that she concealed her sex by extracting the musket ball in her groin herself 'with thumb and finger'.

Whatever the authenticity of detail in her life, there's no doubting the entry in the admission book in the Royal Hospital, Chelsea, where she was admitted as an out-pensioner: 'Wounded at Pondicherry in the thigh of both legs, born at Worcester, her father a dyer.'

However, also aboard before Victorian times were quite a female crew: wives, seamstresses and cooks sailed with the Royal Navy, and Nelson's fleet had skirts below decks during many encounters. At the battle of the Nile John Nichol was one of the gun crew on the *Goliath* off Alexandria:

The sun was just setting as we went into the bay, and a red and fiery sun it was. I would, if I had had my choice, been on the deck; there I would have seen what was passing, and the time would not have hung so heavy; but every man does his duty with spirit, whether his station be in the slaughter-house or in the magazine. (The seamen call the lower deck, near the main-mast, 'the slaughter-house', as it is amidships, and the enemy aim their fire principally at the body of the ship.) My station was in the powder-magazine with the gunner. As we entered the bay we stripped to our trousers, opened our ports, cleared, and every ship we passed gave them a broadside and three cheers. Any information we got was from the boys and women who carried the powder. They behaved as well as the men, and got a present for their bravery from the Grand Signior. When the French Admiral's ship blew up, the Goliath got such a shake we thought the after-part of her had blown up until the boys told us what it was. They brought us every now and then the news of another French ship having struck, and we answered the cheers on deck with heartfelt joy. In the heat of the action, a shot came right into the magazine, but did no harm, as the carpenters plugged it up, and stopped the water that was rushing in. I was much indebted to the gunner's wife, who gave her husband and me a drink of wine every now and then, which lessened our fatigue much. There were some women wounded, and one woman belonging to Leith died of her wounds, and was buried on a small island in the bay. One woman bore a son in the heat of the action; she belonged to Edinburgh.

Dr James Barry, a sketch made in Corfu in 1852

The most curious case is that of Dr Barry, who rose to the top of the Army's medical service with a rank equivalent to major-general. From his sudden appearance in 1809 as James Barry, a medical student at Edinburgh University, through his demanding and distinguished career as an army surgeon and medical inspector, to his final post as the senior of Her Majesty's Inspectors General of Hospitals, he was regarded as a trifle 'effeminate', being a beardless five-foot eccentric. His uniform was always exquisite – sword and plumed hat and exaggeratedly padded jacket – and he had a toy dog in attendance. His medical skills were admired, he dealt with Florence Nightingale during the Crimean War, and he spent forty-six years in the army. When he died in 1865 in London, the death certificate registered him as a male. But the keener eyes of the woman laying out the body knew what she was looking at: Dr Barry was 'a perfect female', and moreover had 'had a child when very young'.

Dr Barry must inevitably have felt isolated at times. It was only in the year of his death that Elizabeth Garrett Anderson passed her Apothecaries' Examination, on her way to becoming Britain's first practising woman doctor. And the army – rather more keenly than the rest of society – still saw medical matters as a male pursuit, especially where soldiers were concerned. Mid-Victorian England had also shifted public attitudes to the ideal female towards a creature who had the vapours and who was politely ignorant of anatomical details. Even when it came to nursing, the Queen's army had adopted a position of priggish hostility to the women who traditionally followed the flag.

Women have always nursed the wounded – but their proximity to the battlefield has depended on society's view of their vulnerability or their status. In Afghanistan, even as late as the 1980s, a woman wrapped in a blue *burkah* described her helplessness to me after her husband was injured by a land-mine during the Soviet invasion.

'He's lost an eye and an leg,' she said. 'He lay bleeding for hours in our fields, because I couldn't go to him. It wasn't allowed – it's Islam. We women had to stay in our quarters whatever happened. So he was nearly dead when he was brought in. I feel it's my fault – a woman should be able to help even if you have to go into a minefield.'

Nevertheless, for centuries soldiers were lucky if they received any medical care at all. As there was little enough interest taken in keeping them healthy when not actually fighting, there was even less when they met a bullet or a bayonet. The rag-tag baggage-train which accumulated round any army might have a few motherly souls prepared to tend injuries; but designated 'nurses' were not to be found among the wives, sutlers, *vivandières*, washerwomen, seamstresses and whores who otherwise sustained a successful campaign. Nursing was the province of the religious. And nuns and baggage-trains were mutually exclusive. However, it was the fusion of a saintly image with militaristic discipline which laid the foundations of modern nursing.

Florence Nightingale in about 1845, wearing white cap, white collar and black dress

Aged sixteen, Florence Nightingale wrote that 'God spoke to me and called me to His service', though it was many years before she knew exactly what she was meant to achieve. However, for a well-brought-up middle-class young lady in the 1840s she showed an unconventional interest in hospitals. Her family and friends were perfectly normal in indulging in Victorian fits of the vapours as Florence began to tour wards, develop a fascination with drains, and read official reports on the Sanitary Condition of the Labouring Classes. Hospitals were vile places. They stank, they were verminous, their walls and floors and ceilings were coated with putrid matter, and they were unquiet: drink and madness saw to that, with the police having to sort out disturbances among the tightly packed beds in the half-dark. The staff drank, too. And nurses were in many instances synonymous with prostitutes. 'It was *preferred*', wrote Florence, 'that the nurses should be women who had lost their characters, i.e. should have had one child.' But salvation, in the form of the Institution of Kaiserswerth on the Rhine for the Practical Training of Deaconesses, came in 1851, and so began the extraordinary labours which led to one woman revolutionising the role of the nurse – and also the image.

When Miss Nightingale's nurses set off three years later for the appalling hospitals on the shores of the Bosphorus, where the British army was losing more men to disease than to battle during the Crimean War, they were not a bevy of crisply uniformed ministering angels. Admittedly, twenty-four came from religious institutions, almost wholly interested in the patient's soul and distinctly indifferent to his body, especially the parts that were either intimate or dirty: flitting about like angels without hands, was Florence's judgement on them. The other fourteen described themselves as nurses, and were best described as the least worst of those who presented themselves for interview. All were well past their prime, which subsequently led to a letter from 'The Bird', as Florence became widely known, in which she stated that in future 'fat drunken old dames of fourteen stones and over must be barred, the provision of bedsteads is not strong enough'. However, all had been provided with a uniform, which in the glorious tradition of uniforms did not actually fit: the result was fourteen women of assorted size in a grey tweed dress, grey worsted jacket, plain white cap, short woollen cloak and 'a frightful scarf of brown, with the words Scutari Hospital embroidered in red'. Though not an ideal uniform, it served the Nightingale purpose of delineating the nurse from the casual camp-follower, yet avoided imitating the nuns; the short cloak appears to have been the forerunner of the distinctive red cape still worn by British military nurses today.

The hell that was Scutari tested everything that nursing would ever be faced with. The Barrack Hospital sat on a cesspool; mud, muck and mighty rats were everywhere, and the odd dead horse turned up in rubbish heaps. Supplies were badly administered, stolen or non-existent. The injured came in a never-ending stream. The nurses endured dreadful conditions – the first party of Anglican nuns found their bedroom occupied by a recently expired Russian general. The doctors were suspicious to the point of hostility to nursing sisters. Paperwork dominated while patients died. Religion and class both raised their heads as the purpose and form of a nursing service went though its birth pangs.

Who should do the cleaning? Who runs a hospital – medics or managers? Who holds the purse-strings? Is it a vocation to scrub floors – and earn a pittance? What's the status of a nurse? Even the Crimea had its quota of fraightfully naice ladies who deemed a smile and a few pious words more appropriate than a scrubbing brush and a blood-spattered apron. Over the decades after the Crimea, Florence Nightingale planned, plotted, badgered and campaigned. What emerged, in both the training and ethos – even in the uniforms – was a secular and civilian service, but one which was rooted in religious tradition and military discipline.

Curiously, she never wore uniform. Popular pictures of 'The Lady with the Lamp' were nearly all the product of artists' imaginations, and some of them show a small but elegant figure walking the grim hospital wards in tight corset and swishing crinoline skirt as worn by every fashionable woman in the 1850s. The crinoline was a cage of whalebone or wire, or hoops of steel springs, so unwieldy that precious ornaments, table lamps and small children could be knocked for six if the wearer twirled unexpectedly. Miss Nightingale had no truck with such frippery, writing that 'a respectable elderly woman stooping forward, invested in the crinoline, exposes quite as much of her own person to the patient lying in the room as any opera-dancer on stage.' However, though she also thought the sound of 'rattling stays' disturbed the sick, her list of requirements addressed 'To the Nurses about to join the Army Hospitals in the East' included among the Flannel Petticoats and the Upper Petticoats a Pair of Stays.

It's fairly certain that her own dress was usually black, trimmed with white collar and cuffs, accompanied by the small cap worn by all Victorian ladies. Not consciously a uniform – but one which survives in those few hospitals today where Matron still rules.

The nurses were all civilians, and therefore did not qualify for any military decorations. In 1855 Miss Nightingale was presented by Queen Victoria with a jewel designed by Prince Albert: the cross of St George bearing the word 'Crimea', surmounted with a diamond crown. The lady nurses were each given a circular gold brooch, enamelled in red and green, with a diamond crescent in the centre – not from the Queen but from the Sultan of Turkey, who sent a sum of money to the British government to pay for them.

Dorothea Dix, Superintendent of Women Nurses for the Union forces during the American Civil War, 1861-5

By the turn of the century, notwithstanding the reservations of die-hard army officers about loose-moralled hangers-on in the wards, the Nightingale influence was worldwide. Training schools flourished, women had joined the staff of military hospitals, and the American Civil War had found Dorothea Dix as Superintendent of Women Nurses confronting and overcoming the same prejudices as had existed in the Crimea, and Clara Barton gaining fame and admiration through working on the actual battlefield. The status of the profession had risen.

Grumble as they might, forty years later in South Africa at the time of the Boer War the British officers, seeing their men plagued by dust, flies, bugs and fleas, were soon faced with the familiar statistic that more of them were being carried off by dysentery and cholera than were being shot by the enemy. The services of over fifteen hundred army nurses – working well away from the battle zone in military hospitals – were deemed a necessity. Nevertheless, there were still many prejudices to overcome. Far from being allowed to hover with their lamps over the beds of wounded soldiers at night, the nurses were shunted off to their quarters at sunset and only gained access to the hospital wards if summoned and given a military escort. Lurking in the military mind was a centuries-old suspicion that women who hung around beds were up to no good. Added to that, the senior army surgeon had made it perfectly clear that he didn't approve of 'lady nurses' in any circumstances. And then there were the social butterflies of Cape Town. Once again, the professional nursing staff found themselves up against the ladies 'who dispensed smiles and visits', giving rise to an early version of a long-standing hospital joke: from a military hospital in the Cape Province came the story of the patient besieged by nursing do-gooders, who eventually wrote a card to hang above his bed: 'I am too ill to be nursed today.' I last heard this going the rounds in Belgium, in a hospital full of survivors from the Zeebrugge ferry disaster in 1987; the Prince and Princess of Wales had just beaten the Prime Minister to the main ward, whereupon a patient was reported as having pasted on his bed-head a notice reading: 'Too exhausted to be visited by Mrs Thatcher.'

Left: Clara Barton, American Civil War battlefield nurse and founder of the American Red Cross

The Boer War gave impetus to the formal establishment of Queen Alexandra's Imperial Military Nursing Service in 1902, for the first time recognising these women as members of the forces rather than regarding them as civilians; even so, they were technically 'in' the army, but not 'of' it. The uniform was a long grey dress covered by a white apron, with floaty white veil and scarlet cape approved by the Queen herself – who was a stylish Dane. That the effect should be both distinctive and elegant was a necessary factor in a society where clothes spelled status, and upper-class women spent a good deal of time with their maid heaving on the strings of the newly fashionable S-shaped corset, aiming for a tiny waist between low bosom and humpy hips. In formal photographs, the newly militarised QAs display enviably nipped-in waistlines, attesting to the powerful presence of whalebone beneath, but at least they had only a few variations to their basic uniform for different formal functions; society *grandes dames* changed up to six times a day. As for practicality, skirts were still full and long, the cap-strings were fiddly, and corsets have never been comfortable. However, the desired effect was achieved: striking, stylish and respectable.

Below: Members of Queen Alexandra's Imperial Military Nursing Service in India, 1911, with full skirts and well-corseted waists

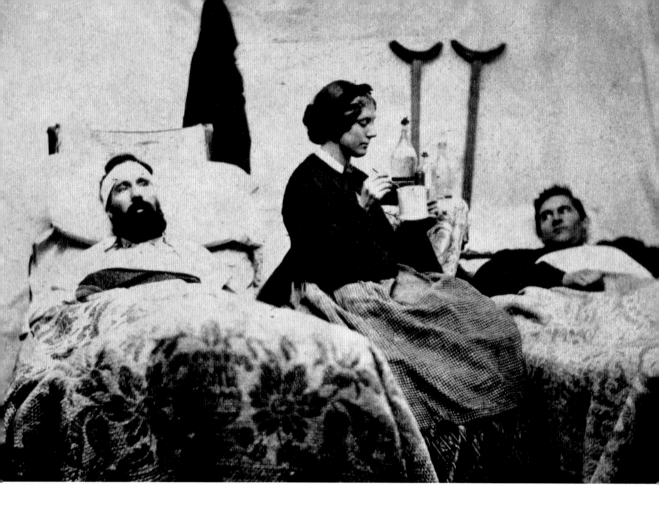

It took decades for Victorian women to establish their presence as nurses amidst Britain's military operations, and the perfectly dressed military surgeon Dr Barry had taken it for granted that he'd be the sole female soldier on a battlefield. However, just as he came to the end of his extraordinary career in 1862, newspapers were carrying numerous reports of the American Civil War in which instances of women's participation as would-be combatants were so frequent that they merited scant attention. Several hundred women appear to have been discovered through injury or death, others were surprised by their male colleagues and discharged, and yet more seem to have made it through the war undetected. The *Harrisburg Patriot* reported from a local army camp in 1861:

> On Monday afternoon two gentlemen – solid-looking farmers – arrived in Camp
> Curtin, who sought an interview with the officer of the day, and informed him that
> they were in search of a girl who had strayed away. The officer thought a military camp
> a queer place to hunt for stray girls, especially as it reflected on the virtue and dignity
> of the men at arms, nevertheless the gentlemen were at liberty to make a search. As

the old song says, 'they hunted her high and they hunted her low,' but they did not hunt her 'when a year had passed away,' for lo! In less than an hour she was found on guard doing duty as a sentinel, in the uniform of Capt. Kuhn's company of Sumner Rifles, of Carlisle – We do not know what name she enlisted under to protect the honor of her country's flag, but her real name is Sophia Cryder, and her residence only about a mile from this city. She had been in Capt. Kuhn's company a week, is a plump lass of only sixteen years of age, and had so completely unsexed herself that she could safely bid defiance to any one not acquainted with her to detect her. How she shirked an examination, which is said to be made with great strictness by the medical men of Camp Curtin, we are not informed.

She is represented as a girl of unblemished reputation, and did not, as generally happens in such cases, enlist to be near the object of her affections, but merely in a wild spirit of adventure. It does not speak well for the modesty of Miss Sophia, however, to say, that she was in the habit of accompanying the men on their excursions to the river to bathe; but she may have done this to ward off suspicion especially as she took precious good care to keep out of the water herself. This is the first case of the kind that has been brought to light, but we are informed that the most reckless dare-devil attached to the Seventh regiment of the three month's volunteers was a woman – *mother of four children.*

Miss Cryder was taken home, where she can reflect over what she did not see.

The following year the *Semi-Weekly Dispatch* reported the enlisting in the 107th Pennsylvania Regiment of an eighteen-year-old boy who 'bore a softened and pleasing expression'. The other recruits thought he had better

conquer his timidity before he could be considered a man and a soldier. The young recruit, however, soon undeceived them, and he could smoke a cigar, swagger, and take an occasional 'horn' with the most perfect sang froid . . . The regiment finally departed for Washington, and we lose sight of our recruit until within the last week or so, when his reappearance was hailed with some surprise by several officers of a recruiting station in this place. He gave no explanation of the reason for his return, but it has been ascertained, since reaching home, that he has abandoned male attire, donned petticoats and frock, and is a girl again! She says she is determined 'to try it again'.

Comparing such women to Joan of Arc and Edward III's queen, Philippa, the *Semi-Weekly Dispatch* felt that they were being wrongly overlooked:

The same love of country and desire for fame actuate our female volunteers, who don male attire and present themselves at the various recruiting stations in the North for enlistment. In most cases their sex has not been known at the time of enlistment, but in every case, as far as we know, after reaching the seat of war, the poor, proscribed sex of these candidates for military glory has been discovered, and they have been returned to the obscurity of their former life.

Concealment was made easier by the non-standard array of clothing which was the lot of the ordinary soldier. For centuries, battlefields had been colourful and confusing: loyalty, fashion, hierarchy, pride and practicality all fought for consideration in the matter of uniforms. Artists frequently depicted orderly encounters in which colour and style easily defined friend and foe, when the reality was a kaleidoscope of individualistic tradition. Mercenaries, bodyguards, privately raised regiments, local militias and standing armies all brought their own standards of dress to a war. And the primary function of a uniform's colour had nearly always been to act as a badge of allegiance for the common soldier, rather than to distinguish him from the enemy.

Towards the end of the seventeenth century in Europe, some kind of standardisation began to appear with the rise of permanent or national armies. Even so, once these armies intermingled mistakes were easy. In the early eighteenth century the French – on the whole – wore white, and the Austrians pearl-grey. However, the Austrians had the habit of whitening their coats with pipe-clay, leading to an intentional – and successful – muddle, narrated by the French Colonel de la Colonie: 'I became grimly aware of several lines of infantry in greyish-white uniforms on our left flank. I verily believed reinforcements had reached us . . . So in the error I laboured under, I shouted to my men that they were Frenchmen and friends. Having, however, made a closer inspection, I discovered bunches of straw attached to their standards, badges the enemy are in the custom of wearing in battle, but at that very moment was struck in the jaw by a ball that stupefied me.'

Even as nations strove to achieve standardisation internal rivalries between regiments reasserted themselves, fuelled by insistence on arcane traditions and determination to avoid uniformity while dressed in uniform. Anyway, uniforms were intended for show – to show others that you were impressive and proud to declare your allegiance.

So, for women joining up, disguise was not too difficult. Added to this, armies were chaotic and mobile, and concealment could be effected in a heaving mass of unregistered fighters. Medical examinations were usually cursory, and anyway, there were other women around in the baggage-train. However, in the nineteenth

century, as the Victorians began to build barracks for a standing army and to introduce a much more regulated life for a soldier, the women began to be edged out. Camp-followers were gradually replaced by army-run support systems. The useful rabble was made redundant. Garrison towns operated rules and regulations, and the services began to take an official interest in running soldiers' private lives. And in the navy, the call to 'show a leg' was no longer relevant: the habit of having women stay on board while ships were in port was ending. Seamen would no longer be allowed an extra hour's snooze if a hairless leg was shown to the bosun's mate on his rounds, for the ladies were now being turfed out of their hammocks for good. The military was becoming a world apart, entirely male, and not so interwoven with its supporters and relatives – and its women.

Sarah Rosetta Wakeman, alias Private Lyons Wakeman, enlisted in the Union army on 30 August 1862. She told the recruiters she worked as a boatman – which was true – but omitted to mention she was a woman

And the military were beginning to *look* a world apart: the common soldiers were starting to appear uniform in their uniforms, and the officers were turning into peacocks. In the nineteenth century gold braid and copious frogging, feathers and fur, tight breeches and elegant boots all made their way into various European uniforms; sex appeal arrived as well, for showy plumage called attention to a profession which stood for manliness and adventure, a masculine approach to life and a slightly monastic existence in barracks and mess and club. Women were meant to admire – but that was all.

Even so, by mid-century serviceable khaki had been adopted by the British in India and another fifty years saw the entire army clad in 'dust colour'. Elsewhere in Europe, however, right up to the early days of World War I it was still possible to find gorgeous colours and showy outfits, to the detriment, for instance, of the ordinary French soldiers who faced German machine-gunners in 1914 while wearing their traditional, highly visible scarlet trousers.

Meanwhile, in the twentieth century the military had discovered once again that it needed the services of women. It reinvented the baggage-train and camp-followers, but this time in uniform.

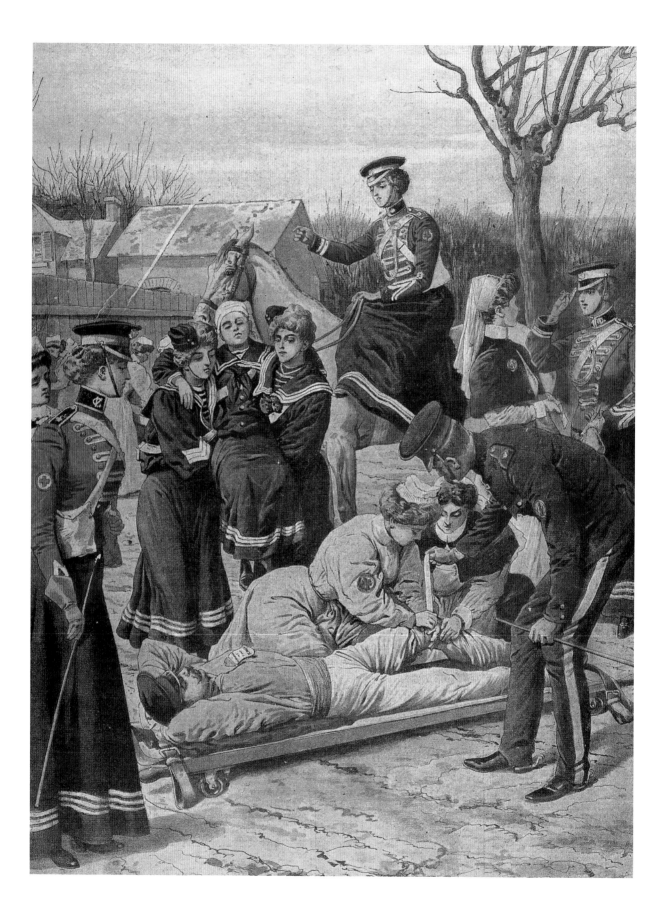

CHAPTER TWO

DASHINGLY
TO WAR

'YOU KNOW WHAT she's like — she was a fenny, you know.' Grown-ups speak in riddles, and as a child I wondered what the raised eyebrows and shrugged shoulders beneath the hats of the Conservative Party Tea Club meant. When I was a little older, but none the wiser, the word appeared again – this time in an announcement by a particularly stuck-up but dim school prefect: 'Well, my auntie was a fanny, so she was *very* important in the war.' The mysterious word had altered slightly in pronunciation – and we suggestible teenage girls suppressed giggles as we guessed at its possible meaning.

The First Aid Nursing Yeomanry was not part of our lives. World War I was in the far distance. Indeed, World War II had happened before we were born, and we were not part of the *Boys' Own* world which consumed Biggles or How to Escape from Stalag Luft III or Instructions for Building Your Own Miniature Submarine. Uniforms had been

Opposite: The First Aid Nursing Yeomanry training in 1909

put away by our parents' generation and Civvy Street embraced, and the phrases such as 'Can I do you now, sir?', which left adults shaking with laughter from memories of wit on the wireless, belonged firmly to an incomprehensible period. But with two generations still alive that had seen two world wars, phrases and habits died hard. And the certain something about a FANY lingered on, and seemed to be rather envied.

The organisation appeared to have slightly romantic roots: Sergeant-Major Edward Charles Baker was a British cavalryman who'd been wounded while fighting in the campaign in the Sudan at the end of the nineteenth century, and he dreamed up – perhaps he dreamed about – a unit of ladies on horseback, riding with the skirmishing parties and swooping down upon the field of battle to carry injured men to safety. How he presented this idea to stolid Edwardian army types is not clear, but in 1907, having left the army and while working for the Armour Meat Packing Company at Smithfield Market, he managed to form a group of mounted auxiliaries to the Royal Army Medical Corps, some of whom were nurses. In his newspaper advertisement for recruits he'd stated: 'Our mission is to tend Britain's soldiers on the field and prove ourselves worthy country-women of the first and greatest of Britain's army nurses' (the eighty-seven-year-old Florence Nightingale had just been awarded the Order of Merit by King Edward VII – the first time it had been given to a woman).

From the very start they had a certain air about them; first aid allied with horsemanship added up to An Accomplishment, something a nicely brought-up gel might acquire, and so the first-ever officially recognised uniformed women's service was born. The ladies were turned out smartly, perched decorously side-saddle in dark

The FANY, riding astride, with their horse ambulance at a military tattoo

blue riding skirts with a striking military-style scarlet tunic and cap, though they soon adopted khaki for the skirt and swapped the cap for a topee – a tropical sun helmet.

According to an article in the *Daily Graphic* on 25 February 1909:

A mere male member of the *Daily Graphic* staff yesterday invaded the sanctum of the First Aid Nursing Yeomanry Corps in Holborn. On giving the password to the pretty sentinel on duty at the door, he found himself in the presence of a busy band of aristocratic amazons in arms. Their purpose was peaceful. In their picturesque uniforms, they were engaged in recruiting work. There was a constant stream of Lady callers, most of them Society folk, whose patriotism had impelled them to enrol in the Corps which is being formed to enable women to help their country in wartime. Surrounded by gaily garbed sergeants and corporals, Lady Ernestine Hunt, the eldest daughter of the Marquis of Aylesbury, who looked dashing in her uniform of scarlet tunic and dark skirt relieved with white braid, was hard at work.

Miss Grace Ashley-Smith was an early recruit. A Scot from Aberdeen and a first-class horsewoman (ladies with their own horses were particularly sought after), she wrote a training manual and recruited vigorously:

I hunted round for recruits and pestered all my friends to join. That was the first step. The second was to weed out others, amongst them a soulful lady with peroxide hair, very fat and hearty, who insisted on wearing white drawers with frills under her khaki skirt. She also insisted on falling off at every parade and displaying them. She was so breezy and warm-hearted that it cost me a pang, but she had to go; no woman's movement could have survived those white frilly drawers on parade.

In 1909 there were about a hundred members of the Corps, and Sergeant-Major Baker had promoted himself to the honorary rank of captain. The women had to undergo a course in first aid and home nursing, horsemanship, veterinary work, signalling and camp cookery – and provide their own uniforms. They took part in military tattoos and paraded with their horse ambulance before graduating to riding astride – a rather thrilling innovation which saw them wearing a button-through khaki skirt which divided to reveal a pair of elegant breeches. There was an annual camp, again remarkable for the fact that women were living under canvas, just like the military. However it's unlikely the military would have recognised the activities: 'Hunting for Casualties' and 'Wounded Rescue Races'.

Interviewing some of the original members for a history of the unit, Dame Irene

Ward recorded one of them saying that 'We were stared at so much, that you simply had to have a sense of humour to carry on.' And they were sometimes mistaken for suffragettes – once, in London's Tottenham Court Road, a crowd of thirty factory girls started booing and shouting, throwing things and calling, 'You————— suffragettes!' Then one pointed to her Red Cross badge on her sleeve: 'You would not believe the sudden silence, the shame-faced Sorrys and the melting away of those girls in less than 2 minutes.' A Miss Bannatyne remembered:

> As to the general public, when they first caught sight of us, they just did not know what we were, and every body stared in amazement, and it took some courage to walk or bus by ourselves. At times we felt like freaks. But it was not long before the Press started writing about us and putting up photos of which there were plenty. . . . I have even had sentries on duty and soldiers in the street, when they saw my pips, give me, or rather the uniform, a salute and very gravely I would return it.

Nursing was a tough, disciplined business, thanks to the Nightingale legacy, and it's not surprising that there seems to have been no formal link between the military nurses and the Edwardian ladies who joined the FANY in the first decade of the twentieth century. The image of rather well-bred ladies dashing about the battlefield on horseback sat ill with trained nurses encouraged to see their work as a vocation. Nor did the FANY appeal to another determined woman who felt that 'women could do things which tradition had supposed they were incapable'.

Mabel Annie Stobart was an adventurous character who'd spent part of her life in the African veldt and in British Columbia. Not in the suffrage movements, but claiming to be a 'feminist' – describing her husband as a 'masculinist' – she had her inspiration in 1909. This was a year when there'd been widespread fear in Britain that a German invasion was imminent, and while the Votes for Women movement was demanding a share in government, Mrs Stobart thought that this should be complemented by women taking a share in the defence of their country. She'd seen a popular play in London by Guy du Maurier called *An Englishman's Home*, and though unimpressed by its theatrical qualities ('crude, inartistic, melodramatic and far-fetched' – Mrs Stobart was not one to mince words) she pondered its theme:

> An Englishman's home was invaded by the enemy and women could do nothing even to staunch the wounds of their men-folk. I forget the details. But I asked myself what could *I* have done? What could all those 'Votes for Women' claimants have done? What was there we could do or should be allowed to do in case of foreign invasion? I found that, in schemes of defence, no provision was made for the help of women. A great deal

CORSETS TO CAMOUFLAGE

has been made of Florence Nightingale's victory, but its present-day results were small, and only, at the best, affected trained hospital nurses.

Galloping round Hyde Park with the FANY didn't seem the right answer to Mrs Stobart. She joined for a short time; but it was too fanciful for words, in her view. So the Women's Sick and Wounded Convoy Corps was born – and got several years' training under its belt in moving casualties from the front clearing stations to hospitals in the rear. In 1912 it went to the aid of the Bulgarian army in the Balkan War, and two years later, on the first day of World War I, Mrs Stobart went into action again. She'd been at a meeting attended by many prominent suffrage campaigners in Kingsway Hall in London. She was asked what she intended to do. There and then she decided to form women's units 'to do women's work of relieving the suffering of sick and wounded, or of any other service that might be required'.

They may have worn grand feathered hats and sweeping skirts, but the women who felt the need for action in 1914 had been pushing against convention for many years. The suffrage question was being debated from America to China and there was growing agitation in many countries for improved education and employment opportunities for women. Those who found themselves on the springboard at the outbreak of war, like Mrs Stobart and the FANY, had experienced skirmishing in the undergrowth of discrimination and inequality. Nevertheless, across Europe the majority of women were still untouched by radical ideas, none more so than the woman who was quintessentially a put-upon wife and second-class citizen but whose death initiated profound change for millions.

CHAPTER THREE

SARAJEVO: A BULLET THROUGH THE CORSET

Y OU'RE SITTING IN a bone-rattling car on a hot day in June, the whalebone corset pinching under your elegant gown. There's been a bit of a scene at the town hall in Sarajevo, and your husband – a difficult man at the best of times – has been furious and rude to everyone. Yet again, you've had to calm him down. Lunch at the town hall has been slightly tedious, and you've spent rather a long time upstairs making pointless small talk with a group of ladies in their quaint national costumes – while listening to your husband barking at officials below: he apparently didn't think much of a welcome which included a man throwing a bomb at your car on the way to lunch.

Rather abruptly, you find yourself emerging into the sunshine and putting on the expected smile for a man with one of those new-fangled film cameras before getting back into the open car – a bit nervous now, and your husband still grumpy. Your

Opposite: Queen Victoria and the Prince Consort at Aldershot *(detail), painting by G. H. Thomas, c. 1866*

corset is digging in, and your husband is taking up much of the seat in his bulky uniform. You ought to be wearing uniform too – but they say you're not grand enough, not the 'right' sort of person. And so you're off to make history and to become the first person to die in the War to End All Wars – even though you're not in uniform . . .

The Archduchess Sophie with her husband Franz Ferdinand, heir to the throne of the Austro-Hungarian Empire, bowled along the riverside road. Drawing level with a stone bridge, their driver was confused about the route. A Serb student, Gavrilo Princip, stepped forward and fired two shots, killing both of them; Sophie herself died within seconds. Yet her death is mentioned as an afterthought, an 'also', to the incident in Sarajevo in 1914 when Franz Ferdinand was assassinated, thus precipitating the slaughter of millions. He was the symbol of imperial power and rank; she was the lady in the feathered hat.

The Archduchess Sophie and her husband, the Archduke Franz Ferdinand, leaving Sarajevo Town Hall in June 1914, minutes before their assassination

Her name, therefore, is not automatically associated with war. She played the role of wife, and the world of politics and the military were closed to her. As a good wife, and Sophie was almost alone in her affection and support for the inadequate and difficult Franz Ferdinand, she dressed the part, did what was expected of her – smiled and waved – and was a loving mother to their two children. In this, she reflected the millions of women who were about to be touched by war.

And yet Sophie in 1914 was more acutely aware than most of her position as a second-class citizen – without a uniform. Her husband, as Inspector General of the army, had been watching the Austrian troops on manoeuvres, and although it had become fashionable for royal ladies to be seen on horseback in dashingly tailored military uniforms, viewing the soldiers as their 'honorary colonel', Sophie had not been awarded this courtesy. Queen Victoria had begun the trend, described by A.B. Tucker in *Royal Ladies and Soldiers* in 1906:

> In the early days of her reign, the late Queen used, when reviewing her own troops, to wear a military cap edged with gold lace and a blue cloth coat. On the occasion of the inauguration of the Victoria Cross, 50 years ago, Her Majesty wore a round hat with a gold band, and on the right side a red and white feather. Her dress consisted of a scarlet bodice made like a military tunic, but open from the throat. Over her shoulders she wore a gold embroidered sash, while a dark blue skirt completed her costume.

The idea had come from Germany, and among that vast spider's web of inter-related royal families in the nineteenth century there was a raft of queens and grand duchesses and princesses all perched side-saddle on pawing chargers, wearing epaulettes and medals and very glamorous braided tunics. Whether they should have completed the ensemble with the *Pickelhaube* is questionable; the spiked military helmet didn't quite go with the sweeping skirt. Nor did the busby sporting a death's head emblem, as worn by Prussian princesses.

However, Sophie could only dream of such finery, for as the twentieth century began social precedence and rigid convention ruled in Europe, no more so than in the stuffy confines of the Austro-Hungarian court. Being born the Countess Sophie Chotek von Chotkova und Wognin might sound grand, but for the ancient – though rather crumbling – Hapsburgs in Vienna Franz Ferdinand's decision to marry a mere Czech countess from Bohemia had been greeted as if he'd dragged in the local washerwoman. Sophie endured years of exquisite humiliation as she was left out of formal court gatherings, stopped from walking next to her husband in royal processions, put to the back of the queue behind higher-ranking ladies, shunted out of carriages in royal processions, and given a series of niggardly titles culminating in

'Highness, with the qualification of Princely Grace' all of which added up to being addressed as The Not Quite Royal Enough Person. Behind her back, they hissed loudly about '*die böhmische Trampel*' – the Bohemian oik. Her marriage was designated morganatic – in other words, her children would not succeed to the throne. Honorary colonel of a regiment of the great empire? Pretty uniform with epaulettes? Not a chance.

However, the day in Sarajevo had looked quite promising: Bosnia was going to treat them both in a manner that befitted an imperial couple, and Sophie was dressed to the nines when she joined her husband after the morning military display to accompany him into the town. She was a column of delicate pale drapery, cinched with a broad sash to which a large tassel was attached. It's highly unlikely that she had discarded her corset, as 'advanced' ladies had begun to do a few years earlier, following the revolutionary exhortations of the young Paris couturier Paul Poiret.

CORSETS TO CAMOUFLAGE

After two children and with a tendency to plumpness, a woman of her class would never have risked such unbecoming behaviour; however, she showed the new shape which was a liberation from the S-bend contortions of the Edwardian era. Her corset would have been long and straight, defining her waist and influencing her stride – straight-backed and slightly stiff. She carried an elegant matching parasol and a delicate handbag, but wore no gloves. No heavy jewellery either, only a gold lorgnette hanging on her fashionably flattish bodice. And a hat which had required the sacrifice of several ostriches. Forty-six years old, and finally beginning to act like a future emperor's wife, Sophie was restrained yet fashionable. Her outfit clearly required the attention of others, and she would not have done much of the dressing herself. Upper-class women had a gaggle of servants – a Lady's maid, for instance, went everywhere with her mistress – and the imperial party occupied the whole of the hotel at Ilidza, just outside Sarajevo. Dressmakers, seamstresses and washerwomen all gained employment from a rich woman's wardrobe, and there was always someone to stick a foot in the small of her back and heave on the corset laces. And despite the recent introduction of more fluid and practical fashions in Paris, formal clothing for the establishment – as ever – would be slow to adapt, so the decorous and sweet pea-coloured figure alighting from an open touring car in front of Sarajevo's town hall fulfilled the expectations of the crowd.

Her husband was in uniform, bulging everywhere, even though he too had the benefit of a corset, the essential accessory for military grandees squeezed into sharply cut tunics. Franz Ferdinand was bedecked with a row of medals, as befitted an archduke, and, hand on sword, sweated under a cocked hat smothered in light green feathers. There was no hint here of the khaki and grey which would fill the fields of Flanders in the coming years. Earlier, the officers round him had glinted and flashed in the Bosnian sunlight, as the show of military brass and scarlet and plumes and swords wheeled past at the manoeuvres. This was what armies were all about. Men with spiked helmets, gold braid and epaulettes. Lively horses with expensive tack, all silver chains and jogging tassels. Thrilling gallops as artillery pieces clattered and flashed around the field. This was 1914, and warfare was paraded as glamorous and manly, a fitting scene for an archduke to view. The archduchess, pointedly, had not been invited.

When the imperial couple met up for their drive to the town hall, small crowds watched the smart cars navigate the narrow Sarajevo streets. The city boasted imposing Hapsburgian buildings, and a number of Turkish confections from its days as part of the Ottoman Empire – mosques and bath-houses, as well as a central bazaar. But much of Bosnia was an imperial backwater, with raw poverty in the mountain villages. Rural life might look picturesque, and the mixture of religions had brought some literacy, but there were also violence and harsh tradition, with women seen as wholly subservient, possessing few legal rights and bearing children year in year out. To the south, in Montenegro and Albania, girls were still sold into a marriage arranged at their birth, leading some foreign travellers to describe them as 'breeding sows'.

The diversity of Bosnia's ethnic mix was caught by the film camera following the royal couple in Sarajevo: a few men in the old Turkish fez, others with heads topped by the traditional white felt plantpot-shaped hat of peasants; women in traditional embroidered Slav costumes or baggy Muslim trousers, with quaint head-dresses and clunking jewellery. Many were merely wrapped in layers of dull, flea-infested material, the shawls and headscarves of the poor. The archduchess may have felt second-class in her chiffon and feathers, denied an elegant uniform; but she shared her inferior status, her position of deference and her exclusion from the military with the Bosnian peasant women she was waving to. Even though the century was over a decade old, and women in some European countries were agitating for the vote and beginning to shed their whalebone underwear, much of the professional world was still barred to them, politics belonged to men, and soldiering excluded women. Hundreds of thousands of men were under arms in an increasingly uneasy Europe, but the only women in distinctive uniform were nuns, nurses and nannies. And after the kerfuffle next to the bridge, when she took a fatal shot in the abdomen, Sophie was sent back to Austria to a second-class grave. Her husband's coffin bore all the insignia of the imperial house; on hers were a pair of white gloves and a little fan, and it was carefully laid to rest several inches lower than his.

Three-quarters of a century later, I wondered how the city of Sarajevo remembered the couple. 'There's a small museum,' I was told, right on the corner next to the bridge where the Serb student Gavrilo Princip had taken aim. 'And Tito's regime stuck a plaque on the wall and plonked a pair of metal footprints into the pavement' – so you can stand on them and imagine just what it was like to be a mere six feet from the shiny car, with its grand occupants, and fire the fatal shots.

It was not the best of summers to be a tourist. In 1992 I first spied the old town hall from behind a large metal rubbish skip, which then sprang two small holes with a strange soft pinging sound, as compacted stinking food waste and a couple of dead dogs slowed the bullets' trajectories.

Keeping the town hall in sight, my cameraman and I hurtled behind a low wall, for the town hall was spectacularly on fire. All around us fluttered glowing pieces of paper, with some thick, parchment-like pages curling languidly as they danced down from the second and third storeys. For the town hall had become the Sarajevo

University Library, repository of some of the more precious books of the unique culture which had seen Ottoman Turkish Islam put down roots in Orthodox Christian Europe. The pink and beige horizontally striped building on the riverbank now presented a ripe target for the Serbian gunners a couple of hundred yards away. For weeks afterwards, enraged Bosnian Muslims told of conspiracies by the Serbs to destroy their culture deliberately 'with special incendiary bombs'. In reality the old town hall was a sitting duck, and the precautions against fire minimal. Because there were snipers about we failed to get round to the front of the building, to see the steps where the archduchess had waved at the people lining the riverbank road. Bits of the central dome's highly decorated support arches were crashing down on to the mosaic floor. The Sarajevo Fire Brigade made valiant efforts, but arcs of water squirted from the numerous bullet punctures in the hoses and there was little that could be done.

By chance half an hour later, due to random explosions which sent us scuttling – as fast as weighty flak-jackets allowed – down a side street towards the river, we came across the Princip Bridge ahead of us, confirmed by a yellow tourist sign spattered with shrapnel holes. The stone bridge had wonky, ugly modern railings atop two elegant arches, connecting to territory that was still Muslim on the other side of the river, but something of a free-fire zone for the Serbs.

A short crawl down the pavement saw us within a few yards of the museum – and some feet from our noses were little heaps of grit and rubble, where a paving-stone had been. Sure enough, not even front-line gunfire had stopped history being rearranged again in Bosnia. Determined Muslims had crept to the corner and hacked out the Princip footprints; and the wall plaque was peppered with holes. The exact spot where Sophie and Franz Ferdinand had met their deaths in 1914 was now littered with shrapnel and lumps of building, and iced with glass.

Every so often figures skittered between buildings, some in tattered bits of uniform, others merely clutching the ubiquitous AK47 rifle. Men at war. Although in 1992 most of the women were unseen, hidden in the basements, trying to scrape together oddments of food and cook them without the aid of gas or electricity, or constantly creeping on all fours below window level in apartments overlooked by snipers, there was the occasional figure to be seen dashing amongst the ruins: a woman in camouflage with a semi-automatic rifle.

War changes lives, whether or not you fight, but in the intervening years since Sophie Chotek had dreamed of parading in scarlet and gold women have found themselves increasingly putting on uniform. And their endeavour to do so has mirrored the wider change in women's rights.

CHAPTER FOUR

WE THINK YOU OUGHT TO GO

THE DAY AFTER war broke out Grace Annie Stobart, the assertive founder of the Women's Sick and Wounded Convoy Corps, acquired an office in St James's Street and formed a Foreign Service and a Home Service. The Foreign Service had women doctors, nurses, cooks, interpreters and 'all workers essential for the independent working of a hospital in war'. Recruiting began at once, and the response with regard to both numbers and money was miraculous.

Mrs Stobart went off to see Sir Frederick Treves, chairman of the British Red Cross Society, and – consistent with prevailing attitudes – got squashed. He said that there 'was not work fitted for women in the sphere of war'. She ignored him and immediately left for Belgium and France, setting up a hospital in Brussels for French and Belgian soldiers, under the friendlier auspices of the Belgian Red Cross.

Her sense that women should be prepared – though for what, it was not clear –

Opposite: Women demonstrating for the right to enter war service at the time of World War I

FANY drivers in
France, 1917,
wearing the
impressive fur coats
that were part of
their uniform

had been an emerging concern of many Edwardians. In the years before World War I there had been a growth in organisations across the country where women could learn first aid and simple nursing. The Order of St John and the Red Cross set up a network of local branches, and from these the Voluntary Aid Detachments (VAD) evolved, working closely with the newly formed Territorial Army from 1909.

Some of the well-heeled young ladies who had joined the FANY had access to papa's Motor Vehicle, and on the outbreak of war their driving skills were offered to the government. Who promptly turned them down. But, as with Mrs Stobart, the rebuff merely strengthened determination, and the Belgian and French armies welcomed their offer. Although they were a tiny organisation ('thirty-five gentlewomen') they were of serious intent by then. Off they went across the Channel, kitted out in rather more elegant khaki than others – and famously topped with huge fur coats like mammoth hamsters. They'd discarded the tropical topee – somehow not quite right for a hospital in wintry northern France or Belgium – and showed a tendency to augment the whole effect with silk scarves and snazzy gauntlets.

Some served with the Red Cross in hospitals, others set up soup kitchens and canteens, but it was as ambulance drivers that they made their name. Initially, they were the butt of those who regarded them and many of the other volunteer outfits heading for Flanders as a bunch of lah-de-dah amateurs, but they gripped the wheels of their unwieldy ambulance vehicles and chugged through mud and shot and shell to gain a reputation as tenacious and dashing – and perfectly willing to perform under fire.

They grew in numbers and spread their wings. One part of the organisation, Unit V, was fully integrated into the Belgian army, carrying on working through ninety-nine air-raids and a sea bombardment. They served in all the Belgian hospitals, and some French. (This unit mounted the Guard of Honour for Edith Cavell, the nurse shot by the Germans in 1915, when her funeral cortege left Brussels.) Their routine was to have one FANY on telephone duty to take calls from incoming ambulances, while another girl stood duty out in the open square, ready to direct the unloading of casualties. It was not unknown for the hospital staff to have taken refuge in the dug-outs, while the FANY staff brought in the wounded and gave first aid as they waited for the medics to return to their posts. Not for nothing had they adopted the motto: I cope.

By the end of the war they were regarded as an elite and had garnered an impressive number of decorations, including the first-ever Military Medal awarded to a woman and numerous awards from the Belgians and French. The four hundred women on active service on the Western Front received altogether ninety-five decorations plus fifteen Mentions in Despatches.

The effect on people at home was more than just the impact of individual acts of heroism. Women weren't supposed to have joined a world where medals were pinned to female chests in recognition of bravery absolutely equal to that of the fighting men, and praise had usually been voiced only for the fortitude of women at home confronting the general enlistment of their men; newspapers were generally full of stirring words to stiffen the sinews of being a housewife at home. The *Lady* magazine asserted: 'Think what this has meant for women, gentle and simple, in loss, sacrifice and work! For them there is none of the wild joy of contest, the glow of "esprit de corps", the enheartening sense of comradeship that sustain the men. Their lot has been to live through lonely months of hard routine, thankfully undertaken to keep at bay the haunting dread for ever at their hearts.' The behaviour of the not so gentle and simple clearly didn't fit the general pattern; however, it was all part and parcel of emerging emancipation, and grist to the mill of those who'd fought so hard before the war in the suffrage movement.

For the advocates of Votes for Women, the suffragists, and their militant sisters the

Mrs Grace McDougall, née Ashley-Smith, FANY Commandant 1914-20. Her French and Belgian decorations included the Croix de Guerre, the Ordre de la Couronne and the Ordre de Leopold

suffragettes, there had been a sudden reckoning in 1914. The various organisations to which they belonged had divided public opinion bitterly through their passionate and sometimes violent campaign prior to the war. Now, as armies mobilised, there was dispute as to whether women were naturally pacifist, or whether their energies should go into supporting the war effort. The arguments were debated very publicly, but took place against a background of war fervour which took hold across the nation: Baroness Orczy, author of the hugely popular *Scarlet Pimpernel* books, founded an organisation which took up the habit of handing out white feathers to men deemed to be avoiding their patriotic duty. Millicent Garrett Fawcett, President of the National Union of Women's Suffrage Societies, stomped the country and turned up in my home town to ginger up the local suffrage supporters. Sunderland women were exhorted to hold fast to their suffrage ideals: her rallying cry of 'Let us show ourselves worthy of citizenship, whether our claim to it be recognised or not' went down well in a hall filled with solid middle-class housewives and a sprinkling of female academics; however, she urged them to remember that, though war would make women's services more conspicuous and prove them to be 'worthy of citizenship', their work in times of peace was just as valuable – for there was already a nagging fear that women's aspirations would be swept away in the manly world of

General Plumer pinning medals on to women ambulance drivers for bravery during air-raids, Blendècques, 1918

warmongering. She then outlined some of the National Union's plans, which included clubs for soldiers and their wives, the formation of maternity centres and the training of women for acetylene welding. The latter passed without comment in the local newspaper, which had conditioned itself to a regular bombardment of articles from the very active local suffrage ladies.

However, missing from the speeches and tracts and letters to the press from the women who had endured a decade of violent threats at public rallies, physical attacks during demonstrations and force-feeding in prison, was the claim – or even the suggestion – that women should be in the front line alongside the men. The battlefield was male, and with the exception of the historic or eccentric individual, that was that.

Fighting, uniforms, ranks, medals, all were seen from a male perspective. The Victoria Cross, for instance, inscribed 'For Valour' at the personal suggestion of Queen Victoria and the highest decoration for bravery in the British armed forces, had never – *has* never – been won by a woman. There was, however, a curious moment in 1859 when the officers of the 104th Bengal Fusiliers stationed in India made a presentation to a Mrs Webber Harris. The wife of their commanding officer, she had nursed the men of the regiment during a terrible cholera outbreak which at one point claimed the lives of twenty-seven men in one night. She was given a 'gold representation' of the VC and commended for her 'indomitable pluck'.

The difference between valour and pluck underlined contemporary attitudes. The notion of bearing arms appears not to have been taken up in any serious way by any of the suffrage groups; instead, they took official indifference on any aspect of women's efforts for granted, and set to work immediately to plan, organise and execute a vast range of support activities. They were well versed in getting on with things while being ignored. Alongside their efforts, a myriad of individuals and societies threw themselves wholeheartedly into the huge void in society that quickly appeared as hundreds of thousands of men volunteered for military service. However, their contribution was entirely voluntary – for throughout the war, the government refrained from conscripting women.

When, initially, zealous female patriots proffered white feathers in public to those men they believed were avoiding military service, they were doing so in the knowledge that *they* did not have to head for the misery of the trenches:

> *Oh we don't want to lose you,*
> *But we think you ought to go,*
> *For your King and your country,*
> *Both need you so.*

The music hall stages throughout the land rang to these refrains – utterly un-ironic, utterly sincere, and female voices rang the loudest, with no suggestion whatsoever that women should ever fight alongside their men.

As a small child, I climbed the gilded staircase to the grand vestibule of the Sunderland Empire Theatre. Ancient posters and slightly faded photographs jostled between the dusty red velvet drapes. Women with rather odd teeth and a cottage-loaf of hair simpered next to men in starched collars with boot-polish hair. The great stars of the music hall thought Sunderland a worthwhile detour: the stage was huge and the audiences a challenge.

Away from the metropolitan buzz, with its fashionable society and politically activist suffragettes, Sunderland was a typical northern fastness of heavy industry and no-nonsense Methodism. It was relatively prosperous at the turn of the century, notwithstanding the precarious nature of shipbuilding, with men laid off when a new vessel was named and went down the ways into the River Wear. There were also mining, seafaring and glassmaking, and a rugged work ethic amidst the industrial murk (described in Victorian times with the words 'dirt is the distinctive feature; earth, air and water are alike black and filthy'.) But out of the dirt came rows of substantial 'Sunderland cottages' built for the skilled shipyard workers; many of them were owner-occupiers, a rarity for working people in those days. The town also had slums, clustered especially near the riverbanks, distinguished by stinking middens and communal wash-houses which resounded to the pounding of poss-sticks in the tubs every Monday. There was little available work attached to the yards for women. Some worked in the pottery kilns, and some down at the fish quay. But most worked at keeping home and hearth together, a full-time occupation of scrubbing, cooking, possing and pregnancy.

If you could scrape together a few pence there might be a trip to the cinema – just before World War I there were at least half a dozen, including Hamilton's Flickerless Pictures, but they weren't considered particularly 'respectable', especially for ladies. (The middle classes were only drawn to them when patriotic 'Official War Pictures' were introduced, such as *the Battle of the Ancre*, advertised in the *Sunderland Daily Echo* in January 1917 as: 'The first presentation in Sunderland of this noble and wonderful record of the great autumn battle and the historic introduction of the tanks . . . specially selected popular and patriotic music by our renowned orchestra'. There was also the Bioscope, installed on the stage of the opulent Sunderland Empire Theatre, showing 'Britain Prepared' in 1916, 'a stupendous kinematograph review of His Majesty's naval and military forces'.)

But in an age before radio and television, just twopence could bring you to the music hall and into the presence of glamorous international stardom – in the flesh, on the Empire's stage – as long as you didn't suffer from vertigo, squashed high up in the gallery tucked under the ornate ceiling. If you were flush with money fourpence would get you a little more room in the balcony below, where you could peer down on the nobs in the Grand Tier, who'd paid two shillings and sixpence. Vesta Tilley, along with Marie Lloyd and Hetty King, was one of that small group of women able to throw off the constraints of respectable womanhood via the stage. In 1907 she topped the bill at the opening of the Sunderland Empire, having just returned from one of her many successful American tours. Tilley was billed as 'London's idol and ideal male impersonator' and one of her most popular acts was Tommy Atkins. At other times she was scarlet-coated, or wore khaki with a Sam Browne belt: the very idea of a woman in a soldier's uniform belonged solely and rather outrageously on the music hall stage. Audiences not only loved her songs, but gawped at the audacity of her appearing in gentlemen's outfits. The very idea of a woman in trousers! Even lady cyclists and horsewomen had the decency to wear long divided skirts. But Tilley's daring was appreciated and her performance was described by the *Sunderland Daily Echo* as 'exquisitely artistic'. (Such praise was not to be sneered at, for in 1908 Charlie Chaplin got not a mention in its columns when he appeared with Fred Karno's comedy troupe.) Five years later, Marie Lloyd faced the Empire's audiences and encountered their growing reputation as a tough bunch of punters. The greatest of all music hall stars, she apparently found them rather 'difficult'.

In 1914, Marie Lloyd and Vesta Tilley represented exceptions to a woman's lot in life: they earned large sums of money, led independent lives, made indirect references in public to sex, and wore unusual clothes, at least on stage. They were the nearest that working people came to unconventional women. And though in no way 'role models', they wielded influence. In wartime, along with the hundreds of artistes who toured the nation's theatres, they belted out the patriotic songs with both fervour and pathos, and brought home popular sentiment about the war which never failed to stir those in their Sunday-best shawls and straw hats up in the gallery:

> . . . *on Saturday I'm willing, if you'll only take the shilling,*
> *To make a man of any one of you.*

In Sunderland, eighteen thousand men took the King's Shilling and enlisted; by 1919, a third had been killed or wounded. Over half a century later, I still heard elderly people talk of Tilley and Lloyd – 'Them canny women in their trews, gorrup like an army lad' who seemed the glamorous, public-spirited glow-worms in the dark of the war.

The daring Miss Vesta Tilley on stage, in uniform, 1907

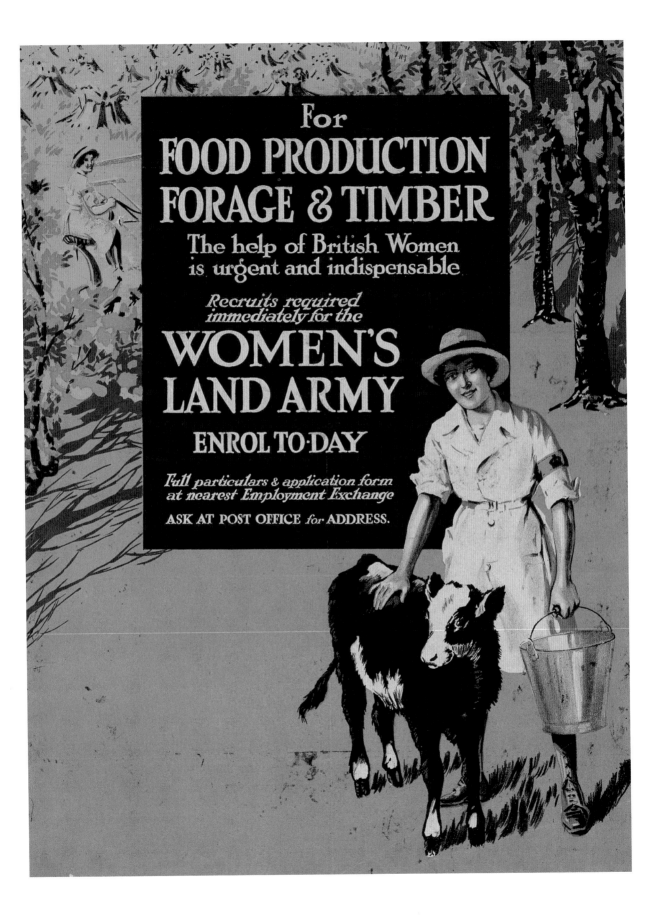

CHAPTER FIVE

YOUR COUNTRY NEEDS YOU

AVING EXHORTED THE men to go off to war, what should the women do next? With no encouragement from the authorities, but fired with patriotism, hundreds of thousands of women – especially leisured middle- and upper-class ladies – saw some kind of opportunity to enlarge their horizons.

On the home front life began to look like a march-past of alphabet games, with W for Women everywhere: WAF, WEC, WEL, WFL, WFC, WTS, WVR, WL, WFGU... Educated women were experts at voluntary work and charitable organisation. Many had no other outlet for their talents and energy. Marriage, with only a few exceptions, put an end to professional work: husbands felt shamed by a 'working wife', and they were supported by employers who dismissed women when they married.

But in 1914, with more women – admittedly small numbers and among the better

Opposite: An exhortation to join the Women's Land Army: 'Large numbers of girls of education and standing have taken up work on the land . . .'

off – learning to drive, taking up sport, dancing the Tango and the Turkey Trot and getting a whiff of politics, it was clear to the activists that knitting socks was not enough. Another popular song at the time described 'Sister Susie sewing shirts for soldiers' – surely Susie needed to join the WAF, the Women's Auxiliary Force? Dressed in a blue jacket and skirt with khaki facings, Sister Susie could be gainfully employed as a part-time seamstress, diversifying into first aid, cooking and canteen management, hospital visiting, stewarding in air-raid shelters and growing vegetables for hospital kitchens – and be addressed as Sergeant Susie. Without any prompting, uniforms proliferated, along with quasi-military ranks and structures. It was unconsciously recognised that uniform has its own power, commands respect and endows the wearer with a status – even for the newly employed conductress on the Clapham omnibus or the volunteer turnip-hoer in a Norfolk field.

The field was led by the Women's Emergency Corps, a novel combination of militant suffragettes, feminists and establishment dowagers. And drawing on the previous decade's experience in the suffrage movement, there was a strong feeling that, while the traditional voluntary help of women in time of crisis should be made available, there was also an argument for women who went to work being paid; though often it remained just that – an argument. The Corps quickly diversified into the Women's Volunteer Reserve and the Women's Legion, and khaki became the smart colour to be seen in, although newspaper cartoonists had a field day initially, especially as the WVR had taken to saluting their officers. Hysterical, thought the press. The jackets had a military look about them, all pockets and buttons, and the skirt length was just a smidgeon variable. It seems to have been a personal choice: older ladies didn't show ankles, but the younger spirits flashed their black stockings above their laced boots or sensible shoes; some wore puttees. And all wore hats, dimpled pudding basins with brims – so now I know where our school hats originated.

The aim of the WVR was 'to provide a trained and efficient body of women whose services could be offered to the country at any time' – a wide brief, and one which could be used to assist women whose lives were being affected by absent husbands and loss of income. Dame Helen Gwynne-Vaughan recalled:

> The members wore khaki, did a good deal of drill and were sometimes exaggeratedly military in their bearing, but they did much useful work in canteens and elsewhere, often undertaking scrubbing and other unattractive jobs in their scanty leisure from paid work. Most of them were wage earners who gave their services on night shifts or from six to eight in the morning before hurrying to their offices and workshops. They may be regarded as having made the first reconnaissance in the direction of work for the Army outside hospitals.

The Glasgow Battalion of the Women's Volunteer Reserve Army being inspected by Field-Marshal Lord French in 1915

And they were followed by the Legion, founded by Lady Londonderry, who gained access to military cookhouses, again extending the army's recognition of jobs which women could usefully do in the services. The Legion both cooked for the army and catered for the mass movement of troops, and also for the increase in wartime industrial employment.

It took only a short time for the editors of women's journals to realise that advice on suitable dress for new surroundings should be offered, backed up by advertisements such as this from the *Lady*:

> 'War work' is rather vague. If you propose to help in a canteen, you will find a trimly-cut coat-overall the most practical, worn over a short skirt and shirt. Certainly pockets are an advantage, almost an essential, and you will find that they are a feature of the strong brown twill skirts which munition-makers and women gardeners are wearing. Beal's specialises in a splendid earth-brown cotton twill skirt of this sort – only 8s 9d; write to Regent Street for patterns.

More adventurously, there were despatch riders – a small number of women familiar

London girls training
in the Land Army –
about to learn how
to spread manure

with motor-cycles, who confidently acquired breeches and high boots and gauntlets. There was no doubt that a uniform presented women in a public role 'ever so respectably' – even if they were paying for it out of their own purse. However, expensive tailored outfits costing perhaps £2 each – two weeks' pay for a Lancashire textile worker – left many unable to afford to join.

Specialised groups spotted their own niche in the paid volunteer market: the Women's Emergency League spawned the Lady Instructors' Signals Company, which attached itself to the British army in Aldershot, and eventually the School of Women Signallers put out advertisements for 'giving classes in semaphore flags, morse flags, flashlight, buzzer, telegraph sounder etc.'. (No one should sneer at the ladies with their semaphore flags, for I last saw the military using them as two huge American warships steamed past each other in the Adriatic during the Kosovo conflict in the late nineties. The captain of the ammunition supply ship remarked that it was 'a kinda neat sort of communication, no noise, no fuss, and no chance of the enemy listening in'.)

Letters between two of the signalling officers convey the rather odd relationship which these quasi-military World War I outfits generated, as Mrs Brunskill Reid (lieutenant) engaged in a dispute with Mrs Agnes del Riego (her commandant) over a small disciplinary matter: the commandant's letter claims the wartime high ground:

Now, it must be distinctly understood that I have neither *time* nor inclination to worry over any petty nonsense at the moment. This is War time. There are important matters which demand *immediate* attention and it can but be obvious to anyone that these must come first. Let us rise above all narrow-mindedness because our Country demands of us bigger things, and, in so doing, prove that women can be large-minded enough to work in accord and harmony for a great Cause.

We meet again at 2 p.m. on Monday to plan out this work. Unless I have all along been mistaken in you (when you realise what is wanted) – you will be at your post, putting Country first. Believe me, my only desire, dear Lieutenant, is to be at one with my Officers, as are my Organising Secretaries and myself.

Rather endearingly, the commandant scrawled under her signature that the letter had been written in 'frantic haste'.

Away from the delights of morse and buzzers, there were horses to be seen to in the army camps: these were the responsibility of the Women's Forage Corps. At its peak it had eight thousand women baling hay, driving horsed transport, chaffing, mending tarpaulin sheets and making sacks. Forage rated as a serious national resource; when a shortage occurred in May 1917 rationing was introduced, and announced in severe terms in the press. The *Sunderland Daily Echo*, for instance, reported: 'The rationing regarding horses is to start at once. No-one will be allowed to feed a horse on oats or grain without a licence, and the Food controller is engaged upon drawing up a scale of rations. Nothing will be allowed for pleasure horses.'

In these circumstances, and after widespread thefts, the Volunteer Reserve provided forage guards for the dumps scattered around the country, and Miss C.F. Shave received her orders from the Forage Committee in Whitehall:

> The Colonel asks me to tell you that you will be required to leave for Ringwood on Tuesday next. . . . Your uniform will be supplied to you at Ringwood. You must provide yourself with a mackintosh, not a raincoat, but a coat that is absolutely waterproof. If you do not already possess one the Colonel would prefer you to obtain an Oilskin from Messrs. Moss, Bros., King Street, Covent Garden. I can give you an order whereby you will obtain it at a cheaper rate. You should also supply yourself with a Fork, Knife and Spoon, or as many of each as you like.
> The Colonel asks me to tell you to be sure and take all the warm underclothes that you can, a warm woolly scarf, and if you have such a thing, a rug or thick blankets. If you have a dog you may take it with you (not Toy dogs).
>   Yours faithfully,
>   D.A.F. Codd, Captain & Adjutant.

Captain Codd's attention to detail suggested he knew something about fashion – not for raincoats, but for toy dogs: an impeccably bred pooch had for some time been the indispensable accessory, with *Vogue* magazine stating: 'The Pekingese now Claims to be the Smartest Dog in Dogdom'. Highly recommended were the Boston bull, the Maltese terrier, the Yorkshire terrier, the French bull terrier ('the height of fashion a few seasons ago') and the English spaniel ('in dainty sizes which fit snugly under the arm'). Captain Codd clearly viewed snug-fitting spaniels as highly inappropriate for guarding forage.

Down at Ringwood they perhaps could have done with a nice large Alsatian, as the commander of the guard there, Doris Odburn, remembered: 'The dump was completely open so that anyone could have access to it. It was therefore somewhat farcical that every week I received a top secret envelope from the War Office with a pass word for the day, which I only communicated to the sergeant and guards actually on duty. They were armed with truncheons and whistles but I doubt if they would have been at all effective against an attempt at theft or sabotage.'

Less popular was the call to work on the land: farm work was not a rural idyll of gentle haymaking and picturesque ploughing with placid Clydesdale horses. It was a poorly paid slog with antiquated equipment, which had lowly status compared to factory work, and few women were involved. The Women's Farm and Garden Union existed to look after their interests, and as the war progressed, increased food production brought yet another organisation into being to coax up the numbers willing to speed the plough. The Women's National Land Service Corps was 'a mobile force of educated women to help in recruiting and organising the local labour of women', who would soon discover – dressed in hat, green tie and brown smock – the joys of flax-pulling, egg-collecting and udder-squeezing.

South of London, a motley bunch of girls enrolled in the Women's Defence Relief Corps and found themselves 'harvesting, hoeing, binding and shocking'. Oh, how they took to it, one of them wrote in the *Lady* in 1915:

> Many of us were Cockneys who didn't know wheat from barley, And we were all sorts – housemaids, schoolmistresses, singers, painters, writers, women of leisure, factory packers, sick nurses and shop assistants.
>
> It is a healthy occupation. Singers talked of their delicate throats, painters showed their fine hands, ordinary women spoke of nerves and muscular weaknesses. They all admitted in the end that their health and physique were greatly benefited, that the experience had proved invigorating, that they no longer had any nerves.
>
> The pay is not good. A well paid labourer makes £1 a week, and we have to make sure of that. Women working on the land must remember that they have to be careful not to lower the wages for the men who have gone to fight. They must insist on that £1 a week.
>
> With regard to clothes, we found the most convenient garb was shirt, knickers, gaiters, stout boots, shady linen hat, and a long, loose white calico painter's coat; this served instead of a skirt, and came to the knees. – It can be bought for 2s 6d.
>
> Girls got wet through, more than once a day, and needed a change of underwear, and two, possibly three pairs of boots and gaiters (the latter being leather, they were difficult to dry, and remained wet for days).
>
> If they did not have the stoutest possible gloves (housemaids) their hands were cut and torn. They needed several pairs.
>
> The amazing thing about the whole business was the adaptability of women. Who would have imagined that these delicately-nurtured, highly-educated women would have undertaken the work of farm labourers – and done it?

Proper pay – that wonderful one pound per week – and an outdoor life: the Women's Land Army and the Women's Forestry Corps were next in the recruitment drive in

1917. However, even in their smocks, corduroy breeches and high lace-up boots they were often regarded as little more than second-best as they harnessed ploughing teams, wrestled with Heath Robinson harvesting contraptions and chopped down swathes of English woodland for ammunition boxes and duckboards in the trenches.

Members of the Women's Forage Corps filling a baler with hay for feeding horses

Everywhere, there were exhortations to encourage women to consider donning gaiters and smocks. Lord Selbourne made a speech in which he declared: 'Women must take the place of men upon the land, so that the men can be spared to fight', and newspapers backed him with descriptions of women ploughing and scattering manure and asseverations that 'the reluctant farmer is looking about him to make sure of the necessary labour'. Really? Most farmers actually thought male pensioners more suitable, leading, reported the *Sunderland Daily Echo*, to a sharp set of exchanges among the members of the Durham County War Agricultural Committee:

> The Chairman remarked that there was what he thought an unreasonable prejudice against the employment of women. A considerable number were being trained in the County and there was a great deal of holding back on the part of the farmers.
>
> Mr Spraggon said some were worth 2s 6d – and others were worth considerably less.

The Chairman replied that if they set a low standard of wages, they got a low class of labour. A sum of 1s 6d or 1s 9d a day was a miserable pittance for more or less experienced women workers, who had to walk in some cases 4 miles to their work – and pay for their own food.

Mr Spraggon said he was paying by the hour . . . and some women were receiving 2d or 3d an hour.

The Chairman thought 2d or 3d an hour was a miserable pittance.

Mr Spraggon replied that if they kept watch upon the women, they would see many of them settling [sitting down] behind the hedge.

The Chairman said he was not surprised. The wages were not sufficient to keep body and soul together.

The sunny world envisaged by poster artists was not borne out in the reality of muddy ploughland for the Land Army or axe grinding for the Forestry Corps

The pay for the male farm workers was between 6s and 7s a day – some four times what the chairman had described as a 'miserable pittance'. No wonder there was a certain amount of 'settling behind the hedge'. Along with gripes about pay, there were frequent observations on 'the deadly dullness of village life'. To counter this, upbeat articles appeared in the newspapers to convince women that Land Army work had its advantages: 'The long-standing prejudice against farming work for women, as work essentially rough, vulgar and coarsening, is breaking down. This is in no doubt partly due to the fact that large numbers of girls of education and standing have taken up work on the land during the duration of the war.' The implication was that nice young women should not be snobbish about getting their hands muddied. For the reality was that enthusiasm for agricultural work was mainly confined to such middle-class women, most of whom hadn't a clue about the rigours of back-breaking slog in the fields. Their poorer sisters had a better grasp of the toil they'd encounter and they resolutely avoided the Land Army. So the appeals were directed towards the sensibilities of the more refined: 'A woman engaged in ordinary fieldwork and dressed in ordinary women's garb is not a sight to attract the fastidious; but that objection again is being removed, and it is to be hoped that the fashion set by the National Service girl will be followed by all women workers on the land. The uniform worn by the girls is not only practical but eminently attractive, and no girl need feel her vanity hurt when she sees herself in it.'

These comments came from the Sunderland Women's Suffrage Society, who, although they added the complaint that the 'wages were insufficient', were regularly at pains to stress the 'attractive – and becoming' appearance of uniforms. And if getting prodigiously muddy in a remote field was just too much for the more genteel to contemplate, the *Lady* magazine weighed in with its own suggestions as to how the more delicate might help:

> The cry of 'Back to the Land' has been answered by thousands of women, who are only too glad to be able to do really valuable work for their country, but many, though willing, know that their physical health is not equal to work on farms.
>
> Grape-thinning as an occupation for patriotic women is exactly suited to them. It helps to provide a necessary delicacy for our wounded soldiers, and it calls for qualities, such as ready judgement and deftness of hand, with which women are specially endowed. One of the biggest grape-growing districts in England is on the south coast round about Worthing, and in the numerous glasshouses there, since the beginning of the war, hundreds of women have been employed as grape-thinners with great satisfaction to their employers.
>
> Naturally, women dress according to the nature of their work. Caps are 'de rigueur', because the hair must not touch the grapes, and fancy can devise any number of pretty cotton costumes.

Such delicacy was not the usual view of work on the land: magazines joyfully ridiculed the meeting of town lass and country lad, with the popular image of a snooty Land Girl confronting a man busy milking and asking: 'Why are you not at the Front?' To which he replies: 'Because the milk's at the back, ma'am.'

CHAPTER SIX

A FOREIGN
CALL TO ARMS

W HILE THE VOLUNTARY, the part-time and the auxiliary were the norm for much of the war in Britain, newspapers discovered the excitement of women at front lines elsewhere. Ten years earlier, intrepid travellers such as Edith Durham had encountered in the rural Balkans the tradition of 'Albanian Virgins' – women whose families lacked a son, or who refused to marry the man chosen for them. In return for forswearing sexual relations, they gained considerable independence in what was then still a near-medieval society. These women wore men's clothes and carried rifles like every other Albanian male. For British readers, eastern Europe was expected to be full of interesting customs.

A mixture of breathless wonderment, much allied to the word 'plucky', infused the wartime reports from Russia, Ukraine and Poland. There were instances in the

Opposite: Maria Bachkarova of the Russian Women's Death Battalion, captioned in Le Petit Journal *1917, 'A lady I for one would not wish to meet on a dark night'*

*An Albanian virgin –
sworn to virginity, so
equal to men*

military of 'personation' – with females only discovered when compelled to undergo medical examination. Reports of 'hundreds' of women concealed in the Russian army hinted at a rather exotic and raffish fighting force, but one which was distant in custom and attitudes and would have little relevance to the British Tommy. Certainly there were individuals who distinguished themselves, particularly in the Cossack regiments, but initially many of the tales had the ring of heroic romance. Undoubtedly, the horrendous conditions which nurses found themselves in as they accompanied fighting units led to a number becoming involved in actual combat; however, it was the Russian Women's Death Battalion which eventually delivered to British readers well-documented evidence of women in the front line. Katherine Hodges – later an ambulance driver in France – was in Petrograd (St Petersburg) at the Anglo-Russian Hospital when she was asked to inspect the Death Battalion based in the city.

Every sort and class of woman seemed to be represented. They had not sufficient military uniforms, but they were all in breeches or trousers of sorts, some of them clad in the most amazing hotch-potch of garments. They were young and old, peasant and aristocrat, a most extraordinary mixture.

After the inspection we had an interview with the woman commanding. She asked us if we would stay and join the Battalion to organise a motor-unit for it. We told her we would let her know the next day. After thinking it over very carefully we decided that as she had no cars as yet, merely a vague promise for the future, and as we should have to teach the women how to drive and such mechanical knowledge as we possessed, all in Russian, we thought it was no use attempting it.

The Woman Commandant told us she did not expect women to be any real use as active combatants, but that her whole idea was to restore the morale of the ordinary troops by the force of example. This, I fear, did not work out according to plan for I was told, possibly untruly, I don't know, that when the Battalion left Petrograd for the Front there was a dreadful scene at the station, several of the women being badly man-handled, some deaths occurring as a result. I also heard that every woman carried cyanide potassium, to take if she was made prisoner & feared rape or torture.

Mrs Pankhurst was another observer who passed through Petrograd, drumming up support for the Allies with the same zeal she had brought to the suffragette movement; she too – 'a famous Englishwoman' – was saluted by the Battalion.

A few months later, the reservations voiced by Katherine Hodges were confirmed by another English nurse, Florence Farmborough. Having been a governess in

CORSETS TO CAMOUFLAGE

Moscow when war broke out, Florence spent three and a half extraordinary years as a Red Cross nurse serving with the Russian army. She had a keen eye and remarkable mastery of the military realities around her, and also spoke excellent Russian. In the summer of 1917, while with the Russian 8th Army in Romania, she too heard that a women's battalion had been formed – news that thrilled her and the other nursing sisters, though Florence remarked that a woman soldier 'was no unusual sight in the Russian Army'. Two weeks later her admiration was dimmed when news came from the Austrian Front that things had gone badly, and three women were brought in wounded:

Florence Farmborough nursing on the Russian Front in 1915

> The size of the Battalion had considerably decreased since the first weeks of recruitment, when some 2,000 women and girls had rallied to the call of their Leader. Many of them, painted and powdered, had joined the Battalion as an exciting and romantic adventure; she loudly condemned their behaviour and demanded iron discipline. Gradually the patriotic enthusiasm had spent itself; the 2,000 slowly dwindled to 250. In honour to those women volunteers, it was recorded that they *did* go into the attack; they *did* go 'over the top'. But not all of them. Some remained in the trenches, fainting and hysterical; others ran or crawled back to the rear. Bachkarova retreated with her decimated battalion; she was wrathful, heartbroken, but she had learnt a great truth: women were quite unfit to be soldiers.

Maria Bachkarova – or Botchkareva – had led a turbulent life, and had had two violent husbands before she joined the Tsar's Imperial Army in 1914. She seems to have been accepted without undue objections, with her shorn hair and regulation boots, trousers and blouse, and after initial harassment and ridicule was seen as 'a comrade, not a woman'. Her battalion, formed in 1917, attracted worldwide attention and brought forth comment, praise, analysis, shock and disapproval. Nevertheless, its main purpose was not to show that women could fight. Morale was breaking down in the Russian army, and there was disarray after the fall of the Tsar. She argued that 'What was important was to shame men and that a few women at one place could serve as an example to the entire front . . . the purpose of the plan would be to shame the men in the trenches by having the women go over the top first.' A third of them were killed or wounded and many showed great bravery, but they failed to goad the entire front line into action. And when the Bolsheviks came to power some months later, the women were told to go home 'and put on female attire'.

However, worldwide, the battalion's poor military showing seemed

secondary in its impact to the very fact of its going into battle, and a world at war chewed over the social and sexual implications of women willing to bear arms. And at least Bachkareva came from exotic Siberia; Flora Sandes, on the other hand, came from Poppleton in Yorkshire.

I first heard of her when I was in Serbia in the early nineties, wedged under a table in a Croat village for several hours while under tank fire. Our Serb interpreter, crammed into a kitchen cupboard under the sink, passed the time between explosions pouring scorn on anyone being capable of heroic feats of valour other than the glorious warriors of the Serb nation. This involved embarrassing questions such as: 'What do you English know about our heroes?' A long silence followed while a tank shell whirred overhead and I searched my memory to locate the pantheon of Balkan warriors on the tip of every British schoolchild's tongue . . .

'Erm . . .'

Another shell found its mark and we all shrieked. A minute later, while bits of suburban villa crackled with licking flames a hundred yards away, Balkan history was back on the agenda. 'What about Vlora Sandees?'

'I'm afraid we didn't do much about Yugoslavia, sorry Serbia, in history,' I replied.

'Sandees was English.'

'Really?'

A tank squealed as it wheeled down a side street and we all cursed the lack of a cellar in the house in which we'd sought refuge.

'Sandees won the Karageorge Medal,' continued our interpreter. 'She fight for Serbia in First World War – you English are all like her?'

Several shells and much mayhem followed, so I was saved from parading my ignorance.

Flora Sandes began conventionally enough – though she had always said her prayers as a child with the fervent request that she should wake the next morning as a boy. She was the ninth and youngest child of a vicar who was originally from Ireland, and she'd had some nursing experience with the FANY and St John Ambulance. Travel delighted her, and she'd once taken a trip – by bicycle – through Central America to visit one of her brothers who was engaged in the building of the Panama Canal. His wife had died, and Flora undertook to bring her very young nephew home, which she did, young Dick spending the first part of the journey through the jungle in her bicycle basket.

Like so many others, at the outbreak of war in 1914 she offered her services, brandishing her first aid certificates. 'I'll go anywhere and do anything,' she said. And like so many others, she was ignored by officialdom. The Red Cross asked if she could join an ambulance unit heading for Serbia. She was thirty-eight and wasn't exactly sure where Serbia was, but left immediately, her baggage including hot water bottles, insect powder and a violin. In her own words she 'was not a trained nurse, but had been for three years an active member of the St John's Ambulance Brigade, so had some idea of the rudiments of first-aid'. Nursing, she thought, was 'surely the most womanly occupation on earth'. Later, she said she had not a thought in her head about becoming a soldier.

Eighteen months later she was carrying a rifle in the Serbian 1st Army, the only British woman officially enrolled as a soldier in World War I. Her transformation, she thought, was not particularly dramatic: 'I seem to have just naturally drifted, by successive stages, from a nurse into a soldier. . . . When the Brigade holding Baboona Pass began slowly to retreat towards Albania, where there were no roads, and we could take no ambulances to carry the sick, I took the red cross off my arm and said, very well, I would join the 2nd Infantry Regiment as a private.' To her Serb colleagues, she was well qualified to serve: she could ride and shoot and drive, spoke French, German and passable Serbo-Croat – and she was English (though speaking with an Irish accent), symbolising a hoped-for promise of support from the Allies, later backed up by her extremely successful fund-raising trips back home.

She had found a true vocation in the army; passionate about the cause of the Serbs, educated and intelligent enough to understand the anomalies of her position and to rationalise it, she fought fearlessly, shot men in combat, was wounded several times, and rose through the ranks to become a sergeant-major and later a captain. As in Russia, there were a number of peasant girls in the Serbian army, including a woman sergeant in Sandes' own regiment. However, the complexities of her position – whether she had become an 'honorary man' and if she needed to prove her claim to serve next to men by being stronger, more enduring and keener to fight than other women, and perhaps some of the men – were the talk of both the Serb army messes and the drawing rooms full of London ladies who'd heard her talk of her experiences. She slept alongside her unit, and was adept at dealing with the sexual approaches and innuendo that inevitably arose. Her method was to cut a figure as a proper serving soldier, trusted by her comrades in arms, and therefore accepted as a person worthy of respect. Rather than being seen as a woman doubtful about her own sexuality or orientation, she mainly had to contend with suggestions that she was just another version of the traditional camp follower, a trollop in uniform. And once a soldier, she reacted with great irritation to the suggestion that she should revert to being a nurse – saying that as a soldier she behaved as one, caring for the wounded only 'between shots', and that as regards the wounded 'we have Red Cross men for first aid'.

Her memories are remarkably matter-of-fact and unromantic, though they ring with the realities of grubby warfare:

> So brutal does one unconsciously become, that when we used to creep out at night on a bombing raid, we always congratulated ourselves on being the most successful when the crash of our bomb was followed only by a few groans and then silence. Were there a tremendous hullabaloo, we used to say that in all probability it meant only a few scratches, or the top of someone's finger – a very sensitive place – taken off.

She endured the hardships of the ordinary soldier and indeed seems to have relished them, carrying her carbine, revolver, water bottle and cartridge belt, and dressing in regulation tunic and helmet. 'We all wear those iron helmets; I hate mine when it is very hot, but love it when we get shelled, which happens pretty often, with very slight cover, and stones and shrapnel come pattering down on it; I only wish on those occasions it was big enough to crawl right under like a snail's shell.' However, her bravery was unquestionable, and she continued to serve even after she was seriously wounded by a bomb on the battlefield in 1916.

> I dare say you've heard that I got knocked out by a Bulgar hand-bomb, so I never got into Monastir after all; but I've had a very good run for my money all the same, as I had three months' incessant fighting without a scratch . . . The Serbs are fine comrades. We thought once we should all get taken, but they wouldn't leave me! I've had ever so many cards from them asking when I'm coming back, but as I have twenty-four wounds and a broken arm the doctors seem to think I'll have to wait a bit.

While recovering from her injuries she was awarded the Order of Karageorge, receiving the medal while still in bed; and she did go back, remaining on active service

CORSETS TO CAMOUFLAGE

in the Serbian army until 1922. Confounding much of the gossip, she married a Russian émigré officer, but for the seven years during which she was enlisted she was always to be seen in breeches and military tunic, with high-laced boots and army cap.

Living in Belgrade at the start of World War II, at the age of sixty-four she was called up and went off in a lorry with other reservists, even though she had severe disabilities as the result of her earlier wounds. Captured by the Germans, she was taken to a military prison hospital. When a friend visited her and gave her women's clothes, she quickly changed from her uniform and walked straight out of jail, gaining several weeks' freedom until she was rearrested. Her reputation in Serbia was immense, even among the Germans. When they occupied Belgrade, she and her husband Yurie were interned for a short time and she was ordered to report to the local Gestapo. The door was quietly closed behind her and a bottle of schnapps produced, before a taxi was summoned to conduct her home. In 1944, as Russian troops and Yugoslav partisans were poised to liberate the city, the German official made his usual routine visit. Clicking his heels, he said stiffly: 'I will see you next month, madam,' to which she replied: 'No, I'm sorry, you will be leaving – I shall be staying.'

Her family never commented that her military service seemed in any way 'odd', and she herself would talk freely of her time under arms, her sword and medals to hand. She remembered being very conscious of the change to her persona brought about by the clothes, from nurse in skirts to soldier in uniform, writing: 'It's a hard world where half the people say you should not dress as a man and the other half want to punish you for dressing as a woman.'

Those who knew her well later in life, such as Dana Stankovic, describe her as 'a very strong lady, terribly good fun, and a very womanly woman, her hair white from the first bout of typhoid in Serbia'. Looking back on her life, having lived in Belgrade until the end of World War II and then retired to Suffolk, she could recall the frustrations she recorded on returning to civilian life: 'I cannot attempt to describe what it now felt like, trying to get accustomed to a woman's life and a woman's clothes again; and also to ordinary society after having lived entirely with men for so many years. Turning from a woman to a private soldier was nothing compared with turning back from soldier to ordinary woman.'

Sergeant-Major Flora Sandes in Salonika in 1917, recovering from her wounds and wearing the Order of Karageorge

CHAPTER SEVEN

WAY BEHIND THE FRONT LINE AT HOME

ORLD WAR I saw an intense variety of views set out about the role of women: while Flora Sandes was proving that practical difficulties could be overcome, others were busy touting the strength of women in their domestic stronghold, sending their men to war with uncomplaining determination:

There is only one temperature for the women of the British race, and that is white heat. ... We gentle-nurtured, timid sex did not want the war. It is no pleasure to us to have our homes made desolate and the apple of our eye taken away. We would sooner our loving, positive, rollicking boy stayed at school. We would much prefer to have gone on in our light-hearted way with our amusements and our hobbies. But the bugle call came, and we have hung up the tennis racquet, we've fetched our laddie from school, we've put his cap away, and we have glanced lovingly over his last report which said

Opposite: Recruiting for the Women's Army Auxiliary Corps in Trafalgar Square, London 1918

'Excellent' – we've wrapped them all in a Union Jack and locked them up, to be taken out only after the war to be looked at. . . . We are proud of our men, and they in turn have to be proud of us. If the men fail, Tommy Atkins, the women won't.

Tommy Atkins to the front,
He has gone to bear the brunt.
Shall 'stay-at-homes' do naught but snivel and but sigh?
No, while your eyes are filling
We are and doing, willing
To face the music with you – or to die!

Women are created for the purpose of giving life, and men to take it. Now we are giving it in a double sense.

Seventy-five thousand copies of the pamphlet from which this is taken, entitled 'A Little Mother', were sold in less than a week in 1916.

However, it wasn't such sentiment that finally prompted the government to take the giant step and open up the services to women; the appalling casualty lists told their own tale, and more men were needed at the front. In February 1917 the *Sunderland Daily Echo* ran a headline: 'Women as Substitutes'. The article beneath stated that 'Lt General Sir Neville Macready, the Adjutant-General, has devised a scheme whereby women will be substituted for men wherever possible in the Army, both in France and in England, and to release to the Army numbers of men now employed in clerical and other departments.'

Within weeks, the Women's Army Auxiliary Corps was marching and drilling, as thousands of women responded to the posters for 'cooks, clerks, waitresses, driver-mechanics, and all kinds of domestic workers'. At no point was there the slightest question that the Corps was anything but a support unit; the notion of fighting, of being on the front line in some kind of combat role, never arose. It was not part of the debate about what women could contribute to the war; Russian and Serbian women may have been carrying rifles, but such behaviour was foreign in all its meanings to those involved in the formation of the WAAC – and those being recruited. Emmeline Pankhurst, a veteran of suffragette violence, was advocating that women be employed so that 'clerks and cashiers and men behind the counters' be freed up to become soldiers. Despite her fervency ('Sex has nothing to do with patriotism or with the spirit of service'), she did not advocate that women should take up arms. So the call to the services promoted traditional help, in the form of cooking and cleaning and clerking, with the promise of some technical skills training. There was also the lure of 'good wages, quarters, rations, and uniform'.

Whether the uniform was alluring is open to question; a number of the new recruits, like Miss L. Saunders, a teacher, were unimpressed:

> I was sent to Hastings where women were being issued with the uniform of a coat-frock, army shoes and a hat etc – We disliked them all but realised we now had to obey orders.
>
> The coat-frocks were fawn or khaki-coloured with brown collar and cuffs and much longer than we had been used to wearing – we disliked them on sight – and the hats too, but now we knew were an 'Army' and not an individual. The thick shoes too were clumsy-looking and much thicker than what we had been used to. However, we were keen to help win the war, so we dressed as ordered and realised our feminine ideas on dress were now of no account.

The uniform had had the benefit of some female thoughts from the most senior women brought in to organise the women's services, Mrs Mona Chalmers Watson and Mrs (later Dame) Helen Gwynne-Vaughan: 'Unwisely', said Dame Helen later, 'we thought that breast-pockets would emphasise the female form and decided against them; . . . The skirts were full and considered most daringly short, as they were twelve inches off the ground. At first we had little, tight-fitting khaki caps with khaki crepe de chine veils at the back. Later, they were replaced by round, brown felt hats – known to their detractors as "baby boys" from their resemblance to the hats worn by children.' But there were problems, according to Dame Helen: '. . . the women provided their own underclothes, and, while these were often excellent and usually neat and appropriate, instances occurred when they were in rags or hardly existed at all.' She had encountered the common fact that many women from poor backgrounds wore the very minimum of underclothes – knickers were an upmarket item.

Overall, the idea was that the women should look as military as possible – but the War Department was very wary of giving them traditional ranks and badges. Fleur-de-lis and roses with crossed stalks were deemed suitable, rather than the usual crowns and laurel leaves. 'Regrettable,' was Dame Helen's view of the titles given to officers: 'officials'; 'other ranks' women soldiers were to be 'members' while NCOs became 'forewomen and assistant forewomen'. In France a need arose for some term for the rank and file, the 'private', and Dame Helen recalled: '"Worker" was decided

A government recruiting poster urging women to join the WAAC – mainly for uniformed domestic service

WAAC drivers in
Dieppe, 1917

upon at a conference at GHQ, the suggestion that "amazon" was appropriate being mercifully disregarded', and she added, 'I suspect these titles were given "to keep us in our place".'

And all these women were legally civilians: what had been formed were the Women's Services, and women were not being integrated into the armed forces. Besides, the War Office determinedly referred to them as 'camp-followers'.

Quite a number of the women who joined up had had other wartime jobs, often in factories, and the chance to join 'the army' offered a glamour that had hitherto been lacking; whether they had their dreams fulfilled is doubtful. Olive Taylor, after domestic and munitions work in Lincolnshire, volunteered the moment she saw a poster and was sent to Aldershot:

> When first called on parade while still in civvies, one of our number – a very prim lady – turned up with an open umbrella. She said she had never gone out in the rain without an umbrella. The barracks were very spartan and food poor and there was very little of it.
>
> A sergeant of the Coldstream Guards was awarded the doubtful honour of teaching us to march. I don't suppose he really wanted that position, but he really inspired us with his 'Put some swank into it, girls' and soon he had us smart as a regiment of guards and was quite proud of us. We would do a seven-mile route march during the morning and be given two halves of a potato and a little gravy for lunch, along with a little boiled rice and two stewed prunes, and then be on another long route march, before bulling shoes, buttons, badges and chin-strap ready for the next day.

The pay, for women who'd been lucky to earn £1 a week – or even less – in domestic service seemed reasonable, but it was hardly riches: even the junior officers were only on just over £2 a week. Olive earned a mere 10s, out of which came laundry, breakages, and 'all our underclothes, including even corsets, by hook or by crook – three sets of everything . . . so we could never have a treat'.

However, the mere fact of belonging to something officially recognised as of national importance, and being paid by the government, was a novelty to thousands of women. Hitherto women had usually only been recognised through their family ties, existing as someone's daughter, wife or widow; they still had no vote and they had little connection to officialdom. As for appearing in public in uniform, the sight of lines of women in khaki caused no little amazement. Corrall Smith, an enthusiastic girl who thought her own uniform 'topping material – and looks jolly when worn properly', observed some of her friends drilling in Hyde Park watched by 'two very grandes-dames who were looking on with puzzled faces. After a few moments, one put up her lorgnette and turning to her companion said "What on earth do those creatures in khaki think they are doing?", and her friend replied "Don't know I'm sure, but they are something connected with the Salvation Army" – however this is exceptional and mostly the public are awfully decent and kind.'

Olive Taylor discovered a different attitude during a rare outing from another camp, near Woolwich:

Some of us looked forward to going into Woolwich and perhaps enjoying egg and chips, but we were subject to such insults in Woolwich that we never tried again. Here we learned for the first time that we were regarded as scum and that we had been enlisted for the sexual satisfaction of soldiers. This, after the way we had worked ever so hard, and put up with so much deprivation for our country's sake, was absolutely terrible. We were broken hearted about it and never went into town again. What a treat it would have been to be able to enjoy egg and chips, something some of us had never even tasted.

To add insult to injury, in the military camp there was rigid discipline which prevented casual socialising by Olive and her friends:

'Out of bounds' was three miles away and one was not allowed to speak to a soldier within bounds. This was a very serious offence and repetition of it could get a girl dismissed the service for unsatisfactory conduct. So if a girl became acquainted with a nice soldier she had to run three miles, say 'hello' and run back again. There were some very nice boys among the Irish Guards, but we could never trust a Coldstream Guard. They would even threaten to throw us into the Brookwood Canal if they couldn't have their way with us and they seemed to have only one thought in mind. What did it matter to them if a girl lost her character and ended up in the workhouse with a baby?

WAACs – by now renamed Queen Mary's Army Auxiliary Corps or QMAACs – in the Signals Office at Le Havre, 1918

Moral panic seized the authorities regularly when considering the impact of women in the army. As hundreds were sent across the Channel to work in offices and canteens in France the generals worked themselves into a tizzy, observed by the redoubtable Dame Helen Gwynne-Vaughan, newly appointed Chief Controller overseas.

> I soon discovered that the objection to the employment of women was almost universal. The Services, of all professions, had naturally the least experience of working with women . . . then there was the question of the relationship between the women and the soldiers. At an early conference at GHQ it was agreed that they were bound to make friends and to walk out together. It was better that they should do so openly with the full approval of the authorities than surreptitiously as an exciting adventure. Nevertheless, a general officer protested that 'if these women are coming, we shall have to wire (off) all the woods on the Lines of Communication'. That was more than I could stand, and I answered: 'If you do, sir, you will have a number of enterprising couples climbing over.' The woods remained unwired.

Notwithstanding the fact that the women were putting up with poor rations and very basic accommodation – lack of beds and surfeit of rats seem to have been a common complaint – and working long hours, the general public back home was very open to the suggestion that northern France was heaving with sexual liaisons. *The Times* carried an article casting aspersions, and it reached Aileen Woodroffe at her VAD (Voluntary Aid Detachment) post in No. 30 General Hospital in France:

> I travelled on a tram today with some of the WAAC. They do not do well running about on the loose, not speaking the language, being rather conspicuous and exceedingly stupid and giggly . . .
> The article in *The Times* describing a WAACs camp is really here – quite close; they really are a quaint lot of females, but a tremendous boon and joy to the men stationed about here. It is really rather amusing to see the couples 'roamin' in the gloamin', after 6 o'clock, and having ham and eggs together, what the natives think of the proceedings, I can't imagine, but the fact that it is a recognised thing to have a WAAC friend is no doubt quite helpful, as there really is nothing for these wretched men to do after hours.

After some months, the *Daily Sketch* tried to calm matters down with a measured article: 'One hears wild and varying stories about the relations between the rank and file of the WAACs and regular army. Joining the WAAC isn't like taking the veil or starting on a career of unbounded sky-larking. Army men and Army girls meet on ordinary ground and are friends in a normal above-board fashion as girls and men are friends in civil life.' Perfectly reasonable, but certainly not the stuff that was doing the rounds as common gossip: the whole enterprise was rumoured to be a disaster, with hundreds of women said to have been sent home to give birth to illegitimate babies. The best bit of scuttlebutt was a widely believed story that a soldier had to be posted as a guard outside 'the WAAC Maternity Home'.

Dame Helen tackled head-on the problem of men and women alongside in war, and saw it primarily as something which bothered the public more than the serving personnel. Pregnancies were dealt with in a low-key manner, and sympathetically, with the women being discharged on compassionate grounds; this was despite the background in 1917–18 about which she said that 'the occurrence of pregnancy was a reliable criterion of the "moral" position' – in other words, there was no getting away from the public's judgement that pregnancy indicated how women were conducting themselves, regardless of the circumstances. She saw the association between the women and the troops as 'inevitable' and endeavoured to make it 'ordinary, friendly, fraternal' rather than something that happened by stealth, 'an exciting adventure, stimulating passion':

No doubt the association of war and love is one of the oldest in our make-up and goes back to the roots of the subconscious and the earliest combats of two males for the

The RAF and the WRAF 'associating' on an outing in France, 1918

female. Possibly the unconscious desire to leave offspring when life is to be risked is also a factor. At any rate, it is clear that, in war, the man is more ardent, the woman more vulnerable. Administrators had to be warned to keep a vigilant and kindly eye on these possibilities. It was not, as might at first have been imagined, the pretty and attractive girl who needed their special care. She was accustomed to admirers and already knew the technique. But the older, plainer woman might find it intoxicating to be the cause of competition, and gratitude for this fillip to her self-respect might be her undoing.

Despite the sensible and level-headed approach of Dame Helen, there was still much gossip back in Britain: and she was none too impressed when a committee of five ladies selected by the Ministry of Labour arrived in France to investigate 'immorality'. After much nosing around, they were reduced to producing a report which revealed that the WAAC were 'a healthy, cheerful, self-respecting body of hard-working women, conscious of their position as links in the great chain of the nation's purpose, and zealous in its service'. Anyway, Dame Helen had been brandishing statistics: under three per thousand single women had become pregnant since joining the army. It was a figure considerably lower than in civilian life back home.

Pregnant or not, the women were not intended to be in the front line. However, by 1918 there were frequent air-raids well behind the lines, raising for the first time the spectre of women – other than medical personnel – becoming battlefield casualties. Dame Helen recorded in her diary:

> On the night of 21st–22nd May, Camp II, Abbeville, on the Montreuil road, was hit by the largest bomb that had been used up to that time. So extensive was the crater that the Commander-in-Chief himself came to see it. The huts were blown to pieces, only the mess hut and cookhouse being left. Uniforms were scattered far and wide, some garments landing on the branches of the trees. The women themselves were in open trenches and were none the worse. I was able to be at the camp early and was proud to find that, in spite of their disturbed night, every woman, – how clothed I will not attempt to say – was in her office or cookhouse at the normal time. From that incident arose a tradition of the Corps that, whatever happened, Queen Mary's Army Auxiliary Corps [recently renamed thus – a much-desired seal of royal approval] reported punctually for duty. During the day the area controller issued fresh clothing.

Eight days later an aerial torpedo exploded in a trench, killing eight QMAACs outright; one died later of wounds and six others were injured. There was a funeral with full military honours the next day, aeroplanes flew overhead, and a large number of soldiers and several officers fell in behind the members of the Corps who

followed the gun-carriages. Dame Helen found the press waiting back at HQ 'all wanting a story and prepared to execrate the enemy for killing women': She continued, 'Up to this time the only women of the Army killed in theatres of war had been hospital personnel under the Geneva Convention. It was an entirely new idea that since we were replacing combatants, the enemy was entirely in order in killing us if he could.' However, she had no desire for headlines which concentrated on gender, and impressed on the journalists that in the circumstances the enemy could be excused.

QMAACs among their bombed Nissen huts at Abbeville after the air-raid of 22 May 1918

Back in Aldershot, twenty-year-old Olive Castle was busy being a military waitress:

Mountains of washing-up, and cleaning after every meal, windows and muddy floors to be scrubbed, 500 pairs of army boots in all kinds of weather, every day, four times a day – you can imagine the state the floor was always in. We had no kneeling mats of course (not in the Army!) so we did it all on our hands and knees. We took turns in doing that job, and that was what I was doings at 11.05 am on Nov 11th, 1918, my overall filthy with mud from the scrubbing, when the official wire came through and the Colonel summoned all the cadets on to the parade ground in front of the mess-room for a very important announcement. He quietly told them the news of the signing of the Armistice at 11 o'clock . . . We all tried to 'do our bit' to help in the time of our country's need. Nothing spectacular, perhaps, just jobs which needed to be done at the time.

If the WAACs were well distanced from the traditional image of soldiering, then the women who joined the WRNS were equally far from the life of a sailor. Any girl with traditional aspirations of gadding about piratically on the high seas in war would have got as far as Lowestoft in 1918. Clerks, canteen assistants, storewomen and messengers – no wonder the WRNS eventually acquired the unofficial motto 'Never at Sea'. Ports and harbours were the only water they saw, and there was no intention ever to have them near ships, never mind on them. Superstition, prejudice, and lots of argument about 'skirts and ladders' kept the Wrens ashore.

The Admiralty, immensely amnesiac on the subject of women aboard ship in the preceding centuries, had not even tolerated female civil servants on the outbreak of war. Vera Laughton Mathews, who later commanded the WRNS in World War II, was testily informed in 1914, 'We don't want any petticoats here.' They finally caved in three years later and advertised for 'Women in the Navy . . . the members of this service will wear a distinctive uniform, and the service will be confined to women employed on definite duties directly connected with the Royal Navy.'

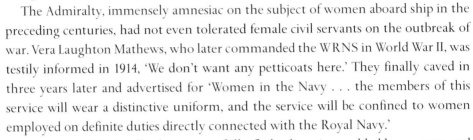

A recruiting poster for the WRNS – 'Mobile' and 'Immobile', although neither category went to sea

Admittedly they were a fully-fledged service, and led by women, and the first senior administrators had had the good sense to argue against the title Women's Auxiliary Naval Corps. However, a large number of them had the rather odd designation of 'Immobiles', meaning that they served in their own home towns; the 'Mobiles' joined the Senior Service not to see the world, but merely to see another part of the British coast, or possibly a 'balloon station'. Here they wore navy blue, their skirts several inches nearer the ground than those of their army colleagues. A sailor's blue and white collar was eventually added because the girls disliked their plain collars, and would insist on borrowing from their navy boyfriends. One small group was trained as wireless telegraphists at the signal school at the Crystal Palace, known as HMS *Victory VI*, where in January 1918 Vera Laughton Mathews, then a young officer, presented herself to the commanding officer. She described him later as having a 'really progressive mind', and, indeed, he was preoccupied with matters which seventy years later the services in the Gulf War had still not resolved, remarking: 'Well, Miss Laughton, you and I are both in the same service and there are certain things which have to be discussed. Now regarding the matter of lavatories . . .'

Just occasionally some of the WRNS worked aboard ships in harbour, their soufflé-like caps emblazoned 'WRNS' rather than the sailors' 'HMS'. But most were as nautical as a fishwife as regards life on the ocean wave. On the other hand, their officers did pull off one small coup, acquiring rather amazing large tricorne hats to

go with their well-tailored suits. Not that this was entirely accidental: there was already a certain distinction between the services, and women who went into the WRNS were regarded as a cut above the WAAC. Class differences, after several years of war, were as distinct as ever, and army recruitment had drawn heavily on working-class women. On the other hand, the WRNS often came from families with a long naval tradition, and soon found themselves wrestling with rules which forbade them from socialising across the ranks with the Royal Navy – whose officers were their brothers, fathers and cousins. Dame Katherine Furse, their first Director, who had years of administrative experience as co-commandant of the Voluntary Aid Detachment, soon sorted out these awkward social hiccups, though she had a keen sense of the need for propriety among her 'gels', recalling with a certain satisfaction in her memoirs that her girls were sometimes referred to as the 'Perfect Ladies' – and also the 'Prigs and Prudes'.

If life on the ocean wave was just a dream for the WRNS, so was the notion of being a magnificent woman in her flying machine. But life in the Women's Royal Air Force at least permitted women to enter the world of 'string-bags', 'pups' and 'moths'. Flying had already garnered its own aura of romance – dashing pilots in fragile biplanes, the freedom and progressiveness of those who were 'air-minded'. When the RAF and the WRAF were created simultaneously, in April 1918, there was a spirit of cooperation in that women were welcomed who, in addition to the usual clerical and storekeeping tasks, would take an interest in what went on behind the propeller.

Wrens were known as 'Perfect Ladies', whether officers in tailored suits and tricorne hats (left) or 'other ranks' in soufflé-shaped caps (above)

When she was about eighty, Mrs P.L. Stephens from Yorkshire recalled her days as one of the first members of the WRAF: 'How good it was to be young at that time,' she said, and remembered leaving munitions work in Lincoln for 'something more exciting':

Looking one day at the notices at the local Labour Exchange, I saw a most unusual one: 'Wanted, female motor-cyclist, for RAF Scampton Aerodrome – apply within'. I promptly did so and the man said 'I'll 'phone the Drome now, so wait'. Quite soon, a Sergeant arrived on a motor cycle with sidecar, and after looking me over said 'Hop in – I'll take you up to the Camp and give you a try-out'. I said 'No, *you* hop in the side-car, and I'll drive you to Scampton'. So, I was signed on, and found myself the only

British Women! — the Royal Air Force needs your help

as CLERKS, WAITRESSES COOKS, experienced MOTOR CYCLISTS & in many other capacities. Full particulars from the nearest EMPLOYMENT EXCHANGE. ENROL AT ONCE IN THE

W·R·A·F· WOMEN'S ROYAL AIR FORCE

girl amongst some few hundred men — attached to the Transport Section. There were five other motor-cyclists, and they did not give me a warm reception — thought I'd be a nuisance, I suppose, and they did *not* speak to me at all for some considerable time. All I said to them was 'Just leave my machine 3764 *alone* and don't take it when your own is out of order — because mine *won't* be!'

. . . No uniform at that stage was provided, so I had to buy some khaki breeches and shirts which I tried to conceal under a rather old and grubby rain-coat! I loved my job – worked hard and was very happy – taking officers to the Station, collecting them from there, delivering goods to Married Quarters, taking the Pay Sergeant to collect cash from the Bank for the men – On Sundays I had to collect the Padre from a near-by village, for Church Parade. I think he was always rather nervous whilst in my care as he usually found other Transport to take him home afterwards.

Sometimes my task was grim – to take the M.O. to a crash within reach of the Aerodrome. Once nothing left save the young Pilot's cap badge – he was very young and a great favourite – I remember the Adjutant broke down and wept when the M.O. told him there was nothing to be done – Scampton was a RAF Training Station and there were many casualties . . .

Once I had to go before the CO on a 'charge'. The charge? Pilots had followed me in their planes, flying very low over the hedges bordering the road on which I was going on duty (no-one in the side-car) into Lincoln, and they waved to me – and I – of course! – waved back. This behaviour had resulted in a cow being killed that cost £20. What had I to say? Nothing. I was a docked a day's pay, and the CO before discharging me remarked 'No further proceedings, on the understanding that you wave to me when next I salute you from my plane.'

A good number of women who joined the WRAF had already served in the WAAC or WRNS and they transferred to the new service. Somehow, the British class system wormed its way into the image of the new services – the WRAF women were considered 'nice', just as the Wrens were 'perfect ladies'; the WAACs, on the other hand, were just 'women'. The nice air force girls got a new uniform, which took an age to be distributed. It finally turned out to be very like the WAACs', but grey-blue. However, at least a tradition had begun of women being involved with actual aircraft, for many worked on the machines, and some were offered flying instruction, giving a boost to what was already significant participation by women in aviation, and eventually leading to some of the first women in the services taking up combat operations towards the end of the twentieth century.

By the end of World War I over a hundred thousand women had been enrolled in these auxiliary bodies, and a vastly greater number had put on the uniforms of the various voluntary organisations. In nearly all instances they had managed their administration themselves, without resorting to having male superiors. They had had a very public role, their dress marking them out as taking part in national affairs, and some had been paid by the state – a novelty at the time. They'd made a significant contribution to breaking the image of frail, dependent women who were frightened by the drums of war.

A class in engine theory for WRAF motor transport drivers, 1918

CHAPTER EIGHT

MUD AND BLOOD

VICTORIAN PRUDERY AND snootiness about nursing had ebbed away as the twentieth century began. Caring for the sick and wounded in war had become acceptable again, with the added imprimatur of the great Nightingale. The FANY and Mrs Stobart's nurses had beaten almost everyone across the Channel on the outbreak of World War I, though there was little appreciation of the horrors they'd face. However, more than an inkling of this soon turned up on the home front.

In my own town of Sunderland 400 miles north of the trenches in Flanders, it arrived by train only weeks after the declaration of hostilities. On to the platforms came the cot cases and the sitting cases – wounded men who were just a fraction of the massive disbursement of casualties nationwide. The first party of one hundred men went to the Royal Infirmary and were immediately subjected to the

Opposite: The Sisters, painting by Edmund Dulac: Land Army member, nurse and munitions worker

ministrations of girls from my old school, who were already knitting socks and making shirts for the Durham Light Infantry. 'Some comforts and luxuries not provided by the hospital regime' were delivered. Senior girls were sent to help in the Red Cross Auxiliary Hospitals and crosses of flowers were taken to the graves of two Canadians and an Australian who died in the Infirmary.

The girls of the Church Schools Company embodied the determination and patriotism that flamed up in 1914, exhorted by their redoubtable headmistress, Miss Ethel M. Ironside, late of Cheltenham Ladies' College. Three months into the war she wrote that the girls were to pray that God would defend the right, and that when peace came the school would have nothing to look back upon of which it need be ashamed . . . and to keep perfectly serene and full of hope. Women at home, she continued, must make the men in the services feel that they realised 'the glorious stock from which they are sprung, a breed which through all the ages had stood for valour and for courage that laughs at difficulties'. Later, for good measure, she named the school houses after Royal Navy ships – HMS *Tiger*, *Panther*, *Swift* and *Drake*.

None of this was in any way exceptional; Sunderland was typical of the phenomenal reaction to the advent of war. The huge response to the need for men to be nursed and cared for was manifested immediately, and ranged from teenagers doing needlework at War Hospital Supply Depots in County Durham to the departure of the first QAs for France a mere fortnight after the declaration of war.

The first ship which crossed the Channel in the vanguard of the British Expeditionary Force also carried Maud McCarthy, matron-in-chief to the British armies in France. Australian-born, she'd already served in South Africa during the Boer War, and ahead of her were five years running a nursing operation that extended south to the Mediterranean, sustaining a reputation that 'defeat was unknown to her'.

But at a time when few women, with the exception of the moneyed upper class, travelled abroad, most of those QA sisters who crammed into the first troop trains would not have had the slightest idea where they would eventually serve. World War I saw hospitals and casualty clearing stations in Egypt and Gaza and Jerusalem; in Basra and Baghdad in Iraq (then Mesopotamia); all through Serbia and Macedonia and in Sofia, Bulgaria. In Dar-es-Salaam – capital of the former German East Africa – with mosquito boots, veils, thick puttees and quinine essential, and in Tbilisi in the Caucasus. And on the hospital ship *Kalyan* anchored in sub-Arctic waters off Archangel, with sheepskin coats, serge gloves and fur ear-muffs very necessary. The scale of operations was astounding, as were the challenges confronting women brought up in late Victorian and Edwardian society. Sybil Harry wrote from the Salles Militaires Hospice Unité:

Saumur 22/10/14

It would amuse you to see some of the improvised utensils in the wards – I don't think the hospital has more than 5 small basins for the 200 wounded! As to a bucket it is unheard of, and we use anything from teapots to dustbins. Hot water is as scarce as whisky, and one only gets about I pint daily, so the cleaning has to be done cold. There is no installed hot water system or lights of any sort. The water is heated on gas rings, and the wards by tiny oil lamps I am sure were used by Henri II who lies buried near here.

When the operations are after dark, it is a perilous procedure to get your case down a flight of stairs & thro 3 large wards, with a match. I have sworn at the men until I have got an oil lamp from the office, which is now placed on the stairs. I do so long for some reliable bearers. These are awful, & so rough. When they are tired, they dump the stretcher on the ground, regardless of place, and sit on the side. The orderlies are soldiers too mad or too bad to fight, so their capabilities are what you would expect. They never cease smoking, they shave not, neither do they wash, & their garments are anything to be found. We have just trained one he should not expectorate *on the floor*, but I know he does it the minute we leave the ward. All these little things provide amusement but are most irritating at the end of a worrying day, however there is a war on and one must not grumble. Visitors to the Cardiff Hospital cannot get an idea what war is really – if I told you some of the things that come in here, you would be horrified and it's just as well that England has not seen yet these remains of what were bright young men brought in to die in a few dreadful hours.

The military nurses were in the vanguard in the first few weeks; large numbers from the Territorial Reserve followed. So did a number of individuals who were utterly convinced they were going to do good, never mind their lack of qualifications, permission or any knowledge of bed-pans. Most were rather grand and, contrary to the scepticism of the officials, proved themselves to be a very tough bit of the upper crust. Foremost, in all senses of the word, was Millicent, Dowager Duchess of Sutherland and daughter of the 4th Earl of Rosslyn, who spent several weeks intimidating army officers – mainly German – as the British Expeditionary Force ran into serious trouble and trench-lines began to define the battlefield. A former Victorian society beauty, also a published poet and a keen rider to hounds, Millicent was resourceful and flamboyant. She crossed the Channel, clad in elegant cap with the red cross prominent on her cape, and descended on the unsuspecting front lines – only to find herself under bombardment and on the wrong side. Totally unflustered, she marshalled her team of eight nurses and a surgeon, treated wounded French and Belgian soldiers in Namur while the Germans looked on

flummoxed, and then got everyone safely back to England by dint of doughty common sense and all the social clout she could muster. The authorities were embarrassed, but their grumbling came to nought as Her Grace raised money, collected her supporters, and headed back to Calais to run one of the best Red Cross hospitals throughout the war. She was only outdone in style by the younger and prettier Duchess of Westminster, who ran a smaller hospital at Le Touquet. Not content with touring the wards with her wolfhound in tow, she and her lady helpers used to greet the wounded on their stretchers having donned tiara and evening dress – the duchess was a firm believer in positive morale-building. (Her hospital made a specific contribution to medical history in the war, for it gave the post of registrar to Charles Myers, a former editor of the *British Journal of Psychology*; he'd been told he was too old to volunteer, so he arrived to be taken on by the duchess. However, as casualties mounted he was commissioned, and took on specialist work in other hospitals where he coined the term 'shell shock'.)

Back in Britain, there was a host of women volunteering; several thousand of them belonged to the Voluntary Aid Detachment, the VADs who'd been trained by the Red Cross and St John Ambulance. In blue dresses – or grey for St John – with a prominent red cross on their starched white aprons, these middle- and upper-class girls who were usually occupied with tea-parties and visiting and were now oh-so-keen to 'do their bit' flocked to local hospitals and embarkation ports; initially, however, both prejudice and the feeling that the war would be brief left the War Office unconcerned about using them.

Just two years earlier there were only 553 qualified women doctors in Britain, and they'd been traditionally corralled into looking after women and children. Medical

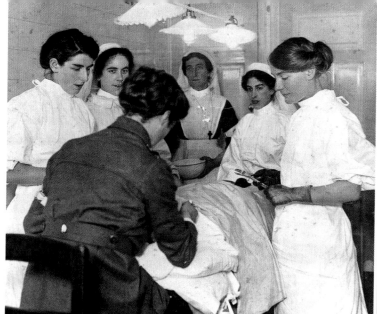

schools were bastions of prejudice, so it was not surprising that these educated and intelligent women who'd survived pompous surgeons and hostile professors were made of the right stuff when it came to war. They also knew that they'd be wasting their time in taking on the War Office. Dr Louisa Garrett Anderson and Dr Flora Murray went straight to the French Embassy in London, were not properly understood because of their rusty grasp of the language, and breathtakingly contrived to head for the Hôtel Claridge in Paris four weeks later as the Women's Hospital Corps. They were seen off by Louisa's mother, Elizabeth Garrett Anderson, who must have felt such pride to see her daughter as chief surgeon leading a trained team, dressed in green-grey uniforms with matching hat, back to the city where, in 1865, she'd become the first British woman to qualify as a doctor. Had she been twenty years younger, she said, she'd have led them herself.

Up in Edinburgh, Dr Elsie Inglis had offered to supply qualified women doctors and nurses but been turned away by the War Office with the cutting remark: 'My good lady, go home and sit still.' She did no such thing, and started raising funds to set up her own operation, the Scottish Women's Hospitals. A seasoned campaigner, Dr Inglis had been involved in the suffrage movement and was aware of the power of publicity; she'd already established two hospitals in Edinburgh before the war, and was a born organiser. Dr Inglis reckoned that the only way to make proper use of women's skills was to create hospital units staffed entirely by them, giving women the chance of performing surgery – and to offer these units to other governments (the British, even though mid-war they bowed to the inevitable and used women doctors, still withheld officer status and refused to employ them on the front line). She was incredibly successful, and though hers was only one amongst many women-

Women doctors had to overcome huge prejudice. Dr Flora Murray (above left, seated) administering chloroform to a wounded soldier, with Dr Louisa Garrett Anderson on her right, Paris, 1914.

Above right: *Dr Elsie Inglis, seen here in her Scottish Women's Hospitals uniform of 'Hodden grey', operated in the Balkans*

Above: A VAD
Motor Driver
(detail), can in hand,
painting by
Gilbert Rogers

Right: St John's
Ambulance nurses
waiting in Etaples to
meet Queen Mary,
1917

only outfits it was the largest and best known, sending over a thousand women abroad.

At the Abbaye de Royaumont in France, a deserted Gothic fright and home to a lot of bats, her organisation soon set up well-equipped wards, with many of the two hundred beds individually sponsored: my local newspaper, the *Sunderland Daily Echo*, received regular reports on the Abbey, which contained 'a Sunderland bed in the Millicent Fawcett Ward'. Miss Marjorie Starr wrote home to Canada of her life there as a VAD in 1915:

Monday 13th September: Nothing different today. Same old rush, two operations. We had a great old time with one poor man this morning. He has all the tendons and nerves of his arm mixed up, and had them operated on again, so they had to be dressed, and the agony was so terrible they gave him chloroform, and it took 6 of us to hold him, he struggled so when he was going under. I had to hold the arm for the dressing and got well sprinkled with blood and pus, as he was very septic and thought he was charging the Germans under chloroform, and didn't he yell and use bad language.

Marjorie was one of many diarists who described what had become routine within a few weeks, but which was an extraordinary situation – a meeting of the commonplace and the tragic every day.

22nd October: We had two deaths in the night, the poor man who had the wound in his brain, and one of the men from my ward, who had also a head wound and was doing so well that he was soon to be allowed up. When yesterday morning he had some sort of fit, and they discovered an abscess on the brain: he went quite mad, and died at midnight. . . . Miller being on night duty had to help carry the body to the Chapel. She says it was rather a gruesome sight. Miss Duncan, the Matron, went first down three flights of steps and through the moonlit cloisters, carrying a lantern, and these three girls carrying a stretcher, draped in a sheet, and a piece of paper pinned on his chest with his name, aged 19, and then the names of the witnesses, who were there when he died. Miss Ivers, the Surgeon, a sister and Richmond, the girl who was an actress with Tree, and played Columbine: one would never take her for an Actress now. I am writing this in a room they have given us for sitting-room. It has a fire-place, and we have a log fire, but at present it is ungetable at, as three rather peculiar girls are sitting round the fire so no one can get a bit of it, but I am not cold, so I don't care. One is smoking a pipe, a pretty young girl, so you can imagine the style. I suppose they are suffragettes. There goes the horn, more wounded arriving.

CORSETS TO CAMOUFLAGE

Marjorie was constantly plagued by aching feet, cold, fleas, mud and loud-snoring colleagues – and gunfire. But she and many of the others were enterprising on their few days off, usually one a month. Sometimes they explored quiet areas of the trenches, or got a train to Paris:

> *7th December*: I got permission to wear my own clothes after a good deal of hemming and hawing on the Administrator's part, one gets thoroughly sick of going about as a Scottish Woman in these ridiculous grey coats, so I felt like a lady again, all but my hands, which simply refuse to look respectable. We always wear uniform as we travel on free tickets, and it saves argument, but I got along alright. . . . We went to dinner at an Italian restaurant, and on to the Opera – Walking about the Foyer and watching the people, I couldn't believe Royaumont was a reality, and that I was a Scottish Woman nursing wounded in an ancient Abbey, where everything is primitive.

There seems to have been no question that any woman who set off to serve abroad would not wear some kind of uniform. It gave status in a world where women were still barred from many professional positions, and here they were working among the military, where rank mattered. It also afforded some protection, and there are numerous diaries and letters which mention with relief that 'the sight of our red crosses' caused men to treat the women with respect. It also differentiated eventually between units such as the Almeric Paget Military Massage Corps and the Hackett-Lowther Ambulance Unit and the First Aid Nursing Yeomanry and a score of similar undertakings. The number of organisations seems bewildering – but they grew out of the terrible realisation that the war was unlike anything hitherto experienced. Looking at the film taken of nurses among the chaos of hospital trains unloading and the urgent crowds of stretcher-bearers, it's blindingly obvious that the cloud of white veils would have had an arresting effect. The men's world was relentlessly dirt-caked and drab; the Flanders earth had seen the last of the gaudily dressed soldier, as the French quickly realised that scarlet trousers upped the casualty numbers. All the nursing uniforms – and there was a striking array of variations on the Nightingale theme – retained the air of the religious allied with the military dedication needed to keep collars and cuffs spotless and aprons starched.

To those who crossed the Channel to nurse in the first few months of the war – eager, sometimes excited, full of ideals – there was a terrifying meeting with reality within hours of setting foot on French soil. Despite the army's strictures that the majority of women should be stationed well away from the front lines, the smashed and mangled results of trench warfare came surging into the casualty clearing stations and the base hospitals. The sheer numbers had never before been anticipated. The railway line which took each new batch of troops forward saw the ambulance train waiting its turn to trundle slowly to the rear, crammed with every kind of injury.

And such ambulance trains were also targets, despite their red cross markings. As early as November 1914, while the casualties of the First Battle of Ypres were being loaded, shells burst over the station. The train windows blew in and some coaches were damaged. The official report on the incident states: 'Although the four Nursing Sisters in charge perfectly well realised that the next shell might mean the complete wreck of the train and station, they remained calm and collected, asked for orders, and continued dressing and attending to the wounded already received in the train.'

Back at the base hospitals, the sisters and the VADs faced the tide of mud and blood and lived in spartan conditions. In April 1916 the *Lady* magazine carried a description of the previous winter from a young woman who had served for a considerable time 'Somewhere in France':

> The snow delighted the New Zealand nurses – but 'nous autres', we all shivered in our warmest woollies, packed them tight in on us like the leaves of a cabbage. 'Positively I shall have to peel myself tonight' vowed one girl. And indeed, it takes a great many woollen garments to replace the furs and fur coats to which we have accustomed ourselves within the last few years. Finally, one gets into one's clothes, laces up one's service boots – how long they are! – with clumsy chilblained fingers, or thrusts and stamps one's feet into gumboots, having first donned three pairs of stockings, one pair of woolly 'slip-ons', or a pair of fleecy soles, and probably padded cotton or cyanide wool round the toes. Then with a jersey, a mackintosh, and a sou'wester over one's uniform, out into the snow to the messroom, with no path yet made. It is one of the few times one pauses to remember that one is on 'active service'.
>
> Going to bed is a prodigious rite and ceremony. After a bath in the camp bath, which seems to possess a centre of gravity more elusive than mercury, one dons pyjamas, cholera belt, pneumonia jacket, bed socks, and bed stockings as long as a Father Christmas's, and then piles on the bed travelling rug, dressing gown, and fur coat. Even in the bed the trials of active service do not end on occasion. We found one girl lying in bed the other night with her umbrella up. The snow had melted and was trickling though the tent, and she was too tried to trouble about having matters righted. 'I'm imagining it is a garden parasol, and I'm in a hammock, and it's June.'

The fur coats suggest a pre-war familiarity with comfort, and the war had proved irresistible to women with education and the ambition to break away from conventional society. Snobbery and snide remarks bubbled around the nursing tents, as the professionally trained nurses – who earned an absolute pittance after years of training – found themselves next to the eager-beaver volunteers. A lot of noses were put out of joint under the starched veils, and there was regular correspondence about correct titles – the amateur VADs being ticked off for responding to calls of 'Sister' or 'Nurse' from the unknowing patients. And there were differences to be observed between the various uniforms alongside the nursing units, as Miss Aileen Woodroffe VAD observed in letters home to her mother: 'Out here you simply couldn't be a WAAC unless you purposed to "walk out with a Tommy" – and all that implies – heaven alone knows the females one has to deal with are quaint enough and quite an unexplored species, but it is still not particularly pleasant to put the VADs on an equality with WAACs. . . . Ye gods, what a snob I become!'

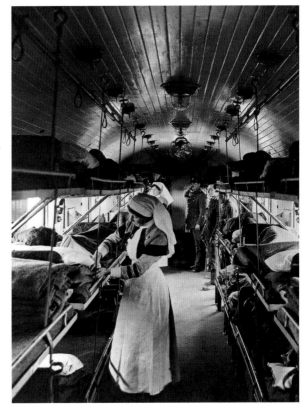

Interior of a ward on a British ambulance train near Doullens, 1918

What was not in question, though, was the way the women rose to the occasion and sustained their devotion to duty. Thousands of words in letters and diaries describing individual experience in the presence of grisly amputations, suppurating gas gangrene wounds and hideously disfigured faces convey a breathtaking patience and a humbling display of care and compassion. From a world of tennis parties and tedious small-talk, respectability and the pursuit of a suitable marriage, thousands of women proved quietly and doggedly that they could see the worst of war and deal with it, up to their armpits in pus and blood, their long skirts bordered with mud and their corsets a snug refuge for lice.

Officially, they were not in the front line, but trains and ambulance ships were attacked and hospitals were shelled. Senior military sisters were moved up the line to casualty clearing stations as the horrors of the battle of the Somme erupted. And there were exceptional people who decided that the best place for their skills was virtually in the front line.

Elsie Knocker was an experienced nurse who had no truck with the do-gooding enthusiasts who held tea-parties dressed in fetching nurse-ish frocks while dreaming about being Ministering Angels at the Front. She was also a driver and a mechanic – and had joined the Women's Emergency Corps in London as a despatch rider. There she met eighteen-year-old Mairi Chisholm, an upper-class Scot whose hobby had been motor-cycling; such behaviour was just about excused as 'adventurous' or 'rather racy', and it was no surprise that they fell in with an equally unconventional man, Dr Hector Munro. He was a gung-ho supporter of the feminist movement — much to the curiosity of the women who joined his Ambulance Unit. Under the auspices of the Belgian Red Cross — the War Office and the British, French and American Red Cross having already said No to Dr Munro, no surprise there — their small party set up behind the lines in Belgium.

Unsurprisingly, they didn't look like conventional volunteers — Elsie and Mairi paid for their own outfits of khaki overcoats, riding breeches and high lace-up riding boots, thereby causing consternation at Victoria Station in London. The rest of the party were 'slightly scandalised — one could see it in their furtive glances . . . it was difficult for these gentle ladies, who wore correct costumes and picture hats, to think there could really be any need for stepping right outside the conventional lines, at all events until they got to the war zone'. When they actually reached the war zone, they swapped easily between nurses' veils and tin helmets.

It took a very short time for Elsie Knocker to realise that the appalling trip back from the front lines, over rutted tracks, fields and sometimes under fire, took a toll of the wounded. She thought an 'Advanced Dressing Station' was needed, and set about presenting her idea to the French senior officer. Admiral Ronarc'h was hugely unimpressed:

> He had never heard anything so absurd. Surely I knew that women were not allowed in the trenches? They had to be at least three miles behind the lines. If I chose to disobey orders I could expect no assistance, and that meant no rations and no medical supplies. The Admiral stated firmly, almost with relish, that because I was a woman (and, oh, how utterly disparaging those two words *une femme*, can sound) I could not possibly stand the strain of Front-line life.

Mrs Knocker, mother of a son, was unfazed, and informed the admiral that because she was a woman she could stand strain and hardship, recalling later that she only just prevented herself from asking him if he'd ever heard of childbirth. With Mairi Chisholm she headed for the village of Pervyse, where they set up a first-aid post in the cellar of a part-ruined building. Their efforts at first attracted amusement and they were called *'Les folles Anglaises'*, but as the months went by, and they remained steadfastly in place despite being under shell-fire, their fame grew. They were virtually the only women in the area — though they encountered kindred spirits in the Polish-French scientist Marie Curie and her daughter, who were driving mobile 'radiological cars' through the battle zones to set up early X-ray posts.

For over three years the 'Women of Pervyse' lived and worked alongside the privations of the fighting forces, until a gas attack in 1918 destroyed their dug-out, nearly suffocating them, and they had to be evacuated. There are many photographs of them, for their renown was considerable, but the idea of women in the front line was still considered, above all else, a brave eccentricity. Elsie Knocker – by now married to a Belgian pilot, Baron T'Serclaes – regretted having to leave: 'I vaguely remember being carried to an ambulance. The driver was saying, "For Christ's sake

Elsie Knocker (left) and Mairi Chisholm (right) with Belgian solders in Pervyse, 1917

hurry"; he wanted to get out of Pervyse and its shells. That is my last memory of the village where I had spent three and a half fantastic years.'

During this time, but far from Belgium, the exploits of the Scottish Women's Hospitals were earning gratitude and praise: they were a formidable organisation. Their thousand women went as doctors, nurses, ambulance drivers, cooks, relief workers and orderlies to Russia, Romania, Serbia, Macedonia, Corsica, Malta and France. The Prefect of Constanta in Romania, who saw their work in his country, commented, 'It is extraordinary how these women endure hardship; they refuse help and carry the wounded themselves. They work like navvies. No wonder England is a great country if the women are like that.'

The Little Grey Partridges was a fond name for these intrepid women in their 'Hodden grey' uniforms with tartan-and-thistle embellishments; in reality, they needed to be tough as old turkeys. The rigours of the campaigns in Romania and Serbia received less attention than the horrors of France and Belgium; indeed, the complicated and ferocious events in the Balkans only earn the term 'side-show' in many historical accounts. Serbia was the small country which had found itself centre stage after the assassination of the Archduke Franz Ferdinand in 1914. A year later, despite being allied with Russia, Britain, France and Romania, it was attacked by the Germans, Austrians and Bulgarians. Short of weapons and ammunition, retreating on two fronts, the Serbian army made for the snowy Albanian mountains towards the Adriatic. It was a desperate situation involving over two hundred thousand soldiers and civilians, including thirty thousand boys under military age; there was panic and privation, the terrain was remote and unforgiving, but the hospital units elected to go with the refugees, testing themselves to the utmost. The very presence of respectable women working independently caused the peasants and soldiers no

'Little Grey Partridges' preparing food at the Scottish Women's Hospitals HQ at Ostrovo in Romania

little amazement, and the Romanian children were apparently fascinated by the stockings which lurked beneath the long skirts. Pure stamina was needed, as the units packed their equipment into any available transport and loaded on the wounded, to head across rough fields in the rear of the retreating army. Katharine Hodges – who was later to visit the Death Battalion in Russia – was attached to the First Serbian Unit as it scrambled through a landscape of burning towns and oil wells and chaotic villages:

> That village was pandemonium all night, guns, guns, guns crashing and Roumanian, Russian and Serbian troops all mixed up in hopeless confusion in the retreat, not knowing where to go or what to do.
>
> At 4 a.m. we started off again, and from then until we got here it was *Hell*. Imagine to yourself an enormous stretch of country like the back of the Downs, only gigantic, and through the centre of it one not very wide or good main road, running to the River Danube and the Frontier, and from *every* direction on this plain as far as you can see, behind and before and all around, streams and streams of carts and horses and women, men, children, herds of cattle and sheep, soldiers, guns, bullock wagons, every conceivable thing, and *all* converging on this one road!
>
> A nation in retreat and only *one* road. The wretched peasants in rough carts made of a few planks roped together, and on them all their worldly goods; furniture, pigs, geese and children all huddled together. Old women and young with babies in their arms trudging along beside them. There were five or six carts deep across the road, we had

awful difficulty in moving at all and every yard we were beseeched to take people. We couldn't, we had wounded with us in most cars and the others were full up with stores, petrol etc. Every hundred yards or so you would see a tragic group of wailing women over one of the wretched carts which had broken, and there were all the things they possessed fallen in the mud and ditch, being trampled on by the passing crowd. It was dreadful.

And then about 10 a.m. a rumour spread that Bulgarian cavalry were coming over the hills at our back, and then panic seized the poor wretches. The soldiers and their wagons whipped up their horses and drove furiously on over everything and everyone. All the people began to *scream* and *scream* and run for their lives . . .

Miss Hodges was later awarded the Russian Orders of St George and St Stanislas, and the Croix de Guerre for her work in France as an ambulance driver. Two decades later, she drove ambulances in the London Blitz.

The letters home from these women are observant and unfailingly cheerful, a testament to their resilient attitude, as they muddled along in various languages and came to grips with different cultures; their work in Kragujevac in Serbia, led by Dr Eleanor Saltau, was a tenacious daily battle as this letter sent by a member of staff in January 1915 testifies:

Patients were sent to us in batches until our wards were full, and we still get them at intervals when we discharge convalescents . . . They come to us in a terrible condition, having had absolutely no nursing. You can imagine from this, perhaps, what the hospitals are like. It is really not the Serbians' fault. The whole country is one immense hospital – doctors, Serbs, and prisoners alike work all day merely to get the dressings done, and the drugs given. There is no attempt at nursing – no Serbian women are trained for it, and they have become apathetic during their three wars [the present one and the two Balkan Wars of 1912–13]. Many are refugees struggling to keep some sort of house together. . . . You must realise, too, that the patients are no slum dwellers, but hate dirt and this utter discomfort. They are splendid men, magnificent when they are dying of fever, but it is a most dreadful waste of fine human beings. . . . Hundreds and hundred of nurses and doctors are needed for Serbia, but especially nurses . . . You see, we are in a very sad country, but it is the pluckiest country in Europe, without exception.

Another letter from this time confirms:

There are quite a number of hospitals in the town, one of them being reserved for fever cases, of which there are a great many. There is a lady doctor working there, Dr Ross, a native of Tain. She has 6 wards to look after, and no nurse, only orderlies . . .

The language question is rather complicated. In the whole company there are three Serbian grammars and several dictionaries, Serbian–German. Nobody has time to study seriously, so it just means that we pick up a few words as we go along. An interview with a laundress usually involves four people. The Matron speaks English, the laundress Serbian, I come in with German and the kitchen maid with German and Serbian. I have been called upon to act as interpreter for the X-ray operator, who knows only a little German. At first, the place was a veritable Tower of Babel.

The ability to take life in one's stride shines through the letters and diaries. On encountering fellow countrywomen engaged in unusual exploits there was no surprise expressed. In September 1916, Ishobel Ross of the Scottish Women's Hospitals recorded in her diary: 'Colonel Vassovitch came into the camp with an Englishwoman dressed in the uniform of the Serbian army. Her name is Flora Sandes. She is quite tall with brown eyes and a strong, yet pretty face. She is a sergeant in the 4th Company and talked to us for a long time about her experiences, and the fierce fighting she and the men of her company have had to face. We felt so proud of her and her bravery.'

Like Florence Nightingale before her, Elsie Inglis and her staff found themselves involved as much with drains as with dispensing drugs. Wrestling with sanitation – or the lack of it where hospitals were concerned – and instilling basic hygiene were essential if the staff were to survive, never mind the patients. A sister in the fever hospital wrote:

Our costume in the wards was hardly that of the stereotyped English nurse, with cap and apron and stiff collar, and our friends would not have recognised us. Instead of the usual uniform and apron, we wore a white cotton combination garment, with the ends tucked into high leather riding boots. Over this, for the sake of appearance, an overall was worn, and our hair was entirely covered with a tight-fitting cap. Round neck and arms we wore bandages soaked in camphor oil, and our boots were smeared with the same, so that no encouragement was given to the little insect by which typhus is spread.

However, when not organising the emptying of cesspits Dr Inglis was able to indulge in surgery – and on adult males. This was an absolute treat for a female doctor in 1915, and something which would still have brought about apoplexy in her former superiors in Scotland.

The war in the Balkans was unforgiving and involved appalling shifts of population and fighting units. Wherever possible the volunteer medical units brought stability and a determination to work with whomsoever presented themselves – Serbs and Turks and Austrians, Bulgarians and Romanians and Russians. However, the units were at times forced to retreat as the fighting engulfed them, and Elsie herself spent time as a prisoner of war, treating Serb POWs under the German occupation.

Her resolutely Victorian Scots background showed itself in a determined discipline, and occasionally in slightly prissy attitudes to her unit members. When she heard members of her transport units swearing she called it 'disgusting and disagreeable', adding that it was an impertinence that she should approve of language she wouldn't 'tolerate in a coster'.

The ability to drive was a passport to female usefulness in World War I, but one which tended to be confined to women from affluent families. Even so, faced with the jalopies and trucks and converted bakers' vans that were pressed into service as ambulances everywhere, their drivers not only mastered their gearboxes but usually got to grips with the rest of the engine – for skilled motor mechanics were not in abundant supply.

Gertrude Holland drove for various units in Belgium and France before going to Serbia, where she worked with the independent unit run by Mabel Stobart. Mabel had seven doctors and ten nurses, and they were gaining a reputation for tenacious determination. During the nightmare retreat from Serbia Mabel herself, fifty-three years old, spent eighteen hours a day on horseback and recalled: 'Whichever way you looked, oxen, horses, and human beings were struggling, and rolling and stumbling, all day long in the ice and snow.' Gertrude witnessed the same wretched retreat:

The founder (in 1907) of the Women's Sick and Wounded Convoy Corps, Mabel Annie Stobart

An awful blizzard began to blow. All day we laboured on & on, slipping & slithering on the icy paths. When night came, we were only half way up the mountain, & the wet and misery was awful, too awful to find words to explain. This terrible suffering made children of us all again. We cowered together, holding each other's hands through the long dark bitter night. The next morning at 8.30 we started off again, thank goodness the blizzard had stopped for a while, & this day was the first of the awful experiences & sights that we became quite accustomed to for the rest of the trek. Dead horses, ponies & donkeys lay by the side of paths and at first I could not imagine as the poor beasts had merely died of starvation and cold, why they should be so cut about, but presently the problem was solved. Often the snow was stained red with the blood of these poor beasts and from as yet warm bodies, the prisoners, Bulgarians, Austrians and Germans who were in front of us, cut chunks of flesh and ate it raw and

Mrs Stobart, then in
her fifties, leading a
column during the
Serbian retreat in
1915

warm. These prisoners were a pitiable sight, they were no longer men at all, but dumb and driven animals and they too fell by the roadside dying from exhaustion & hunger, & their comrades would strip off clothes even before life had really left their poor shrunken frames. It was a common sight to see hands & feet protruding from the snow drifts – the feet never had shoes or boots on – they were far too valuable to be left there. Oh! It was awful, day after day & night after night the same.

One most pathetic sight I saw. It was a Serbian mother staggering along beneath the weight of a highly coloured cradle which was strapped to her back across her shoulders, its occupant, an infant of a few months was feebly wailing. On either side of her stumbled a wee child, not more than five & six keeping up a perpetual cry of 'Leibes – Leibes' (bread – bread). At her breast she clutched a yet smaller child two years or so. Not a particle of food had she with her – not a single bundle of any kind, & there she was, struggling along hoping to reach shelter before the night overtook her, hoping also to get food there too.

The propaganda films of fluttering-veiled sisters and the fond imaginings of many who believed nursing to be a cool hand on a fevered brow held sway with many at home. But as the casualty lists lengthened, and the medical women returned to raise further funds through public lectures, the reality was there – if you cared to address it.

Women such as Elsie Inglis were front-page news when they came home from the front. And in November 1917 a great welcome was being prepared for her in London as she headed back from Bessarabia (present-day Moldova), skirting a Moscow in the grip of revolution and finally taking ship from Archangel to Newcastle. However she had known for over a year, perhaps much longer, that she had cancer. She died in the Station Hotel in Newcastle and the nation mourned as her body lay in state in St

Giles' Cathedral in Edinburgh. One tribute read: 'In Scotland they made her a doctor, in Serbia we would have made her a saint.'

Whether everyone grasped what had been demanded of these women – and how they had responded – is a moot point. General recognition was coming in one respect, however. Just before she left the Balkans, Elsie learned that the bill granting women the vote (though only women over the age of thirty) had passed its second reading in the House of Commons. But she wasn't hugely impressed with the idea that it was women's work in the war which had brought this about: 'Where do they think the world would have been without women's work all these ages?'

Nevertheless, there was plenty of evidence of the remarkable work which had been undertaken, in which the doctors and nurses and volunteer auxiliaries had shown that extra dimension of compassion. Even while the war was on, books and pamphlets and articles were published, vivid and factual. Sometimes the words tumble out across the page with an 'oops, there I go again' schoolgirl innocence, but the facts and statistics which eventually left both sides horrified by the carnage were not ignored by the keen young volunteers. Although a sturdy patriotism informs many letters with an enthusiasm which strikes an unfamiliar note today, it was rare that the women omitted their feelings on seeing so many suffer. And some of the women were seasoned campaigners for the vote, experienced in the cool assessment of a campaign, and much more aware of how institutions functioned than were most of their middle-class peer group.

Meanwhile the debate continued about women's rights, for those who were nursing were still very definitely seen in the 'voluntary' sector of work, and even the military nurses were not actually part of the forces. Many chafed under the 'social discipline' that went with the military orders. Sisters and VADs had all manner of restrictions put on their fraternisation with men. Regardless of their intimate dealings with every aspect of the wounded, the notion that they should have any dealings – however innocent – with healthy and eligible men was thought totally inappropriate. Matrons behaved like Victorian headmistresses and kept a sharp eye on any skirts being shortened – back home the suggestion that cutting a few inches off hems to save on material would help the war effort failed to make any headway in France; ankles were not to be seen, and mud was brushed off nightly. Being posted among hundreds of thousands of men was no free ticket to the marriage market. Not for nothing were women's uniforms a reminder of nun-like qualities.

Even though some of the nursing was carried out within range of enemy fire, and the various independent hospital units were often swept up in moving front lines, the general view was that the world of heroism belonged to the men – until the Germans made a major propaganda mistake. The rules of war were clear to both sides: aid to the enemy has the most severe consequences. However, shooting a country parson's daughter dressed in her dark blue nurse's uniform with a starched white cap broke unwritten rules.

Nurse Edith Cavell, a woman of strong Christian principles who believed that 'Patriotism is not enough'

Edith Cavell had come to nursing at the age of thirty, having trodden the traditional root of the genteelly poor Victorian daughter of the manse. She had had a reasonable education and then taken several posts as a governess. After a holiday in Austria and Bavaria she came home enthusing about a hospital she'd seen, and, having nursed her father through an illness, she began training at the London Hospital in 1896. On qualifying, she went immediately to Maidstone in Kent to deal with an epidemic of typhoid fever which had struck nearly two thousand people; only 132 died and she was awarded the Maidstone Typhoid Epidemic Medal – the only medal she ever received from her country. Work in some of the tougher London hospitals followed, including the Poor Law Institution for Destitutes at St Pancras. She'd spent some time in Belgium as a governess, and in 1907 accepted an invitation to set up a training school on the outskirts of Brussels to provide the country with Nightingale-style nurses, as distinct from the religious sisters who'd hitherto provided nursing care.

The prejudices which Miss Nightingale had met fifty years earlier were alive and thriving in Brussels. 'The old idea that it is a disgrace for women to work is still held in Belgium and women of good birth and education still think they lose caste by earning their own living,' Edith wrote, and persevered in the face of her nurses' newly designed (by her) blue dresses and white aprons being pelted with mud by disapproving Belgians. But the school unexpectedly received that classic stamp of public approval when the Queen of the Belgians broke her arm and one of Miss Cavell's nurses was despatched to the palace. By the time the war was approaching her techniques and influence had spread throughout the country, giving it a firm foundation of secular modern nursing.

Although she was at home in Norfolk visiting her mother when war was declared, she did not hesitate to return. Her hospital – having dispensed with the services of Dutch and German nurses on the outbreak of war – came under Red Cross administration and treated German soldiers equally with Belgians. In the autumn of 1914, in the debacle and confusion following the battle of Mons, many men were cut off from their units and two British soldiers arriving in Brussels asked her for help. Only one was wounded, and the assistance they were seeking went well beyond nursing convention. They were both hidden, then helped to escape to neutral Holland.

Edith had strong Christian principles and addressed problems of loyalty and law with decisiveness. She saw soldiers as hunted men in danger – and believed it to be

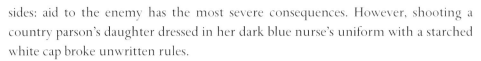

her duty to protect them; nor did she have any illusions about the consequences. So began nearly a year of expertly run clandestine activity, during which more than two hundred British and Allied soldiers were sheltered and conducted to safety. Then she was betrayed by a Belgian 'collaborator', and she and thirty-four others in the 'escape line' were arrested.

During her interrogation, she revealed all. Of the many arguments about her behaviour, it seems logical that she believed the Germans' offer that others would not be

The funeral procession in Dover of Edith Cavell, whose body was taken back to England after she was shot as a spy in Brussels by the Germans in 1915

so badly treated if she were to confess. Not so much naïve, but based on principled Christian honesty – the Germans were surely Christians too? And she willingly condemned herself by making it clear she understood that the soldiers she had aided were 'enemies of the German people'. At her trial she wished not to compromise her profession, so turned up in dress and bonnet to hear that she had been sentenced to death.

Dressed in her distinctive dark blue uniform, she was shot the next day, 12 October 1915, having spoken to an English chaplain the previous evening the words that now appear on her memorial in London: 'Patriotism is not enough. I must have no hatred or bitterness towards anyone.' Her death was a public relations disaster for the Germans, especially in America, and in the eight weeks following her execution recruiting figures doubled.

In the House of Commons, as men rose to comment on the events in Brussels, there was a small sign that Edith Cavell had made a significant contribution to thoughts on women's rights: the Prime Minister, Mr Asquith – no fan of the suffrage movement – made a speech which was noted by the campaigner Millicent Garrett Fawcett, who then commented acerbically:

> Referring to what had happened during the fifteen months of war to justify faith in the manhood and womanhood of the country, he [Mr Asquith] added, speaking of Miss Cavell, 'She has taught the bravest man among us a supreme lesson of courage; yes, and in this United Kingdom and throughout the Dominions there are thousands of such women, but a year ago we did not know it.' Pathetic blindness! Especially as a great deal of it must have been wilful.

A SQUARE MEAL
BUT A YELLOW FACE

I N THE YEARS leading up to World War I James Adie, my adoptive grandfather, was a Baptist lay-preacher who was rather big on the hellfire-and-damnation aspects of life – or rather death – and berating the congregation in the Bethesda Chapel in Sunderland about their sins. Sundays were spent walking – in Sunday-best clothes – to and from chapel, and, in between, contemplating the things one ought to avoid or abstain from (alcohol, moving pictures, fun) while sitting in an over-furnished gloomy parlour in a large and draughty house. The rest of the family had to follow suit, and as a child I heard some of them recalling how it was possible to be both well-off and hard done by simultaneously. But it was not only the family who trooped to chapel: the cook, the housemaid and the tweenies also had piety thrust upon them. Having served, cleared and washed up after the Sunday lunch, they had the pleasure of an afternoon's Bible-reading followed by their outing to Bethesda,

Opposite: The Call to Munitions – dirty, demanding and dangerous

where they sat decorously in the upper gallery peering down on the shipyard management at prayer. (Nonconformism might be the shining light and saving grace of the working classes, but even a Nonconformist God knew about a servant's proper place.)

The tweenies – Mary and Emmy, the between-stairs maids – inhabited two tiny garret rooms, and their day began with lugging buckets of coal up four flights of stairs and lighting a fire in every bedroom by seven o'clock. This was followed by raking out and relighting the huge kitchen range, before beginning a day of washing, dusting and cleaning. Very early on in the war, the tweenies scarpered: one to 'munitions' on Tyneside, the other to a War Hospital kitchen. Cook saw this as treachery; the lay-preacher saw it as the Road to Perdition, and no doubt preached thus to other irritated middle-class Baptists in the congregation who saw their servants' defection as a slide into moral turpitude.

But the tweenies were girls of their time, like thousands of others who had heard about the better-paid jobs on offer in the factories which were burgeoning across the land. Not that there weren't working women before the war – the majority of working-class single girls were in some kind of paid work: the Lancashire mill towns employed hundreds of thousands, the Staffordshire Potteries had a long tradition of working women, and there were more women in industry than in domestic service: However, most work was unskilled, pay was low, and much was piece-work or part-time. Even lady 'Type Writers', who were gradually moving into offices to replace the all-male army of clerks, received measly wages and worked punishing hours. For those fortunate enough to have had an excellent education, a professional career was akin to being an unfancied horse in the Grand National: daunting hurdles, heavy going, and few people to cheer you on. There were women teachers and post office staff – but marriage was seen as the winning post, and the law insisted you were turned out to grass immediately. There were doctors and university dons, but no more than a few hundred – and they needed to be tenacious, and more often than not financially independent, to make their way in their professions.

It made little impact that from the United States at that time came examples of the opportunities – or perhaps necessity – of the frontier lifestyle of the female pioneer. Here there were women stock-raisers, wood-choppers, blacksmiths, commercial travellers, marble-cutters, butchers, bank officials, a reindeer herder and even a lady lighthouse keeper. Throughout the increasingly industrialised Victorian era in Britain there had been frequent complaints that working women would displace men from jobs because they could be paid less; and that employers were all too keen to introduce improved mechanisation, which would push out skilled men in favour of unskilled women. In 1870 the brass workers, the nut and bolt makers and

CORSETS TO CAMOUFLAGE

the chain and nail makers protested that their trades were being invaded by 'those outrageous women who turn at the lathe and file at the vice'. The trades unions voiced their wholehearted support for the men, suspicious that 'to organise was to recognise'.

Nevertheless, when war broke out in 1914 thousands of women found themselves out of work. People took fright about financial security, filled their piggy banks and fretted about prices. Society took on a patriotic and purposeful attitude, eschewing new fashions, ribbons and frippery. Within weeks milliners, seamstresses, laundresses, dressmakers, and cotton and lace industry workers found themselves unemployed. The cost of living began to rise, and men started to volunteer for the army.

Initially, gaps appeared in the ordinary services which kept the community going: postmen and bus drivers joined up, and so did cleaners and railway porters and ticket collectors and lamp-lighters. And it became quite common for wives or sisters to take over in family businesses such as window-cleaning and painting and decorating. Journalists scribbled away productively at the sight of yet another male bastion falling to females: *Punch* magazine squeaked with surprise at the sight of 'the female Jehu', having no embarrassment in alluding to ancient and reckless Israeli war charioteers when spotting a cautious lady taxi driver in London. The newspapers also carried stories of male strongholds successfully resisting the new turn of events.

In the north-east, in that most male of environments, the coal mine, there was double prejudice against women: not only superstition allied with a macho atmosphere, but the memory of Victorian days when the scandal of women and children 'doon the pits' had stood for the worst of the industrial revolution's exploitation of labour. After the Mines and Collieries Act of 1842 they'd been brought up from the coalface and permitted to work only at the pit brow – that is, above ground – but they were few in number. Once the war began 'pit lasses' clad in clogs and shawls reappeared, especially in Lancashire. In Wales and the north-east, however, the men were having none of it. In County Durham there were rumblings at the Miners' Lodge at Houghton and Harraton: a resolution was passed stating: 'We instruct the General Association that whenever female labour is employed in or about mines in the county, the workmen in such mines shall down tools, and that they receive support from the General Association.' In 1917 were was still considerable resistance to conscription amongst miners – who were classified as 'in essential work' – though they'd had to yield to the army some men who'd become miners since the war started. The possibility of more women being put to pit duties threatened to exacerbate an already fraught relationship with the government, which was needing ever more men for the front.

In 1915, when the Minister of Munitions, Lloyd George, finally realised that the

government had to recruit women for the war effort – having spent months ignoring the obvious – there were many good reasons for the sudden tide of clacking heels that headed for the armouries and arsenals and factories dedicated to the production of munitions, which embraced not only shells and weapons and tanks and planes but also tents and boots and uniforms and bandages. Government work meant regular pay and regulated hours. Even if these hours were long – twelve-hour shifts were the norm – at least you weren't at the mercy of 'madam, above stairs' whose social life dictated when the day's work ended.

Huge numbers of women were recruited to make shells and fill them with explosives, and to produce hand grenades and cartridges. The old establishments such as Woolwich Arsenal expanded and new factories were built, creating a migration of young women at a time when it was not usual for them to move away from their home towns. Special hostels were built, and canteens introduced, and for the first time women's working conditions became the subject of official scrutiny. Miss G.M. West was a 'munitions policewoman' in a TNT and cordite factory in South Wales:

> The girls here are very rough, so are the conditions. . . . The ether in the cordite affects the girls. It gives some headaches, hysteria, and sometimes fits. If the worker has the least tendency to epilepsy, even if she has never shown it before, the ether will bring it

out. There are 15 or 20 girls who get these epileptic fits. On a heavy windless day we sometimes have 30 girls overcome by the fumes in one way or another. . . . There are about 3,800 women workers in all sections on both shifts. Some of them come down from the sheep farms in the mountains, and speak only Welsh, or a very little broken English. Then there are the relatives of miners from the Rhondda and other coal pits near. They are full of socialistic theories and very great on getting up strikes. But they are very easily influenced by a little oratory, and go back to work like lambs if you shout at them long enough.

Prior to this, Miss West had worked as a canteen manager at Woolwich Arsenal. There, too, she had found the girls 'very rough', and had observed the much-trumpeted phenomenon of rubbing shoulders with different classes:

As for Woolwich, it is a very slummy part of London, but it is rather amusing for all that. There is a big market place full of costers' barrows, and with street jugglers, palmists etc performing. All along the road to Greenwich are weird little shops, rather like the North End Road. There is also a sort of creche for pipes and baccy. The workpeople are not allowed to take their smoking outfit into the Arsenal, so for a few pence a week they can leave them just outside the gate.

Munitions workers at Woolwich, 'very rough, regular cockney but mostly very nice and amiable'

The girls are very rough, regular cockney but mostly very nice and amiable, but if one does happen to get roused she is just Billingsgate gone mad. If they are aggressive, the only thing is to be equally so, and to give them as good as you get – then they generally shut up and become quite meek.

Such an awful old party has been 'helping' this week – Lady Clarke. She announced that she meant to teach the girls nicer manners. They must say Please and Thank You. Well, presently a girl comes up: 'Pennyworth cheese'. 'What' says Lady C, 'What'? – meaning her to add Please. 'Huh' says the girl, 'there's a way to speak to anyone. Wot Wot! Why can't you say: I beg your pardon Missus?'

'My dear girl' says Lady Clarke 'where *did* you learn your manners?'

'Not where you learnt yours thank the Lord.'

We haven't had much trouble with her ladyship since. She is singularly quiet and inoffensive.

Olive Castle decided to 'do her bit' the moment she was eighteen and went to her local munitions factory, starting in the gun-cotton department and then transferring to cordite.

Lady Parsons, founder member of the Women's Engineering Society

> We all wore khaki overalls with a 'War Service' badge. The work there was quite easy really, simply required speed and careful handling of the wet 'cords' while packing them in trays for drying in the next department. There were two men and four girls in each press-room, the two men doing the heavy work on the hydraulic press. But as time went by, even those two men had to join the forces, owing to man-shortage and I was ordered to be the press hand myself – dreadfully heavy work with those heavy cylinders to haul about all the time, and as I was on the smallish side – 5ft 3 ½ tall – that wasn't much help. Those cylinders weighed ¼ cwts [35 lb] empty and had to be packed by hydraulic pressure ready for the actual press to make the moist cordite into cords. For this job I was given another ½ d per hour, which made my weekly wage about 30s. The work was continuous, seven days a week, so the presses never stopped, night and day.

Many moved on to skilled work, and on Tyneside one of the outstanding advocates of women's employment was gingering up the traditional work-places of the north-east. Katherine, Lady Parsons was a suffrage campaigner, a founder member of the Women's Engineering Society, and the first woman member of the North-east Coast Institution of Engineers and Shipbuilders. A passionate fan of technical skills for women, she was in a good position to wield influence: her husband Charles owned the famous Parsons Engineering Works in Newcastle. Lady Parsons watched with pride as women mastered precision engineering:

> Quite a large number of girls were able to set and grind their own tools, and a small proportion could set up their jobs from drawings. They could mill all the parts of the breech mechanism of howitzers, screwing the internal thread for the breech block, milling the interrupted screw and screwing the cone that fits into the breech block; milling firing pins and all the parts of gun sights; in each case setting up their own work. In a firm repairing guns two girls dealt with guns varying from the 13 inch Naval Gun, weighing 50 tons, to the 6-pound Tank Gun. They could design repairs to guns and mechanism and calculate the factor of safety of a damaged gun by logarithm and slide rule.

Olive Taylor, who later joined the WAAC, started her war work on a farm near the River Humber, then judged that industry would be a better employer:

I volunteered for 'munitions' as it was called, and at the end of 1916 I was sent to a factory near Morecambe Bay. The factory was privately owned and the wages terribly low. We were billeted in sea-side boarding houses, but the landladies who took us in wanted us out before holiday-makers came in. We slept five in a room and never got enough to eat. On an all night shift (seven to seven) we had a few slices of bread and margarine for our main meal which we ate between eleven & twelve. We had to pay the landladies twenty-five shillings out of the twenty-seven we received, and there were no facilities for laundry.

We had to walk three miles each way to the factory, which was a filling factory packed with explosives. Many railway lines traversed the area which was three miles across and nine miles in circumference. Shells of all sizes came in to be filled, many of them nine inches across, 9.2s. The filling was a boring and laborious task. A large amount of powder stood by each shell, and this had to be rammed into the shell using a piece of wood & wooden hammer. Often it seemed impossible to ram in any more powder but with the mallet and stem another small hole had to be made into the powder & more inserted. This was called 'stemming'. Many girls fainted in the TNT room but I was not affected, so was often exposed to that deadly poison. I did, however, begin to faint fairly often, mostly with trapped fingers between the larger shells. Not having enough to eat probably helped to cause the fainting. My perfect set of teeth were ruined & gave me years of pain.

Above left: Precision work on machines milling parts for shell fuses.

Above right: Filling shells involved contact with toxic chemicals that destroyed many women's health

Hands and faces that turned yellow, hair that went a weird shade of orange – at first the rather light-hearted nickname of 'canaries' was used for those in the TNT departments, as everything they touched went as yellow as their skin. In fact they had toxic jaundice, and it produced a range of debilitating symptoms which were sometimes fatal. At Woolwich Arsenal, as Miss G.M. West recalled, not only people turned yellow:

> There is . . . a dog in the Arsenal who lives with the gunners in the testing pits. He has a very beautiful brass studded collar bearing the inscription: I am Barney, the proof butts dog, but whose dog are you? During the air raid of April 3rd 1916, he rushed out to bark at the guns, and fell into the ditch that runs round the Danger Area. The ditch is full of picric acid and the result was, first that he was very sick, and secondly that for months he was bright yellow. No amount of baths would take it off.

Medical workers reported on the symptoms of poisoning experienced by munitions workers, but the work was essential and had to go on

Other factories had a poisonous mix of chemicals to be handled – Miss West found herself policing at Queen's Ferry near Chester where sulphuric acid was turned into nitric acid, and nitric acid into a corrosive substance called oleum: 'The particles of acid land on your face & make you nearly mad, like pins & needles, only much more so; & they land on your clothes and make brown specks all over them, & they rot your handkerchiefs & get up your nose & down your throat, & into your eyes, so that you are blind & speechless by the time your hour is up & you make your escape.'

Photographs of these factories present a scene of monstrous machinery amid heaps of metal shavings, bits of rag, whizzing lathes, ammunition boxes higgledy-piggledy all over the floor, with women wielding hammers and wooden staves and metal rods – and everywhere row upon row of lethal shells. Understandably, there were strict regulations to prevent accidents, as reported in the *Sunderland Daily Echo*: 'A munitions worker who was fined £2 in a London munitions tribunal for carrying two sweets into a danger building, was informed that the sugar might mix with the acids and cause an explosion.' Being fined two weeks' pay was warning indeed, but inevitably there were accidents.

The newspaper reports were terse, for severe censorship was in force, and locations were kept vague – 'a factory in the north-west' or 'the London area'. One explosion that was impossible to conceal occurred at a chemical factory in Silvertown: the entire East End of London and much of the rest

THE LANCET,

Observations

ON

E EFFECTS OF TRI-NITRO-TOLUENE
ON WOMEN WORKERS,

AGNES LIVINGSTONE-LEARMONTH,
M.B., CH.B. EDIN.,
AND
BARBARA MARTIN CUNNINGHAM,
M.D. EDIN.

DURING the past five months we have made careful notes the symptoms complained of by women working on tri-tro-toluene (or, for brevity, T.N.T.) in the munition ctories in which we have been acting as women medical ficers. There some hundreds of women come into contact ith T.N.T. in its various forms. We are convinced that e frequency with which these symptoms occur among the orkers cannot be mere coincidence, and must point to ritation by, and absorption of, some toxic product of the explosive used. The work necessitates intimate handling of he powder, and the more floury or fine the powder the greater the amount of dust in the air of the shop. The symptoms complained of may be roughly divided into two classes—viz., irritative and toxic.

of the capital saw and heard it. Officially 69 people were killed and 400 injured, but the true total was rumoured to be much higher. Across the Thames from Silvertown lay Woolwich Arsenal, and at one point the flames reached over the river to send up a gasometer like a Roman candle. The devastation was widespread and, as with any publicised horror today, the press reported that 'motorcars filled with well-dressed sight-seers slipped along'.

None of those inside the factories, like Olive Taylor in Lancashire, had any illusions about the potential for danger:

> On the evening of October 1st a rocket was seen to leave the middle of the works and go over the sea. At eleven p.m. just as we went to the canteen for our dinners a fire alarm sounded & we saw flames. We never expected any fire to spread, as each building was separated from the next by a long corridor with water sprinklers. Actually we girls hoped it would last for a while as we would not have to resume work until it was safe. However, the fire did spread rapidly and soon huge explosions shook everything. There was quite a lot of panic as the twelve foot high gates remained closed. The police on the gates were never permitted to open them until soldiers surrounded the factory and the line to the camp had been cut. The rush for the gates had the weaker people on the ground, yet still others climbed over them to try & climb the gates while the police tried to hold them back. A few girls were working to dislodge the girls on the ground & carry them into the canteen. I had no hopes of escaping the holocaust, but somehow I was not scared. We were shut in with those explosions for several hours. The buildings had strong walls & weak roofs so that the roofs would go up rather than the walls. Truck loads of benzene & dangerous chemicals were exploding too, and several people threw themselves into a river which ran at the back of the works. We never knew how many died. At the end of the week with the huge place still smouldering, we were paid off and given a railway ticket for home from the Labour Exchange. We were asked if we would return if the factory was rebuilt and only eight of us said 'Yes'.

TNT was not the only unpleasant substance that had to be handled. Here, dusty soda and ash are fed into an ash furnace at a chemical works at Northwich, near Manchester

If it wasn't enough to be surrounded with explosives, there was the threat from above. The throbbing of the huge German Zeppelin airships brought particular terror. Lady Parsons thought they were a specific threat to the psychological state of the workforce:

The funeral of a Swansea girl killed in a munitions factory accident in 1917, escorted by uniformed workmates

Then there were the air-raids, sufficiently alarming to many people leading their ordinary lives in their well-screened houses; but when hundreds of workers were gathered within the brightly lighted shop, and all the conditions were unusual and exciting, a highly nervous mentality was produced. Great judgement and careful handling were required on the part of those in charge of the workers, in order to repress and allay any symptoms of panic.

Lady Parsons was possibly not aware of how some of the women dealt with such feelings, for it was common for the phrase 'two Zepps and a cloud' to be heard in the canteens when a plate of two sausages and mashed potato appeared.

Caroline Rennles was working in a shell-filling factory at Slade Green in Kent when the manager rushed in one day shouting: 'Run for your lives!' as a plane approached: 'They said there was ninety tons of TNT there . . . [the men workers] were all soldiers that had come back from the war, you know, so one or two of them grabbed us kids and they ran as far . . . as they could and they tore our aprons off us . . . and they made us lie flat on our faces and they covered over these white aprons at the back so that we looked like cows.' Being machine-gunned in a field was presumably an alternative to being blown up in a factory.

Mrs Geraldine Kaye became a principal overlooker at a Vickers armaments factory after working at Woolwich Arsenal:

At Woolwich I had 400 women and girls in the three workshops and I used to feel very proud of their wonderful pluck when all our lights were put out when the Zeppelins used to come over.

When I first went to Vickers not only were all the lights put out but all the doors and windows were fastened from the outside so that we could not possibly get out. There was such a great outcry from the women that after a short time all doors and windows were left open so that we could escape if a bomb did hit us.

The Zepp that was brought down at Cuffley flew right over our hostel. Such a lovely moonlit night that I stood on the steps outside and watched her going away and then saw a light falling down on her from one of our planes and presently what looked like a very bright orange stuck up in the sky appeared, and she turned round looking like a cigar lit at one end and then the front end broke off flaming orange colour and presently the rest followed. Immediately from the dark streets near our hostel (which was up on

CORSETS TO CAMOUFLAGE

a hill) there rose a great sound of children's voices cheering and calling. It sounded as if all the children in the world were cheering although one couldn't see anyone.

'Zepps' caught in spotlights were one of the stories I heard as a child. Sunderland, on the north-east coast, though not subject to naval bombardment like Hartlepool, Whitby or Scarborough, had seen these huge, threatening airships coming in from the North Sea. James Adie, taking a walk by the sea with his son Wilfrid in April 1916, watched as an immense silver-grey Zeppelin, engines thumping, floated over the cliffs south of the town. Father and son, both science enthusiasts, were apparently entranced by its appearance and had difficulty relating it to a machine of war. On this occasion it flew harmlessly past, for whatever reason failing to drop its load of bombs.

It seemed strange to me that Zeppelins had visited Sunderland, so far north of the main action in France, though the local shipyard was furiously building merchant navy vessels. However, north of the river in Fulwell there is still evidence of how seriously the threat was taken – a concrete acoustical mirror, 15 feet in diameter, now almost buried amidst semi-derelict allotments. It's a curious device which reflected the engine noise of an approaching Zeppelin, and gave about fifteen minutes' warning of its arrival. A duty observer, or listener, was positioned in a bunker in front of the mirror, and connected by a stethoscope head-set to a 'collector head'. He was thus able to hear the engine thump of a Zepp, loaded with 4000 lb of bombs, crossing the sea at 60 mph. Because it was thought that blind people had more acute hearing, they were often used as duty observers. Most attacks occurred at night, and there were batteries of searchlights and anti-aircraft guns dotted around the coast. But whether the townsfolk benefited from this 'track plotting mirror' is questionable. Solemnly, in the local newspaper, the Chief Constable of Sunderland divulged information which he thought might help the townsfolk in the event of enemy attack: 'Indications that enemy aircraft are in the vicinity are as follows: First, the cutting off of the electrical supply. Second, the noise caused by the explosion of bombs.'

Women did not operate the searchlight mirrors, but they had made them, and were judged by Lady Parsons on Tyneside to have done particularly well:

> On mirrors, women have been working with great success. They back the mirrors and do a great deal of the polishing and fitting. We are all familiar with the beautiful beams of light travelling over the sky in the search for Zepp. and aircraft. Their beauty stirred the imagination of both painters and artists. Here on the Tyne we may feel great pride in the mirrors and searchlight, as most of us know that Tyneside girls polished the mirrors and so added to the brilliancy of the searchlights.

This lyrical view of combat in war, pointing up the curious distance put between the instruments of war and the destruction they cause, is found time and again in arguments today about 'over-the-horizon' warfare, where there is no face-to-face confrontation. And it still seems to be more acceptable for a woman to participate at a distance in the war effort than to skewer the enemy in the guts. Every woman filling a World War I shell or filing a warhead contributed to death on the battlefield, but from afar.

In the letters and diaries of the munitions workers there are scant references to 'the enemy', and little preoccupation with being part of the killing process. A very small number of women record criticism that they had crossed the line from creators to takers of life, but few seemed affected by this argument. Patriotism and a sense of duty were an unembarrassing part of social behaviour. 'Doing one's bit' is the phrase which appears time and again in the reminiscences, coupled with an implied desire not to let down the men at the front – after all, every terraced street, every village had men away at the war. And again, receiving wages and being recognised as useful citizens were a great comfort.

And so, as civilian participants, the women put on uniforms. These consisted of an array of serviceable and wholly unattractive garments which resisted laundering, but introduced trousers as acceptable wear for working women – though usually covered by some sort of skirt or tunic, and topped by a cap resembling a cottage loaf, squashed and primped into individual shape. Drab in the extreme and normally made of very heavy cotton, only occasionally enlivened with a few ribbons, the overalls and smocks were usually worn with pride – signifying the improved status of these women, employed on national work for the government. At least two weddings were recorded at which the bridesmaids turned up in smocks and trousers, while one of the brides wore overalls.

The arrival of trousers caused more comment than the nature of the war work. If women were shifting shells and driving cranes in factories, pure necessity introduced trousers or puttees (military-style strips of cloth wound round the legs) into the workplace. There were some objections recorded in factory reports, but on the whole women found these garments practical and liberating; and, because of the large numbers involved, there was a quicker acceptance than might have been expected among the general public, though occasional attempts were made to retain traditional restraint, as the *Lady* reported: 'The authorities of a London Bank which employs girl clerks have issued an edict that V-shaped blouses and short skirts must be covered by overalls reaching to within two inches of the ground.'

The munitionettes' uniform included trousers discreetly covered by a baggy smock and could not be called attractive – but it gave them status and they wore it with pride

CORSETS TO CAMOUFLAGE

One area of resistance was in France, where husbands and boyfriends at the front got to hear of this major change in women's dress and wrote home angrily demanding that such a revolution be halted. Perhaps this response has roots in the strong sense of what men visualised they were fighting for – the photograph of the pretty young wife in her best dress carried in the uniform pocket, a comfort and consolation during the darkest moments. To hear that this image was being destroyed was doubly disturbing to those in a distant trench, separated from home and family, and longing for stability and a return to that which they held dear.

Inevitably, the middle classes needed to be introduced to the concept of workclothes via subtle suggestion – and smart advertising. From the *Lady* again:

> The 'Munitions Overall' . . . this really capital garment is enjoying enormous popularity, not only with those engaged in munition making but also for the canteen voluntary worker. The problem that first beset all those patriotic ladies who for hours at a stretch may be seen serving out sandwiches and beverages in hut canteens – 'What shall I wear?' – is solved exactly by Shoolbred's Munition Overall. Altogether a first rate investment at five shillings, as it lends itself admirably to gardening and household work as to the war duties referred to.

The more stylish 'Munitions Overall', in fashionable pastel colours, as recommended to the middle classes

Six months later, Shoolbred's in London's Tottenham Court Road realised they were on to a winner, and were producing 'coat-overalls' in eight 'charming shades', including 'heliotrope, biscuit and vieux-rose', accompanied by the hard sell:

> The overall must be well-cut and roomy without clumsiness – a skimpy, or on the other hand, balloon-like garment makes even the nicest figure look ungainly. Quite a host of canteen workers lend eloquent testimony to the virtues of Shoolbred's coat-overall, which, by the way, is in request among lady workers in many different fields of activity – not only 'behind the counter' at soldiers' and munitioners' buffets, but also by actual women workers among the lathes and shells.

At over 5s a garment, Shoolbred's probably didn't get many of their mail-order requests from 'actual workers'. Why spend half your weekly wages on a uniform, when you could indulge in the delights of smart clothes for the first time in your life? The munitionettes had discovered the fabulously liberating business of shopping for pleasure. Girls who'd existed on a few shillings as domestic staff were soon a national scandal as they headed for the milliners and smart outfitters, flush with undreamed-of wages. There was the usual outbreak of British moral panic in the newspapers as money was spent on 'fripperies and luxuries'. Stories circulated about factory girls in furs and silk underwear.

And along with extravagant clothing came the suspicion that behaviour was deteriorating. 'Criticism of finery and 'showy gowns' appeared in newspaper articles. These terms from Victoria's age, denoting outward signs of an inward depravity in the working class, suggested the road to prostitution: maids who dressed like their former mistresses were regarded as a threat to social order. However, the factory girls knew that better clothes gained them more respectability and acceptance; even so, there were regular suggestions in the press that they were taking to a life of drink — if not worse. The fear that 'loose' women would corrupt and deprave, that their increased independence could only lead to sexual promiscuity, raised fears about the future: were women actually going to increase their stake in society — and change their role? The newspapers and social commentators quivered with concern.

The reality was that munitions workers showed fewer, rather than more, signs of drunkenness, and that the supposed explosion of 'war babies', though much talked about, was not backed up by statistics. Many of the munitions workers were married women, not flibbertigibbets, and as the war had taken away their male breadwinners (notwithstanding the 'separation allowances' paid to servicemen's wives) they were frequently supporting elderly parents and other relatives.

Short court reports from the local press highlight the actual daily lives of women on Tyneside: 'Yesterday, a munition worker now earning her £3 a week, said that she had been married 28 years, and had 16 children. Her daughter, who also gave evidence, said that *she* had been married 5 years, and had 6 children.' The mother of sixteen was applying for a separation order. Earlier in the same week, a terse paragraph had stated: 'A chubby infant of 3 or 4 weeks was picked up on the doorstep of Villa Place, Newcastle. It was warmly wrapped up, and on a piece of paper the following: "I am a munition worker, 17 years. My mother put me out. Father of baby killed. Take care of her." And for all that the wages were generous in comparison to pre-war times, they were still much less than those paid to men. Some of the arguments for lower pay were based on the assumption that women ate less than men, didn't drink and smoke so much, and had fewer hobbies and fewer dependants. Now the war was challenging some of these assumptions.

Away from the mighty munitions complexes, the need to bolster the workforce brought a profound culture shock to everyday life. James Adie, having lost his tweenies to munitions and hospital work, was having to oversee the arrival of women at the shipyard gates. The yards of Sunderland, which proudly bore the title of 'the biggest shipbuilding town in the world', were increasing their work-rate to

provide merchant shipping for the war effort and at the same time repair torpedo boats. And those yards were losing their skilled men to the army. Rather reluctantly, the lasses were allowed past the huge gates into the noisy world of shipwrights and platers and boilermakers. About five hundred women were employed, mainly in unskilled jobs, but some managed to get training as riveters, painters and welders, and others scaled and cleaned ships' boilers.

Ships were built in all weathers, with pots of tar boiling, welding sparks flying and metal plates and girders swinging through the forest of scaffolding in which each vessel grew. Injuries were common: Doxford's, one of the main yards, was known before the war as 'The Butcher's Shop'. Men worked with sacks on their shoulders to keep out cold, damp and bouncing red-hot rivets. The women wore stout boots, coarse clothes and the ubiquitous working woman's shawl.

Even so, to have got into the yards – a kind of monastic establishment where ships were cultured mysteriously out of wood and iron behind high walls – was an achievement in itself. However, the determination of the management to use men at any cost, rather than accept women, could be seen when King George V and Queen Mary visited Wearside in 1919. Somewhere towards the end of the shipyard tour, having been introduced to every municipal official and management member, the King finally got to meet a few of the workers, including a shipwright, Mr Chambers. Mr Chambers was eighty-two. Apart from eight years spent in the Royal Navy, he'd hung on to his job in North Sands Yard for fifty years. No one appeared to think this odd, except perhaps for the King, who, the local paper reported, asked Mr Chambers if he suffered from headaches. One would have thought rheumatism, lumbago or bronchitis might have been more relevant, but there's royalty for you.

Alongside Mr Chambers was another shipwright, Mr Corby, a mere stripling at eighty, but with a much more impressive sixty-seven years' service under his belt; and Mr Thomas Hull, a foreman-blacksmith with a measly fifty-three years in the yard. There was clearly a reluctance to give way to 'young lasses' if you could still lift a hammer.

Male or female, they were made of tough stuff – though not necessarily 'healthy' by modern standards. A few hundred yards from the ribbon of shipyards on the river was the Monkwearmouth coal mine. Resistant to employing women at the pit brow, its owners nevertheless lost men to the armed forces: these were miners in physically demanding jobs, working in seams pushing out under the North Sea, and it might have been thought they were fine physical specimens. However, the recruiting officers for the Durham Light Infantry, which formed a 'Bantam' battalion for men under the standard minimum height of 5 ft 3 ins, observed: 'Doctors were horrified at the condition of a batch of volunteers from Monkwearmouth Colliery, whose bodies were covered in carbuncles and sores caused by years of working in hot salt water seeping down from the North Sea far above the mines.'

With hours of work, rough conditions and few if any facilities for rest and food, heavy industry was not an inviting prospect for women during the war. However, they tackled an extraordinary range of jobs, from loading coke in gasworks to cleaning hides in tanning factories. Carrying sacks of flour in mills, loading stores on to trains, heaving milk churns on to dairy wagons – all sorts of work was undertaken which hitherto had been considered 'impossible' for women. Many industries had imposed bans on them doing such work, and there was much debate – unresolved – as to whether women should now be subjected to the grim and filthy conditions prevalent in many workplaces. Nor were their children exempt from the stress of wartime. Half a million were thought to have been withdrawn from school in order to become child labour and supplement the family income. Some, as evinced by the setting up of soup kitchens in County Durham, were not going to school because they were too hungry. In some villages there were reports of children starving.

From the very outset of hostilities there'd been food shortages because of panic buying and rising prices, and by 1917 shortages were common. Queuing was a major wartime chore for women, and by the end of the year limited rationing was introduced by the government for butter, margarine and lard, sugar and meat. However, a few months later meat became extremely scarce, and the Food

Controller decided to allow extra for manual workers, who were divided into three categories: very heavy industrial workers, heavy agricultural workers, and heavy industrial workers (including all women over eighteen). It didn't take an active feminist to notice that those women who lugged heavy shells around in munitions factories had been popped into Category Three which had the smallest ration of meat. And those under eighteen apparently didn't need to eat meat.

Coke heavers at a London gasworks, photographed by Horace Nicholls

Added to this, the women shouldered the complete responsibility for cooking and cleaning at home, which made for a working day of well over sixteen hours. The kitchen range had to be riddled of ashes and lit, coal brought in, and pans put on for hot water. Such food as was available was basic – and took a good deal of boiling. Walter Sharpen, who lived with his family just behind the Sunderland shipyards, remembered what his mother cooked in wartime: 'We were brought up on pans of soup, home baked bread, ham shanks, sheep's heads, tripe, trotters and vinegar. We also ate lots of roast potatoes, sausage and black pudding.' Despite the privations, the munitionettes and other factory workers actually ended the war somewhat healthier than they began it. Canteens provided regular, if dull, fare, and the women got used to thinking about food for themselves – a change from always putting the available food on the male breadwinner's plate.

For those with a little more education, there were all kinds of opportunities for work which was not so arduous but which had still been the preserve of men. Postwomen, female refuse collectors, railway clerks, window cleaners and road-menders became a common sight, and all of them wore some sort of uniform. The papers were full of 'firsts' for women:

> A tin mine in Truro, whose manager is in active service, is now under the management of a woman, Miss Joyce, said to be the only mine manageress in the world.
>
> A blacksmith at Chealyn Hay stated that he had a woman working for him, who was better at the work than many men.
>
> A new departure has been inaugurated by the Rev. G. Hudson Shaw, the broad-minded rector of St Botolph's, Bishopsgate. He has invited Miss Maude Royden to read the lesson at the Sunday service.

However, in London the cabbies were putting up a rearguard action:

Following the decision to license women as drivers of public vehicles, the London and Provincial Union of Licensed Vehicle Drivers has informed the executive of all the tramway car, omnibus, and taxi-cab services of London that a ballot is being taken to decide whether all licensed men shall be ordered to cease work when the first woman driver appears in the streets. The union urges employers not to engage women drivers until the result of the ballot is made known next week.

All Jehus please take note.

Notwithstanding the taxi drivers' views, transport offered great opportunities. Tramcar companies were full of pride and panache at the turn of the century: they had a smart, almost military style in some towns, and an *esprit de corps*. They felt a civic responsibility – and needed it when their trams were involved in rather messy accidents. The war soon spirited away large numbers of their crews; so, with their progressive attitudes, the managers hired conductresses and, in some cases, lady tram drivers, the Corporation of Glasgow Tramways Department leading the way. However, there were growls from the trades unions, who saw women on trams as 'doing dangerous work', though their main objection, as reported in the *Lady*, was that women would probably be paid less, so undercutting the general wage:

The annual delegate meeting of the Association of Tramwaymen protested vigorously against the employment of women. Some women may think this hostility unfair, as this is not to displace male labour, but to set free men for military service. In Newcastle the problem has been faced fairly. The women who have been taken on have been made members of the Union, to prevent the undercutting of men's rates, and it has been demanded that their employment on the tramways should be considered emergency labour.

In Sunderland, ten females – the Corporation liked to call them lady conductors – were already employed by 1915, and eventually all the trams had women taking fares. There were eighty-five of them, dressed in navy-blue jackets and longish skirts, with a riot of brass buttons everywhere, and a cap with a large brass badge. They earned between 6s and 10s a week, compared to the men on 11s to 15s.

Sally Holmes, one of the ten 'lady conductors' employed on trams in Sunderland, was injured by a Zeppelin raid on the city

One effect of their employment was the increase in the number of small boys who turned up in court for the heinous offence of hanging on to the back of trams – ticketless. Pre-war, about half a dozen boys annually had been hauled in front of the magistrates and prosecuted. However, in the first year the women were in place forty-five lads had to be dealt with firmly, along with four accused of 'throwing stones, street refuse, etc. at female conductors and cars'. Clearly the women weren't entirely accepted, and one Sunderland lady passenger, on being told by a lady conductor to go upstairs, responded by belabouring the conductor with her umbrella.

On a Saturday evening in April 1916, the town's electric lights were dimmed twice – the noise of a Zeppelin's engines had been picked up. The airship slowly followed the line of the river and dropped a large number of bombs between the harbour and the town centre. Several houses, a school, a workmen's hall and a church were damaged. Sally Holmes was collecting fares on tram number 10, standing outside the Wheat Sheaf public house, when another explosion caught the tram, set it on fire and wrecked it. She was injured, and the nearby Tramway Offices were badly damaged, with a tram inspector killed and other employees injured. The local hospitals were hard pressed as they dealt with a hundred more casualties. Twenty-two people were killed in this one raid, and for the first time the sharp end of warfare had come to Sunderland's home front, to men – and women – in an ordinary town a world away from the fighting.

CHAPTER TEN

FLU AND FLAPPERS

W ORLD WAR I ended with curtains in Britain respectfully closed, as yet
another neighbour succumbed to Spanish flu. I heard family tales of
people surviving Zeppelin raids, the trenches and food shortages, only
to die like flies in the immense epidemic which swept worldwide as the Armistice was
being signed. When I asked about that war as a child, many people just recalled the
flu – and then said little more, for it had seemed so unfair, invading the home front
just as the awful casualties at the foreign front were diminishing. My maternal
grandmother, Ethel Maud Hedinburgh, took six days to go from a healthy mother of
two to a wraith; she'd had a difficult war, with her relatives pestered and whispered
about because of their (anglicised) name. 'We were followed, the children called us
Huns, and officials kept calling at the house,' remembered an elderly great-aunt, still
protesting loudly that her ancestors were Austrians, not Germans.

Opposite: Women police drilling in 1914. After the war their numbers and status slowly increased

There were photograph albums with unnamed young men looking watchful or cocky in new uniforms, posed in front of a potted plant and a Greek column. Some have a mid-war date on the back, perhaps to mark when the uniform was first put on for the posh photograph, perhaps the day when the name appeared on the casualty lists. But what happened to them – and what stories other soldiers had to tell – was not talked about in ordinary parlours. It was noticeable how the grandparents' generation retreated behind small memories of bread rationing and influenza.

In all the albums people were wearing black. One of the curious effects of the war had been to turn the butterfly colours of society ladies into discreet 'dove grey' or 'biscuit', and the one outfit of Sunday Best for the less well-off into funereal black.

Newspapers had attempted to twitter about fashion throughout the war, and the gossip columns merely embraced wartime elements in their usual round of receptions and weddings: frequently mentioned were 'a quietly celebrated war wedding, owing to the death of . . .' and the usual minute descriptions of the nuptials of the establishment were laced with the reality of Flanders:

> Neame–Strutt Wedding: at St George's, Hanover Square, London. February 1915. A Khaki wedding group: Miss Agnes Strutt . . . was in a dainty wedding gown of white charmeuse and chiffon with a long tulle veil, and Mr Gerald W. Gore-Langton, 18th Hussars, who is now convalescent from his severe wound received in recent action, acted as best man to his brother officer. Captain Beaumont Neame, who only just arrived in London straight from the front one hour before his wedding ceremony, was married in his service uniform, with the soil of France still clinging to his boots.

But next to the society chatter were the all-too prominent advertisements aimed at those recently bereaved:

> Choosing and trying on mourning is a melancholy business, the details of which can nevertheless be mitigated by the deft understanding of customers' requirements on the part of those who are concerned in the selection, and that can only be gained by experience. All William Barker's staff can be relied upon for quiet and unobtrusive attentiveness and consideration, and it is a real relief for those about to put on mourning to be able to leave so much of the deciding to these specialists in black wear.

Everyone was catered for, the department stores such as Barker's in Kensington being particularly solicitous in their targeting of potential customers: 'Sketched – a widow's dress of armure fabric trimmed with bands of crepe, the vest being of peau de soie – altogether simple yet suitable style for the middle-aged woman, at the reasonable price of 4 guineas. (The net veil is in the latest fashion).' Some outfitters had devoted themselves entirely to the needs of the bereaved: 'The House of Black Wear . . . specialising in the matron's wear department – pretty and useful blouses stocked for matronly wearers, well-cut skirts in all dimensions, up to 40 inch waist size.'

Nor were these appeals directed only at well-heeled Londoners: the *Sunderland Daily Echo*, like a myriad local newspapers, was carrying regular suggestions for those about to don widows' weeds: 'Special provision for mourning orders at Binns: At a period when it is difficult to think of details, we can give you every assistance in the matter of dress. We are prepared to take Complete Mourning Orders – Dress-making, Millinery etc, at the shortest possible notice . . . and representatives will wait on patrons at their own homes, if desired.'

And the widows themselves often soon succumbed. It's estimated that one in eight war widows died within a year of their husband's death.

Determinedly, because fashion had lost its drive amid the economies of war, there were plaintive attempts to reflect the activities of the Parisians, struggling with a much-reduced industry since many of the couturiers had gone away to fight and the seamstresses were employed making uniforms rather than tea-gowns. An article in the *Lady* in 1917 ran:

Paris Spring Fashions: Simplicity is the ruling quality in all French women's new clothes, and there is marked avoidance of anything masculine or military. The passing love of Joffre blue and khaki is quite dead, and all the fashions of this spring are very feminine in the new sense of the word. That is to say, they are practical and dainty at the same time. A suggestion of flow in the skirts takes away any boyish touch, yet by being short and still, they are quite fit for muddy and dusty streets. . . . A great many women are choosing the coloured crepe or muslin blouses, or little dresses without lingerie and lace, for this reason [a desire to economise on washing]. It is almost impossible to get washing done satisfactorily, and little of it can be done in the house because of the gas limitation. Even in France, the habit of cleaning with *essence* [petrol] is much reduced, because *essence*, too, is scarce and expensive.

Keeping up appearances, even in adversity: 'Fashionable mourning' garb advertised in The Lady, March 1915

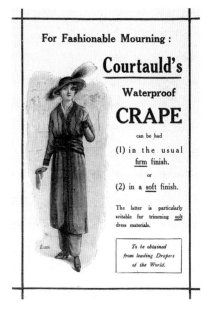

For Fashionable Mourning :

Courtauld's

Waterproof

CRAPE

can be had

(1) in the usual firm finish.

or

(2) in a soft finish.

The latter is particularly suitable for trimming soft dress materials.

To be obtained from leading Drapers of the World.

At least, despite the strains in the economy, clothing in Britain had not been rationed, though there was a weird attempt in 1918 to suggest a National Standard Dress for women. This was a 'utility' garment, designed for every occasion: 'Outdoor gown, house gown, rest gown, tea gown, evening dress and nightgown.' There's a temptation to imagine a committee of men sitting quietly in a panelled room in Whitehall, asking each other with polite bafflement just why their wives needed more than one dress, resulting in a neat memo on which was written: all-purpose gown. Luckily, no one seemed to take this seriously, and such an idea lay dormant until Chairman Mao put his civilians into uniform clothes half a century later. However, later in 1918 there was a move to limit the amount of woollen cloth used in a woman's dress to 4½ yards. One recorded reaction to this appeared in the columns of *Vogue* magazine. Ladies, it stated, should slim and wear silk instead.

But by the end of the war, notwithstanding the exhortations of the fashion writers, women looked different. Skirts had risen – practical working clothes had led the way – leading to a boom in the stocking and footwear industries. Trousers had appeared for rough work, but it would take a few years before they were gently introduced into leisure wear. And whatever shape – or shapelessness – had reigned in the uniforms issued to women of varying shapes and sizes, corsets were still considered essential. Underwear had not normally been issued as official kit, so there were numerous references and grumbles from women in the services about supplying 'the necessary'. Even so, corsets were now being designed to support the body, rather than to mould it into an hour-glass or pouter pigeon shape. And they were being advertised in terms such as 'Specialité – a comfortable model, particularly adapted for War Work and Sports Wear'.

The elements of the garments themselves had become the victims of war: munitions girls were ordered not to wear corsets containing metal, or underwear with metal buttons, because of worries about sparks. Coincidentally, steel was not made available for the underwear industry – corsets not being considered 'essential' by the men who drew up the regulations for rationing the use of metal. Whalebone, an imported luxury, was hard to come by, so curious materials including compressed paper and rubber were introduced into stays – with varying success (warmed-up corsets, especially on munitions workers, tended to rot – and sag – rather quickly).

The mere issue of uniforms had had its effect on how the country dressed: standardised sizes became more common, and the very habit of wearing just one set of clothes led to the middle and upper classes revising their rigid conventions on changing several times a day. The manufacturing firms improved their mass-production techniques and concentrated less on seasonal variations, and their workers became better organised as a result of war work. 'Simplicity' was a word that, before the war, had had no place in the fashion vocabulary. Now, with a shortage of domestic staff to clean, starch, iron, and tug on the corset laces, 'easy to wear' became an essential style.

So what happened to the swarm of tweenies and kitchen-maids and scullery-maids who in 1914 had been employed by the wealthy? After all, when the men returned home the women's services were swiftly closed down. Many of the tram and railway companies, the post office and the local authorities dispensed with female employees in order to accommodate the demobbed troops, in some instances emphasising that only exceptional circumstances of war had necessitated the hiring of women in the first place. The canteens, the knitting groups, the voluntary buffets and the munitions factories all disappeared. The uniforms were abandoned, often with reluctance – they had given status, despite a great deal of mocking commentary from those who thought women were laying claim to an exaggerated importance. There was also anger among those who had worked in munitions when their achievements appeared to count for nothing in official attitudes to their future.

Nevertheless, thousands of women had seen a wider world, and many had gained some insight into how it was run. A qualified number of them were now allowed to vote. Areas thought out of bounds and beyond 'the gentler instincts' and 'fluffy little minds' had been invaded, and masculine work had been undertaken – at very obviously lower rates of pay. Those women still in work were now more aware of trade unions and had much greater experience of organisation than before; they had become more mobile, and had been recognised by the state as having made a contribution to the national war effort. Barriers had gone down and expectations had been raised – not dramatically, but enough for their daughters to know that they didn't have to emulate their grandmothers.

Workers at a Lancashire glucose factory, 1918. When the war ended and the troops were demobbed, most women like these lost their jobs

High hopes and disappointments were intertwined as the labour market adjusted to post-war requirements. In a closely argued report published in 1919, Lady Parsons reviewed the engineering industry and the contribution made by women:

> Great hopes were entertained by many women that a new profession was open to them, where they could earn good wages and where they would have some scope for their skill and intelligence. But with the signing of the Armistice all such pleasant hopes were destroyed, the training schools were closed to women, the trade unions reminded employers of the Government pledge to restore trade union rules, and within a few weeks the demobilisation of women was general.

She mentioned the very small number of factories that were keeping on their highly skilled women and observed:

> It has been a strange perversion of women's sphere – to make them work at producing the implements of war and destruction and to deny them the privilege of fashioning the munitions of peace. The women who worked so hard to win the freedom of the world may not have the freedom at home to engage in an industry where the wages are promising. It is fully acknowledged that men will not go back to pre-war conditions; they must have shorter hours, more leisure, more wages. But as for women, they are merely told to go back to what they were doing before, regardless of the fact that, like men, they have now a higher standard of life, and they also wish to have their economic independence, and freedom to make their way without any artificial restrictions.

Lady Parsons' arguments are a lesson in clear thinking and restrained passion; and many of the diaries and memoirs from the ambulance trains and shell factories have an underlying sense of the change that was desired after so many women had experienced 'something different'.

Those who had thought that the introduction of women into the forces boded a steady career also received a very rude awakening. Their service in the WAAC (now the QMAAC, courtesy of Queen Mary), WRNS and WRAF was abruptly terminated. Despite the best efforts of the doughty leaders of these services, there was the over-riding argument that women were only in uniform to replace men needed for the front – so they were now redundant.

At least shedding the uniform was no tragedy from the glamour point of view. Though the recruiting posters had indicated mildly dashing clothes with nicely tailored jackets and rather saucy hats, the reality had been a 'one fits all' shape, with

CORSETS TO CAMOUFLAGE

Most World War I uniforms for women had been far from glamorous.

Above: *WRAF storewomen issuing kit to new recruits.*

Below: *A WAAC officer*

pockets large enough to hold whole sacks of ferrets, topped by an array of pudding basins, odd caps and eighteenth-century tricornes. But status was shed, too, and with it the sense that women were being removed very definitely from the battlefield.

The nurses, however, managed to retain their role with little difficulty; after all, the British forces were busy across what was still a considerable empire, and the nurses merely followed the flag – with increased status after the passing of the Nurses' Registration Act in 1919. This finally confirmed nurses as professionals, gave them officially recognised uniforms and badges, and stopped any old patient-visitor fluttering around in a nursey outfit, dispensing grapes and rolling the odd bandage, calling themselves 'nurse'.

Ironically, now the women's services had been dispensed with, the military decided to organise distinct branches of nursing, with the Queen Alexandra's Royal Naval Nursing Service being recognised in 1922. Their uniform was to be a blue dress with cap and apron, and, for the officers, a navy dress and a smart navy mini-cape edged in red. The RAF got the Princess Mary's RAF Nursing Service the following year, and the Treasury made each nurse a grant of £8 to cover a vast list of what were deemed essential items, from triangular head-veils and muslin caps, collars and cuffs to long-sleeved 'washing dresses' worn when actually nursing patients. At some point a four-cornered hat had been introduced – no one wanted to offend the three-cornered WRNS – but this seems to have disappeared very quickly, and with thankfulness.

Though nursing was recognised as a necessary arm of the services, during the war minds had been concentrated on the need to maintain morale, and the importance of cups of tea and small comforts for the troops. Every week local newspapers carried reports from local voluntary groups thanking donors for gifts and soliciting more items: in Durham, Lady Anne Lambton's County Work Depot had appealed for garments and treats, in order to send parcels to men on active service: socks, shirts, mufflers, fingerless gloves and handkerchiefs were despatched, along with cigarettes, Oxo cubes and malted milk tablets. Shops spotted a potential market, advertising for women to buy their goods and Send Useful Presents for Our Sailors with the Fleet and Our Soldiers at the Front.

Turner and Co. in Sunderland had an interesting line of suggestions: 'Sleeping Helmets and Pyjama Suits, also the "Chemico Body Shield" – the Greatest Invention of the Age: Will stop Revolver Bullets at six paces, Flying Shrapnel, Bayonet, Sword and Lance Thrust. Has no steel in its construction, and is comfortable to wear. It is your privilege and duty to send one to any near and dear ones fighting.' I suspect the Chemico Body Shield might not have been all it was cracked up to be, otherwise I would have scoured Sunderland to see if any remained for present-day use. Lance thrusts might be redundant, but stopping bullets at six paces . . .?

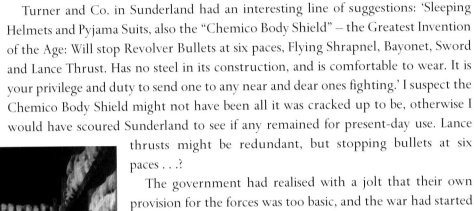

The government had realised with a jolt that their own provision for the forces was too basic, and the war had started without any provision whatsoever for a canteen system. Camp followers and sutleresses had been banished from the battlefield in late Victorian times, and the Canteen and Mess Society was all that existed. In 1914 it had precarious finances and hotch-potch organisation, but as the first troops left for France it was asked to provide a new service called the Expeditionary Force Canteens (EFC). When its first contingent landed in France early in 1915 it consisted of one Ford car – to serve an army of nearly half a million men. With great determination huts were soon erected near the front lines: here cigarettes, ginger beer, tea, coffee and chocolate could be bought, bringing a fleeting taste of home and comfort to men stuck in squelching trenches in the company of rats. The canteen workers doubled as stretcher-bearers when a 'push' was in progress, and they had a high casualty rate. Further to the rear there were eventually large rest houses and clubs, serviced by efficient depots, bakeries, laundries and mineral water factories. Seven hundred of the newly formed WAAC were in the EFC as waitresses, and they had to sit an exam paper which included questions such as:

What change, in English silver, would you give to a customer who spent 4.80 francs and tendered a Canadian one dollar note?

What quantities of the following articles are required to make an eight gallon urn of tea, and how many cups should it realise? a) Tea b) Sugar c) Milk.

How many carriage candles make one pound and what is the price per pound?

Just how important carriage candles were in wartime France was not explained, but the canteen system itself took hold and expanded, following the forces to all the major campaign fronts. British troops in Palestine were supplied from Egypt, being provided in the desert with a number of soda fountain kiosks which offered tea, coffee and lemonade. Many of the supplies came by camel. An ice factory functioned in northern Greece, for the troops around Salonika. In Egypt, an attempt to supply turkeys for Christmas came to nought as hundreds died in the heat. In France the WAAC operated a printing works, producing a magazine and canteen menus which included one in Urdu for the Indian soldiers. And in Mesopotamia the official canteen was a steamboat, carrying betel nut and cummerbunds for the Indian troops and calling at Basra to collect locally made uniforms for British army nurses from its tailoring shop.

After the war the EFC became the Navy, Army and Air Force Institutes (NAAFI) when Winston Churchill, then Secretary of State for War, accepted that a peacetime army needed its canteens too, and that there had to be a nucleus of a service to respond to any future mobilisation. There was endless wrangling over the name, and only the combined efforts of the military and the civil service could possibly have dreamed up something pronounced Naffy. However, it became a source of employment for women, and in the inter-war years they already constituted over half the workforce, clad in unbecoming overalls.

One group to hang on to their jobs tenaciously were, unsurprisingly, the FANYs. They were still a band of volunteers, had friends in useful places like the Guards regiments, and continued to train as a band of drivers and signallers. Called up for government service during the General Strike of 1926, they were recognised the next year by the War Office as an official corps, to be known as the FANY (Ambulance Car Corps).

Much more visible in uniform were the women police, who seemed to have their origins in moral panic. Whenever women had congregated in less than docile groups – raucous munitions workers lurking in pubs and women loitering with intent around barracks and docks and railway stations – there was a fear that things were getting out of control. The troops were seen as vulnerable to not very 'clean' women, and the army, run by organised and tidy-minded sorts of chaps, liked to deal with this problem by providing its own brothels (with due separation of the ranks). As camps and temporary barracks sprang up at the start of the war, women had found themselves barred from pubs in some towns and even subjected to curfew. Those who had left their home towns and villages to live in lodgings or hostels near the ordnance factories were thought particularly susceptible to 'loose living', and much thought was given to how to police them. Little thought seems to have been given to the idea that the women might need some sort of protection from the licentious soldiery.

There had been a few women attached to the Metropolitan Police in Edwardian times, mainly employed questioning women and children involved in sexual crimes, but they didn't wear uniform, and in 1914 there were precisely half a dozen 'policewomen' in the country. As ever, the war's volunteer spirit produced some well-educated middle-class women full of enthusiasm whose intention was ostensibly to 'protect' women, but in reality to control and police them. Women's Patrols began to operate, and some were partly integrated into the police force. They patrolled those traditional flesh-pots, public parks and railway stations, but it was difficult to see whether they were pouncing on couples merely availing themselves of the only privacy they could find or acting as guardians to weak and vulnerable girls. When Scotland Yard hired a hundred women in 1918, the Commissioner of Police announced cryptically: 'I don't think it is quite the thing for a full-blown constable to go and stir up ladies and gentlemen lying about in parks. It had far better be done by women police.' In order to 'stir up' they had severe uniforms with a high collar – basically the male police uniform with a long skirt, ''orrible boots' and hats described by their wearers as 'inverted soup-plates'.

It was all very well to snoop around bushes and boozy drinking-holes for fallen women, but the general public was not quite ready for law and order to be maintained in respectable locations by lady police. Initially the Scotland Yard experiment contained an element of farce, as policewomen patrolled in pairs, followed closely by a pair of policemen: the women had not been empowered to arrest anyone, so they merely apprehended suspects and waited for the males to dash up and complete the official business. Even when they gained more power in law there were only small numbers in each constabulary, and they were very definitely expected to concern themselves with 'women's affairs'.

A column of policewomen in the twenties offers a classic example of a uniform design based on clothes already out-of-date by the time several committees have agreed. In their heavy boots and long skirts they were from the Edwardian era, while the rest of the country was back on a civilian footing and changing shape and style.

Cropped hair, flattened chests, shortened skirts: the era of the 'flapper' was emerging. And though there was no flowering of economic or political freedom for women – the vote was not given to women below the age of thirty until 1928 – the image that many took on was often that of '*la garçonne*', a boyish figure somewhat at odds with the reality of domestic dedication that was being encouraged by the authorities worried about 'liberties' being taken now the war was over. However, more women were taking part in sport, especially tennis and golf, and there were fashionable icons to emulate such as the Wimbledon champion Suzanne Lenglen. More fluid and casual styles appeared, and as the women who could afford it learned to drive, increased mobility and practical clothing went hand in hand. And with fewer maids to look after the wardrobe, getting dressed had to be simpler.

The more daring women plucked their eyebrows and took to wearing kohl, eye shadow and dark lipstick. During the war, there had been few prohibitions needed in the women's services about make-up: 'decent women' never wore more than a hint of rouge and a little powder. Only the canary-complexioned munitions girls were thought a suitable target of the cosmetics industry, with blandishments about the properties of 'Oatine' and 'Ven-Yusa, The Oxygen Face Cream', suggesting that it was 'patriotic to preserve the natural beauty of their skins'.

Underwear, too, was changing. To have abandoned corsets altogether would have been too radical a move – very like the 'bra-burning' of the women's movement fifty years later. So, as the new outlines took hold in the twenties, pencil-straight and sleek, the corsetieres merely adapted their designs and produced a long elasticated tube which ceased to pinch the waist but instead suppressed the bosoms.

The real change that had occurred, though, was to women's aspirations, although the self-confidence gained in World War I might not have been put to good use immediately. Exhaustion and turmoil, the relentless insistence on men reclaiming their jobs, and the desire to return to a familiar and less worrying life – all may have conspired quietly to blunt women's experience. However, many put their thoughts on paper, and as mothers they passed on stories and casual asides which alerted their daughters: if Mum did that, what could I achieve? Neatly dressed housewives who passed a factory and mentioned wielding a spanner or ramming TNT into a tank shell planted the seeds of possibilities in the next generation. While making radio documentaries in the 1970s I met a number of impressive elderly women who smiled serenely at the mention of dismantling car engines or disposing of sawn-off limbs somewhere in northern France. They'd not turned into Amazons or harridans, yet to call them 'plucky' was not enough. They'd not only 'done their bit', they'd pioneered and won through.

CHAPTER ELEVEN

TO THE BARRICADES

M OST OF THE conflicts and confrontations which occurred in the twenties and thirties in Europe saw few women involved with great significance – except for the Spanish Civil War. Sitting, as any child, bored in my school's main hall, and not listening to another interminable ramble from some well-meaning bishop, I'd stare at the walls and the elaborately carved boards on which were inscribed the names of the brainy girls. One name appeared four times as winner of prizes and scholarships: Eileen O'Shaughnessy. Born in South Shields, the daughter of a customs collector, she went to St Hugh's College, Oxford in the twenties, worked as a secretary, ran a business, and later studied for an MA in psychology at University College, London. Then she met Eric Arthur Blair, already a well-known left-wing writer published under the name of George Orwell. Two years earlier, in 1934, to celebrate Sunderland Church High School's fiftieth anniversary,

Opposite: Near the Aragon Front during the Spanish Civil War in 1936 – and all in dungarees

Eileen
O'Shaughnessy
married the writer
George Orwell in
1936, then went to
Spain with him to
support the
Republicans

Eileen had written a poem in which she evoked past, present and future. The third section was called 'The End of the Century: 1984', and it was duly published in the school magazine – and forgotten until the end of the century, when it was unearthed in a battered edition of the School Chronicle and scanned for references to the novel *1984* which added to Orwell's international fame in 1949, four years after Eileen's death.

The Orwells married in 1936, and at the outbreak of the Spanish Civil War that year George immediately headed for Barcelona to fight on the Republican side against the Nationalist forces of General Franco. Eileen followed him and got herself a job with the International Labour Party office in that city; she was one of several British women who'd joined the international effort to help the Spanish Republicans. Here, living a precarious existence in which suspicion and factionalism were rife she worked at coordinating the funds and materials which flowed from England, and at helping the volunteers who arrived to fight.

The Spanish Civil War also drew writers, journalists, artists and intellectuals to its front lines. There were a number of female newspaper correspondents, among them Sheila Grant Duff from Britain and the American Martha Gellhorn; it was in Spain that Gellhorn embarked on a distinguished career which took her to war zones for the next sixty years.

Another American writer, Dorothy Parker, found herself initially the object of stares and laughter as she walked the streets of Valencia. Unwittingly, she'd stumbled upon one of the causes of division and debate between the various factions: she was wearing a fashionable hat. In a society riven by arguments about revolution and change, hat-wearing, somewhat absurdly, had suddenly come to symbolise women's traditional subservience. On the other hand, going bare-headed suggested a lack of respect for Catholic tradition. From the Republican point of view, military caps were much more acceptable.

Amongst the turbulence on the streets and the intense political debate, highly traditional Spain began to see other changes in women's wear as a visible sign of defiance – or allegiance. In the first few heady weeks of conflict the 'mono' appeared – rather nondescript workers' dungarees, but redolent of rebellion when worn by a young woman alongside a man in an identical pair. As life became rougher, and riding lorries and working in bombed-out buildings became the norm for the volunteers, the 'falo-pantalon' appeared – slightly more stylish culottes.

In the early days of the war, Franco's Nationalist troops were faced with women who wished to defend the Republic. They were among the crowds storming the barracks in Madrid and Barcelona, and, brandishing guns and wearing dungarees, they delivered an image of progressive young Spaniards as seen on many of the subsequent Civil War posters. Many women were among the forty thousand international volunteers in Spain, and several of the intellectuals and artists opted for a life of fighting. They included the British painter and sculptress Felicia Browne, who had been visiting Barcelona when the war broke out in July 1936. She was a communist and joined the local militia, only to die when shot in the head a month later at the front near Saragossa, during an attempt to blow up an ammunition train.

The volunteer battalions from the United States were revolutionary in another respect; among the thousand or so industrial workers, five hundred students and teachers and other professionals were several hundred black Americans. Back home, segregation was the norm in most aspects of life, including the military. In Spain, in 1937, the Abraham Lincoln Battalion became the first integrated unit in US history to be led by a black American, Oliver Law, who later died in battle. It was later said that Law was immensely cheered to hear that among the medical volunteers from home was Salaria Kea, the only black nurse in the group.

An anti-fascist poster from the time of the Spanish Civil War

Born into a poor family in Georgia, Salaria was six months old when her father was stabbed to death while working as an attendant at the Ohio State Hospital for the Insane. She and her three brothers moved to Akron, Ohio to be brought up by friends, who themselves had five children, after her mother moved away on remarriage. Since little money was available for schooling, her brothers went to work around the ages of nine and ten. However, Solaria was bright and excelled at athletics, so somehow the family managed to keep her education going. But at high school, when she wanted to play basketball she was told that 'no negro had ever been admitted on the team'. There followed her first efforts to counter discrimination, and with the help of her brothers she got herself transferred to another school, specifically obtaining the right to join in sporting activities.

A determined character and a devout Catholic, when she left school she wanted to make her mark; so she headed for the Harlem Hospital training school in New York to become a nurse. In the early thirties the hospital had a mixed staff but segregation was accepted in several areas, such as the dining room. Again Solaria took part in protests, though they were low-key by later civil rights standards, and many of the older black staff were resigned to the daily snubs and restrictions.

Curious about the treatment of various groups by fascist regimes, and relating it to her own experience, she began to take an interest in events abroad. When the Italian leader Mussolini invaded Abyssinia in 1935, she organised medical supplies in

Harlem and helped despatch a seventy-five-bed field hospital. She wrote later that 'hundreds of negroes in this country attempted to join the Ethiopian forces' but were frustrated by sheer distance. However, within eighteen months the first volunteers were on the move to another conflict involving fascism: the war in Spain. This time she could write: 'I sailed from New York with the Second American Medical Unit. I was the lone representative of the negro race. The doctor in charge of the group refused to sit at the same table with me in the dining room and demanded to see the captain. The captain moved me to his table where I remained throughout the voyage.'

At first she was in a field hospital set up at the Villa La Paz near Madrid, the deserted summer home of ex-King Alfonso XIII. Such was the Spanish peasants' deference to the monarch, regardless of the fact that he'd abdicated six years previously, that they continued to live in adjacent hovels while cattle lorded it in the palace. The Americans soon chased out the cows and goats and set up shop, but not before Salaria absorbed that there could be other kinds of discrimination. Indeed, when the medics started sorting out the plumbing they noted that the locals hadn't known what the elegant bathrooms were for. . . .

Salaria found conditions tough, but was able to work in Spain without restrictions – and she was nursing volunteers of a huge range of nationalities, not only from western Europe but also from Mexico, Cuba, Japan and Russia. In 1938 the unit moved to the front and was based outside Teruel. After a savage winter of fighting, a counter-attack by the Nationalists was about to begin. 'The first two days were quiet,' she wrote. 'From the village each morning the women and children and old men went out to work in their fields. At sunset they returned to their small houses. At evening the third day the fascist planes flew low, dropping bombs. Next day no one went to the field. Most of them were dead.'

The unit shifted to a base hospital and hundreds of wounded began to arrive. The hospital was machine-gunned from the air, and Salaria listened to 'stray bullets as they fell through the olive trees'. Continuous strafing and bombardment eventually led to her suffering serious injuries when a shell exploded in a trench where she was sheltering. She was dug out from under six feet of earth and rocks and had to return to the United States. Once recovered, she enlisted as a nurse in World War II and worked in France. Eventually she married an Irish engineer, John O'Reilly.

Salaria Kea found freedom from racial discrimination in Spain, but could not be unaware of the immense tensions regarding the status of women in that country. The behaviour of the women on the Republican side, and the assault on traditional religious imagery – especially the Virgin Mary – shocked many commentators. Spanish society had been hitherto fiercely conservative, and the London *Times* reporter wrote with amazement in 1936 of a man smashing a saint's statue with a mallet in a Barcelona church while 'women and girls stood about laughing'. Later a correspondent reported from Valencia: 'Corps of *milicianas* (militia-women) have been organised, and women, armed and aggressive, take their place in the front line with men. All that womanhood traditionally stands for is rapidly disappearing. Women of the proletariat are not at all perturbed by the fact that in the region held by the government scarcely a church is open, scarcely a priest appears in public.'

Among the communists, argument raged on as to whether the men's revolutionary attitudes on the front lines were translated into the home. Dolores Ibarruri, known as La Pasionaria – a rousing public orator and symbol of Republican commitment – complained of her own supporters: 'I have known many of my comrades who considered themselves great revolutionaries, but when I asked them "Why do you not let your wives join the party, why do you not see to it that your wives attend meetings?" – they would answer "My wife does not understand anything, she does not know anything, she has to look after the children."'

La Pasionaria, firebrand Republican orator, in Barcelona in 1938

As the war effort got going, Republican women manufactured munitions and drove lorries and military vehicles – but they were paid less than men, annoyed the trade unions, and rarely obtained supervisory positions. And after the initial period of fighting, they were discouraged from joining front-line units and directed into supply battalions; indeed, there was a women's battalion in the 5th Communist Regiment, but it was not intended for combat. And as the initial excitement and confusion gave way to more organised military action, women were pushed aside. The enduring image of the Civil War's valiant young woman fighter was just that: an image. For in reality they were behind the lines, and even disparaged by some of the less liberal rank-and-file who hadn't reckoned on explicit women's liberation accompanying revolutionary action. And where women had been in the front line, they'd been expected to act as women: doing duty in the trenches, and then doing the washing-up and laundry. And when victory eventually went to Franco's forces, all the liberating legislation involving divorce, abortion and employment which had briefly existed was swept away. The position of women under the new regime was made clear in 1939 in a public speech in Madrid: 'The only mission assigned to women in the nation's great enterprise is the home.'

Back in Britain in the thirties, those who had envisaged radical change after World War I were wrestling with the complexities of home versus work. The majority of women were still discriminated against, unable to claim unemployment benefit if married, and barred from teaching and the civil service on marriage – even having to resist attempts to legislate against married women shop workers. Demand for equal pay found its main obstacle in the Trades Union Congress. Fear of unemployment loomed large.

Admittedly, more women were working, especially in the burgeoning light industries, making those domestic items such as the vacuum cleaner, gramophone and radio which the middle classes thirsted for. A small number of women were now prominent in politics, and events in Spain, the rise to power of the Nazis in Germany, and the appearance of right-wing fascism in Britain provoked disparate responses from them and among women's organisations. Mass-Observation, the public opinion research organisation founded in 1937, found that women were confused about the issue of fascism, but on the whole tended to support the idea of appeasement with Germany.

As the possibility of another war approached, there were stirrings in those who'd been involved in the last conflict. They'd fretted in the mid-thirties about the lack of interest from the government in utilising a reserve of women, and had tried to organise voluntary bodies to keep the spirit alive. With Adolf Hitler marching into Austria and eyeing Czechoslovakia, they went into action again – Lady Londonderry, Lady Trenchard, Lady Hailsham, Agatha, Lady Hindlip, Miss Baxter-Ellis, Mrs Harnett and Dame Helen Gwynne-Vaughan. (Though public positions now tended to be held by women of education and ambition, rather than by splendid duchesses of independent mind, class was nevertheless still a very active ingredient in public life.) In 1938 they undertook to bring their three organisations, the Women's Legion, the Women's Emergency Service and the doughty and rather superior FANY, into the new Auxiliary Territorial Service. Dame Helen, who'd been Chief Controller of the QMAAC British Armies in France in 1918 and Commandant of the WRAF in 1919, became the director of the ATS. With bags of experience of the military and an academic mind – though most definitely not a candidate for a military academy, being an authority on fungi – she wasn't keen on the FANY. A certain amount of turf-fighting took place, couched in genteel tones that concealed – just – all the barbs and innuendo of the class warfare system. The FANY, on the other hand, had never been out of training, could drive, and several appeared to have their own transport – a singular distinction for a thirties' woman. Off-duty they dropped rank, and over a drink officers hob-nobbed with privates – who didn't address them as ma'am, shocking the ATS. The FANY were a small unit and saw themselves as a regiment – and, as ever, they had a good working relationship with the Guards regiments. The ATS hierarchy were none too impressed to be told by a general inspecting them at Camberley: 'You know, I have always looked on the FANYs as the women's equivalent of the Guards and as regular army. It must be rather difficult for you now. . . .'

Eventually two interlinked organisations appeared – the FANY in the ATS and the 'free' FANY, a voluntary corps with its own khaki uniform and smart Sam Browne belt. And ahead of the 'free' lay yet another extraordinary war.

The glamour of the FANY, as seen in Everybody's Weekly, 1939

CHAPTER TWELVE

ON TARGET– FIRE

I couldn't go dancing – my dad would never allow that.

I put my lipstick on in the street – after I went out.

In by eight o'clock tonight, my girl, or trouble.

FOR EIRA JONES, Vera Bartholomew and Julie Hutchings – and almost all the other girls who joined the Auxiliary Territorial Service to work on the anti-aircraft and searchlight batteries (ack-ack), life at home was strict, and Dad ruled the roost. Joining up early in the war, they were volunteers, just like all the women in World War I; but although this was essential war work they needed their father's permission, and there was considerable opposition in some families. Mrs Mavis Middleton, then unmarried, was conscripted in 1943; even so, there was still friction: 'I was glad to be called up – my dad was in the last war, my eldest sister was

Opposite: The ATS operating a range-finder on an anti-aircraft gun at night, December 1942

married with children so not working, so I thought one of us must go. So I said to my dad, "I'm going in the army." He said: "No you're not, my girl, I saw them in the last war." And I said: "Just watch me."' Doreen Davis from West Norwood thought her father was very broad-minded: 'Some of our neighbours said to him: "I'm surprised you let your daughter go in the ATS." He said, "Why's that?" And they said, "She might bring trouble home." If you were brought up the way we were – strictly, I suppose you'd say today – then, well, my dad's face came in front of me quite a lot while I was enjoying myself.'

Mary Costello (now Mrs Rulton) was eighteen when the family heard that her brother had been killed at Dunkirk: 'I thought I'd put one in for him when I saw my mother get the news, but I didn't want to go into munitions – I had a friend who went all yellow with the gunpowder. So I joined up – and when I got my uniform, my father took me all round the pubs and showed me off, and he said: "She makes her own mind up" – because there was always a bit of a question about it.'

So young women (though treated as girls) were taking on work which involved discipline and gave them an integral part in the defence of the country: the anti-aircraft batteries were soaking up too many men who were intended for front-line duties, so mixed batteries were created. But the prejudices of World War I were in a lot of the dads' minds – the idea of women in army uniform conjured up something improper ('Those ATS – they're officers' groundsheets') and many of the girls went off to join up with the words 'If you get yourself in the family way, never darken the doorstep' ringing in their ears.

However, both volunteers and later conscripts found themselves with a job which brought them companionship and fulfilment: they acted as height-and-range-finders, picking up the German bombers and plotting their precise position so that the guns would be on target. The idea that they should also man the guns was absolutely ruled out. There are numerous references at the start of the war to the subject of women bearing arms – or being involved in firing at the enemy – and all reflect the attitude that it was an unpalatable idea which civilised people would automatically reject. The remarks usually carried an inference that it would be an imposition on women which would go against their intrinsic nature. Listening to the recollections of the ATS Anti-Aircraft Command Branch members, the dividing line between spotting the enemy and dispatching him seems spurious:

You were a team – we were working at Rhondda with 612 Heavy AA Battery and I was on the predictor. The radar comes through – aircraft approaching – and you were all geared up, terribly exciting – and the Command says: 'Predictor working', and you say,

HQ ANTI AIRCRAFT COMMAND

'On target', and the height-finder girl gives you the height and then, of course – On Target, Fire. And all these big guns roar into the air and you stand there sort of shuddering and thinking to yourself, is it going to come down on top of you? Rather wonderful – a lovely feeling. We shot down a JU88 as it was coming in from the Bristol Channel – and we were marched through Cardiff to celebrate.

Joan Thompson (now Mrs Butler) remembered every moment: 'You were young, we were eighteen girls in a hut, and when it was Duty, you all jumped out of bed, pulling your pants on and trying to get your helmet on – oh, it was great fun!'

Olive Helyer (now Mrs Kinghorn) was defending Plymouth, a long way from home in Norton-on-Tees: 'My mother wouldn't sign for me to go abroad – your parents had a lot of say then – so I joined the ATS. You were frightened, naturally, but after the alarm you just got out of bed with your Dinky curlers in and you got your steel hat on – you didn't have time to take your curlers out. Then you got your battledress on, pyjamas underneath, and said to yourself: "They're coming over here – and we're going to hit them!"'

Edna Smith (now Mrs Starr) was seventeen and a half in 1941:

I had a strict father – and you couldn't do this, you couldn't do that. So I joined up – it was an adventure. When I first started, everything was manual – there was no remote control, and all the orders had to be shouted. So we had to go into a very big field, one of us at each corner and the officer in the middle. And she would come up to you and give you a sentence, and you had to pass it over – hand up if you received it and pass it on to the next – in order to learn to be heard over the gunfire. When I went home on leave my mam said straightaway: 'Do you have to shout like that?' But I said, 'That's what we've been taught – it's orders.' And all our equipment was World War I, because later I found my father-in-law's diaries, and he'd been on the same work, and the little height-finder was in his diary – the same as mine.

Emily Newbold had a German bomber in her sights over Newcastle, but the plane was coming in so low that the guns couldn't fire for fear of hitting houses. She could see the German pilot and his machine-gunner – 'But we had to stand firm, ready for the moment when we could have a go at them.' Bringing down a plane brought not only elation but souvenirs. When Kathleen Duffy's unit brought down a plane, shrapnel from the bomb it had dropped whizzed past her. She picked it up, but dropped it again because it was red-hot. However, the unit retrieved the German black cross from the fuselage and nailed their trophy to a nearby fence, and Kathleen got a bit of propeller.

The food was stodge. Bread was substituted with the infamous 'dog biscuits', filling but teeth-breaking, and the diet was sometimes enlivened by parcels from home: bread pudding and Geordie stottie cake wrapped in brown paper and string. The uniform never quite fitted – skirts too tight, jackets too large and itchy. Vera Bartholomew (now Mrs Greenhouse) had worked in the corsetry department of a large store before the war, when everyone seemed to wear stays (laces and bones and steel bits and all), but the demands of ack-ack action seemed to preclude pulling on such garments in haste. She remembers the big leather jerkins and gaiters, but they were still not enough to keep out the cold on the cliffs above Plymouth, even though the girls kept their pyjamas on underneath. They all survived on large buckets of cocoa. Discipline was strict – and the NAAFI was the only trysting place available. 'Nasty remarks' about the girls in uniform were not unknown – 'You're only here For A Purpose, Aren't You?' – and many of the men treated the girls as a joke when

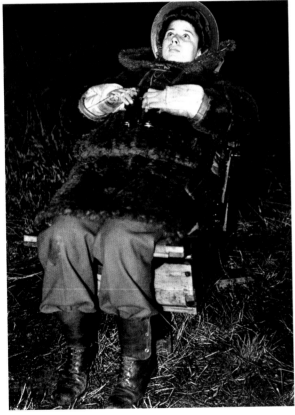

Private Talea Mulla, former mother's help and now, in 1943, an ATS spotter on a searchlight battery, in her teddy bear fur coat

they first arrived. However, most of the men on the batteries were much older, or deemed unfit for service, so the girls would hope that a nearby town or village might have a weekly 'sixpenny hop'.

Elizabeth Oldham (now Mrs Lapham) had volunteered to go on searchlights:

I was in the 93rd Searchlight Regiment – the only regiment manned entirely by women. We were unique, and when I first went home my father walked me all round Stockport, he was so proud. We'd go on duty at dusk and stay through the night. And if there were Hostiles coming over, we'd illuminate them. We spent long hours awake, waiting – but when we got something in our sights it was fantastic. There was always a risk that they would shoot down the beam – it did happen – but we never lost a girl. We were eleven girls, that's all, miles out in the country outside London, stuck in the middle of a huge field. We didn't have any cover, we weren't sandbagged in or anything like that – out in the open and all we had was a steel helmet and a fur coat! Official-issue fur coat – just something you pulled over your head and it came down round your bottom and kept you warm. Teddy-bear fur, actually!

Listening to former ATS members at one of their well-attended reunions in York over fifty years after the war ended, their vivid shared memories and joy in each other's company seemed to me a classic testament to the camaraderie of war. They came from varied backgrounds, were now housewives, grandmothers, widows. They wore smart suits over frilly blouses and carried themselves with bustling pride. They held a commemorative service in the Minster, where they sang robustly, then gathered outside for their traditional march past. Like jolly, purposeful labradors, heads high, they wheeled through the narrow streets. Tourists and young people watched them, possibly trying to guess what made these pensioners swing arms, catch each other's eyes and smile.

At the start of the war Churchill had been one of those most determined that women should not be involved in combat, but he eventually came round to accept that ack-ack duties freed up men and that the work was of 'immense importance'. His youngest daughter, Mary, was a junior officer in the ATS. In an interview in the *Daily Telegraph* in 2002 she described it as 'the biggest experience in my life . . . which gave me responsibilities far beyond my years'. She spent five years in the ATS: 'Uniform is a tremendous leveller, we all looked the same, lovely girls from Liverpool and country bumpkins like me. If you were an officer, you were a real part of the gun team, not just in charge of the girls' shoes and ticking them off.' Being Churchill's daughter, however, caused her some difficulties every time she was sent to a new unit: 'I knew they'd be saying "Here's Churchill's daughter – she won't be scrubbing any floors!" You had to start all over again and make the point that you weren't there to polish your nails.'

She was posted to 481 Battery in Hyde Park, where Mavis Middleton was also serving:

Winston Churchill with his daughter Mary in ATS uniform. She recalled: 'I was catapulted out of my narrow class background and I was independent'

Mary Churchill was our officer, and her dad, when he was ever going off anywhere special, he would come up to the gates – we girls did guard duty during the day – and when he came to the gates, a private detective would get out and say, 'Thee Prayme Ministah' – and he'd get out of one of these huge cars and put his hand up and wave his cigar, and we'd say: 'The old man's going somewhere, he's just come to say cheerio to Mary', and, sure enough, in the papers a few days later he'd been somewhere to meet the VIPs from America or whatever. . . . Wonderful times, in spite of the war. You were young, and you can cope so much better – I'd never have missed it for the world.

UP IN THE AIR
AND ALL AT SEA

THOUSANDS OF FEET above the anti-aircraft batteries – and well away from them – droned the hundreds of planes mint-new from the factories, smelling of varnish. In complete contrast to the jolly companionship on the ground, the women pilots of the Air Transport Auxiliary found themselves utterly alone. Civilians, not part of the RAF, but charged with delivering the ever-growing stream of aircraft spewing out of the factories to airfields all over the country, they clambered into whatever sort of plane popped out of the factory doors.

In the thirties, flying had been one of those pursuits which attracted outgoing women with a bit of money, for it was a sporty adventure relatively uncluttered with male traditions. It had already produced popular heroines such as Amy Johnson, the first woman to fly solo to Australia. But when the Air Transport Auxiliary was formed in September 1939 to free up RAF pilots for combat duty, the impressive

Opposite: The appeal for volunteers – direct and patriotic

group of women who had hundreds of hours' flying time was at first ignored. Protests were made, but it was publicly pronounced by Lord Londonderry, a former Secretary of State for Air, that 'this country has not accepted the principle that women should be exposed to fighting risks in so far as they can be protected from them'. More protests were made and quickly, but grudgingly, the government said they'd take 'a dozen very capable women pilots'. The first group joined to fly Tiger Moths in January 1940. However, there was a huffy correspondence in the magazine *The Aeroplane*, and the editor, Mr C.G. Grey, finally delivered his own opinion:

We quite agree . . . that there are millions of women in the country who could do useful jobs in war. But the trouble is so many insist on wanting to do jobs which they are quite incapable of doing. The menace is the woman who thinks that she ought to be flying a high-speed bomber when she really has not the intelligence to scrub the floor of a hospital properly, or want to nose round as an Air Raid Warden and yet can't cook her husband's dinner. There are men like that too, so there is no need to charge us with anti-feminism. One of the most difficult types of man with whom one has to deal, is that which has a certain amount of ability, too much self-confidence, an overload of conceit, and dislike of taking orders and not enough experience to balance one against the other by his own will. The combination is perhaps even more common amongst women than men. And is one of the commonest causes of crashes, in aeroplanes and other ways.

Mr Grey also had support from some lady readers: 'I think the whole affair of engaging women pilots to fly aeroplanes when there are so many men fully qualified to do the work, is disgusting! The women are only doing it more or less as a hobby and they should be ashamed of themselves!'

Lettice Curtis had just come down from Oxford, where she'd obtained a maths degree, and realised that in 1937 'there was really no work for women like me, except to teach or take a course in Pitman's shorthand and typing'. Yet she was determined not to be a further drain on her family's finances and wanted to earn her own living. One day she was passing a newly built airstrip near her home in Devon:

An aeroplane came flying in, and the pilot came over to talk to me, so I asked: 'Can women fly?' And he said, 'Oh yes, they can.' And that was it. I remember my father putting down his copy of *The Times* and saying, 'I suppose you'll come and knock our chimney pots off.' So I found where to get lessons – about a pound a time in a Moth –

and I hadn't realised it would be so cold, mid-winter: it was freezing. Anyway, I passed everything and got my 'B' licence – the commercial licence. My first job was with an Air Survey Company, map-making – rather boring at times actually, just flying up and down. Then in 1938 we took part in 'Army Co-op', an exercise when we fixed course in a Puss Moth for two hours or so, twice a day, to allow the ack-ack defences to practise ranging and aiming their guns. And then when the war broke out, all civil flying was stopped – so end of job.

Amy Johnson joined in May 1940 – and by then the pressure was on, because the country was frighteningly short of planes and the Ministry of Aircraft Production under Lord Beaverbrook was going into overdrive. Lettice was accepted into the second small group who joined soon afterwards – just 'sort of thrown in', she remembers. Initially she flew Tiger Moths, the greatest inconvenience being her skirt. No uniforms had been issued, and she wore her

ordinary clothes, a navy-blue pleated skirt and a pullover – many of the women didn't own any trousers. You had to get into your Moth, having been given a chit in the morning telling you where you had to go, and off we went. It was your decision about the weather and the flying conditions – you were absolutely on your own. If you had to go to Lossiemouth or Kinloss it took about three days, and you had to decide where to stop – you just looked for an airfield. It was jolly cold as well, so I'd wear a teddy-bear cloth coat on top. When all the paperwork was completed, I went to a tailor and had the uniform made: navy-blue tunic and trousers. But there was also a skirt as well, which we had to take with us, because we weren't supposed to leave the airfield unless wearing a skirt. We had boots and a flying helmet – but as we had no radios I hardly ever wore my helmet.

The factories were churning out planes and obsolete models had to be moved out of the aerodromes, so the women were cleared to fly these and all twin-engined models. Spitfires and Hurricanes, however, were off limits. 'Government policy,' remembers Lettice. 'Women were not, on any account, to fly operational aircraft.' But the need was urgent, with Spitfires and Hurricanes piling up outside the factories and needing to be dispersed to squadrons across the country. There were by now two dozen women pilots – though Amy Johnson had been lost in January 1941 on a ferrying assignment over the Thames Estuary, having taken her own decision to fly in poor conditions.

Very soon the ban on ferrying operational planes had been lifted, and some women went on conversion courses – though not Lettice:

They suddenly produced a Hurricane and said to me: 'Deliver it.' It was very worrying, really – my first one. . . . I thought, God, I daren't say no. There was this tremendous feeling amongst us women that if there was an accident then they'd stop women flying, so you just got on with it. So I went to the other side of the airfield – it was horrifying – and somehow I got into it, looked up 'Hurricane' in my Pilot's Notes, and got it up and flew it and landed it with several bounces at Prestwick. Then we were given Spitfires. Same thing – you just got in, stared at the controls and flew it.

The ground was always in view – if you went above the clouds you were lost. So you flew straight and level, map gripped between the knees – it usually ended up on the floor – with minimum fuel, unarmed, and braving the added hazard of barrage balloons. Lettice particularly disliked bits of the west coast run, weaving around the barrage balloons of Manchester and Warrington and then trying to spot an airfield when smog was blanketing much of industrial England: 'In those days the coal-burning towns were impossible to see, and if the weather conditions changed the smog would rise up and come at you – it was not easy.' On the ground it was a businesslike operation – land the plane, hand over the chit – and no welcome in the RAF Mess: women were not allowed in. Overnights were spent with the WAAFs, quartered a safe distance from the men, in a bed just vacated by a WAAF who'd gone on night duty. The ATA pilots felt slightly on their own: 'You couldn't really talk to the WAAFs about flying or planes or what we did – all they nattered about was boyfriends and dances and that sort of thing.' Eventually the women were at the controls of the four-engined bombers, and life was made a little less lonely by the presence of a flight engineer – though when they landed at Linton-on-Ouse in Yorkshire the engineer, being male, was ushered into the Mess for lunch while Lettice, the pilot, was shown into 'a cupboard'.

By the end of the war there were over a hundred women pilots and a handful of flight engineers – and altogether the thousand-odd pilots of the ATA had made over three hundred thousand deliveries. It was prosaic but, at times, frightening and rather isolated work – a wonderful achievement, but not a jolly in the blue beyond.

The women who already possessed flying experience at the start of the war had similar advantages to the women in 1914 who had learned to drive. Having mastered a relatively new and unusual skill, they were needed – albeit with official reluctance. As a result, the upper and middle class claimed a stake in particular services. And class was entwined with the image of various uniforms.

Somehow the Royal Navy, with its cute tricorne officers' hats and black stockings, managed to project a very definite profile – and backed this up with a recruiting policy which laid much emphasis on having relatives already in the senior service.

'There are naturally many women in the Wrens whose husbands or brothers or fathers – or even sons – are admirals or ABs which is as it should be' was the view of Bernard Stubbs, one of the BBC's 'News observers', writing in 1940 about 'The Navy at War'. However, he was struggling with his traditional convictions when he came to the matter of uniforms:

> To many people, one of the minor misfortunes of war is that it becomes necessary to dress large numbers of otherwise personable young women in uniforms. And it is odd, because standardization of clothing is the one thing women avoid like the plague in peace-time. . . . And many people have wondered if the excellent work women are doing in all three services . . . could not be done equally well without the trappings.

Despite the image on the posters, most Wrens would find themselves driving, cooking or typing

Joining the Wrens still didn't mean a life on the ocean wave, even though official government publications and posters liked to give the impression of an exciting sea-going job: 'The small craft of many of our harbours and inland waterways have Wren boats' crews; not the summer yachtswomen of peacetime but girls who can man a boat on the dirtiest winter night and still find it the most enthralling job imaginable.' The reality was anchored on shore – clerical and store assistants, drivers and cooks. But as the war progressed a long list of technical posts was added, and girls might get themselves qualifications in meteorology, communications and radar. At Portsmouth Bernard Stubbs, having observed Wrens ciphering and 'working on complicated naval ledgers', had what he called 'the most novel of all my experiences with the service: I was invited to lunch with the Wren officers in their mess . . . and so, for the first time in my life, I had lunch in an officers' mess which consisted entirely of women. For some time, I felt uneasy and self-conscious. . . .' Eventually Mr Stubbs steadied himself by remarking that they talked about ships, mutual friends and Hitler – 'much as it would have been with the men'. Phew.

The government, meanwhile, was happily trumpeting the officers' responsibilities in a booklet: 'Two thirds of the WRNS officers are replacing naval officers in shore jobs, in convoy-rooms, plotting-rooms, naval control service offices, as junior accountant officers, secretaries, torpedo assessors, gunnery school assistants and in numerous other ways. The remaining one-third are employed in administrative duties. Where will it end?' Hard to tell if the booklet was written with enthusiasm or faint apprehension. There was a little quote appended from a House of Commons debate, in which Captain Pilkington, Civil Lord of the Admiralty, remarked: 'I have no doubt that if you gave the WRNS half a chance they would be perfectly prepared to sail a battleship.' One can just about hear the chortles on the back benches.

Nevertheless, a tiny handful of the seventy-five thousand Wrens managed to get on to boats' crews, messing about with engines and boat-hooks and generally attracting attention: 'Cor, look, stokers – cooee, stokies!' Among them was Rozelle Pierrepont, who was eighteen and had wanted to be a radio mechanic but ended up a stoker. She was the daughter of Earl Manvers, and had a pretty jolly hockey-sticks approach to her tasks:

> We get up at 5 a.m. here [WRNS Training Depot, Mill Hill], and scrub or polish or sweep the decks till 7.30, then we have breakfast, and after that continue to scrub etc for 2 or 3 hours. After lunch we have lectures on nautical subjects, and squad drill which is no end of fun! . . . We were given our kit yesterday, and mine is most elaborate! Besides the usual Wren uniform mine included 2 pairs of bell-bottom trousers, 2 seamen's square-necked blouses, a very thick seaman's jersey, a lanyard and a most formidable-looking knife!

To this was later added 'Two boiler suits, to wear in the engine workshops – they don't fit anywhere, and we look like grizzly bears in them.'

Officers had to buy their own uniforms, though they received a grant, but at least they could head for a tailor and get something that fitted. As for ratings, there was a long list of Free Issue – two jackets, serge, double-breasted etc. – and an underclothing grant of 45 'payable on production of the following articles: 2 pairs pyjamas or night-dresses, 3 vests or combinations, 3 brassieres or bodices (or two pairs of corselettes), 2 suspender belts or corsets, etc'.

Puttering across Southampton Water and down the south coast, ferrying admirals out to ships, and doing a lot of rowing – and bailing – when their motor-boat, *Anndora*, was yet again in for repairs, the girls had a lively time. They tackled various engineering jobs, and knew they were a very select group even when in dungarees and covered in oil. However, Rozelle's mother was busy writing letters to her commanding officer, wanting to know about likely hazards for these Wrens and eliciting soothing replies: 'Dear Lady Manvers: In reply to your letter of Saturday last, I can assure you that your daughter is safe from floating mines, it being the policy to refrain from sending any boats into dangerous areas. Your daughter is well looked after and happy, and you can rest assured that she will not be sent into any danger.' Even so, the *Anndora* was more of a colander than a craft, and after a particularly whizzing trip across to Ryde, when the engine burst into flames three times, she developed a nasty leak in the engine room. Rozelle and the girls wielded fire extinguishers and bailed: 'Tragedy . . . poor *Anndora*. We only just got back in time, for shortly afterwards she sank, and when we arrived the next morning, only her bows were to be seen above the water. We were all terribly sorry to lose our first boat – but hope we shall be given one with better engines.'

On land there were air mechanics, radio mechanics, ship mechanics and meteorologists; also torpedo Wrens undertaking 'a study of the torpedo itself, how to dismantle and reassemble it, make necessary rudder adjustments – and how to master the mechanism of the depth-charge. Needless to say, each step means hard work and taking of stiff exams, but the period between each grade is lessened for the duration and a girl can attain in a comparatively short time a rank which would involve many years of hard work for the man in peacetime.' Clearly the navy was keen to be seen as encouraging, and the official recruiting literature grew more excited:

> Boarding Officers: qualifications are: good sea legs and a liking for the open air, for the Boarding Officer goes some miles out to sea, often with a gale blowing. As she goes aboard, the White Ensign is hoisted in acknowledgement of her rank. Many a hard-bitten skipper has been shaken as no attack on the voyage has shaken him by the arrival of a trim Wren Boarding Officer – but all acknowledge that these women know their job, and carry it out well.

Hearty stuff – you can almost hear the words booming out to cinema audiences as they watched the latest newsreel films while nibbling at a tiny toffee from their sweet ration. At least in this war the 'women knew their job' and appeared to have progressed from merely being 'plucky'.

There were opportunities abroad as well – and before the fall of Singapore to the Japanese in the spring of 1942 the first Wrens had been posted there as wireless telegraphists. Time for more booming phrases: 'Now Wrens are scattered over the globe in more than thirty naval establishments overseas, and here again the numbers are growing continually in response to the cry of Send Us More Wrens.'

Some, however, joined up because of the very atmosphere engendered by war – not patriotism, but a sense of disarray in life, with all the old certainties swept away: Phyllis Damonte worked in a sweatshop in the East End of London and saw it burn in the Blitz. She'd joined a concert party to entertain the air-raid wardens – and now there were no more concerts as the raids intensified.

> Feeling very despondent and unsure of my future I accepted a proposal of marriage from the only eligible man I knew of near my own age. We had had a casual relationship for some time. I was nearly twenty, he six years my senior. I grabbed at his proposal as though it was a lifeline – as indeed it was. In my despair I looked upon

the outcome of the liaison with hope. I didn't love him, and with hindsight I know he didn't love me. Young boys and girls were getting married by the dozen in those early days of the war – it was the thing to do. Death was just around the corner, if not for him then maybe for me. Kim gave me an engagement ring which he had bought from a Jewish lady in need of £10. He was already in the Navy. . . . We had a June wedding with no trimmings. I don't remember what I wore – I'm certain no special trousseau was bought. . . .

The bombing seemed to go on and on. I think we were all beginning to get beyond it. . . . I had to apply for war work and was sent for an interview and written test for work with the Victualling Department of the Admiralty, as a temporary civil servant. I didn't pass the test with flying colours, but with war well under way was found good enough to become a Grade III clerk. I found digs with two maiden ladies not given to smiles. At work we victualled the ships in readiness for the D-Day landings.

When it was obvious we were going to win the war a memo came around the office asking for volunteers to go to Ceylon (Sri Lanka) as members of the WRNS. I immediately applied and was accepted. I was running away from the man I didn't love and had no intention of ever being his wife again. So I was going to hide in the uniform of a Wren until I could sort myself out.

Little by little, the navy pushed back the barriers to women which had been erected around the fleet in Victorian times – but only by a few inches. There was absolutely no demand from any quarter that women should serve at sea, though every so often a skirt was allowed passage and finally they actually worked at sea, as reported by the *Sunderland Daily Echo* in May 1943: 'Six members of the WRNS of Great Britain have just completed a round trip aboard a big transport as the first women ever to take over the vital job handling signalling and communications on a large liner.' Even so, not quite the same as handing out the ammunition at Trafalgar.

In the WAAF, they at least got their hands on the aircraft. A whole raft of trades – acetylene welder, fabric maker, flight mechanic, fitter – opened up to women fully integrated into the RAF, clad in battledress tops and trousers, or sheepskin jackets, leather jerkins and boots, the practical and individual clothes that the air force prided itself on and which served them well on the dozens of remote airfields which dotted the country. However, most opportunities were clerical or domestic, and operational flying was not on the horizon for WAAFs.

Nancy Mullet was a shorthand typist when war began, and joined up to find herself doing the same job in uniform next to male typists – but earning two-thirds of the pay of an airman. She felt it an injustice, particularly because the men didn't need to

have shorthand. But it was not an issue which the services were in the least minded to address, even though there might be agitation in civilian factories. The dreary work was enlivened by lots of dances and entertainments laid on at the RAF camp at Innsworth in Gloucestershire. However, things were not allowed to get out of hand: 'If after a dance an airman escorted us back to our billet, there was a line painted around the building, about three yards from the walls, which airmen were not allowed to cross. No sheltering in the shadows!'

RAF and WAAF flight mechanics working together on a Beaufighter, 1944

Nancy was desperate to look smart, quoting a pre-war saying: 'To be poor and look poor is the devil all over.' She wasn't quite sure why she joined up, and was not encouraged after a medical in a draughty church hall 'where my specimen of urine was passed straight into a small milk-pan so that the Red Cross nurse could immediately boil it on an ancient gas stove – I think to check for diabetes'. She quite liked her blue uniform, after she'd shortened the skirt hem from the regulation 12 inches off the floor, taken it in to stop it looking baggy, adjusted her jacket, narrowed the waist and otherwise done a complete make-over on it. She thought her helmet particularly useful: 'The steel helmets served a very good purpose as far as the WAAF were concerned. Our uniform hats had voluminous tops, so we steamed them, up-ended them and placed our tin hat on top to flatten the crown.' She was rather puzzled by her greatcoat, which had a white wool lining: a colleague informed her that this was so it could be spread on the ground so that aircraft could find you if you'd baled out. If only – behind her typist's desk, like thousands of others, Nancy was unlikely to bale out. The why and wherefore of bits of kit was always something of a mystery, none more so than the sanitary towels which were supplied free – when the girls had expected to have to buy their own, being rather a luxury to those who came from poor homes. Nancy and the others believed the story that they'd been paid for by the philanthropist Lord Nuffield, personally. And that similar benefactors had paid for deliveries to the ATS and the Wrens. True? The girls couldn't think who to ask.

For the WAAF officers there was training as meteorologists, as accountants and in Intelligence, and there was keen competition to join. It seemed a progressive and 'modern' service, with lots of decent middle-class girls. Indeed, joining up involved a certain amount of string-tugging, much to the wonder of the Labour MP Dr Edith Summerskill, who tabled a question in the House of Commons asking if, because of over-subscription, 'family connections were needed to get in'. She was told, 'Yes: family connections take precedence, and having a fiancé in the RAF makes a girl more acceptable.'

Once in, officers needed a good tailor, and there were ingenious responses from the hard-pressed clothing industry to supplement the basic uniform: the manufacturers were unable to use the latest invention from America – nylon – because the war was swallowing up the precious material for parachutes and tents and glider tow-ropes. The introduction of food rationing in January 1940 was followed by clothes rationing eighteen months later. 'At least the servicewomen get something decent to wear', was a frequent grumble as the majority of the population embarked on the national experience of 'make-do and mend'. And, indeed, the list of kit was impressive in length, if not in quality and style, including one cape/groundsheet, greatcoat, respirator, steel helmet, cap with badge, two jackets, two skirts, two brassieres, two suspender belts (or two corselettes to women of bust sizes 40–44), two blue overalls and buttons, button-stick, two tins anti-gas ointment and about another thirty items.

The corset with money pockets, specially designed at the request of the ATS and WAAF: it enabled the wearer to take off her uniform jacket with impunity

The corsetry industry was nothing if not robust in the face of shortages and austerity, having to abandon frilly edgings, lace and embroidery, and in 1940 bringing out a special design of corset for the WAAFs and ATS 'at their request'. It had been noted that, when working, servicewomen often removed their jackets, and there was nowhere a woman could safely keep any money – hence the Corset With Pockets! But for all its efforts to produce war-friendly underwear, the industry soon found that the steel that had replaced whalebone in stays was not regarded as 'essential' – bullets and shells had priority. And, as in World War I, whalebone wasn't something on the list of essential imports, either. Lingerie reverted to the plain and serviceable, and the corset got a bit floppy. However, the aching backs of the factory workers slogging over their machines for long hours needed some sort of support, and there was public demand that something should be done. Step forward the Corset Guild of Great Britain, who in 1943 petitioned Downing Street on behalf of the women of Britain and their sagging spines – and succeeded in getting measures introduced to support the Support Industry.

Life on RAF stations had its own tensions and excitements, and long after the war I heard it said (not too unkindly) that former WAAFs were always the life and soul of a party – because they always think they're in the middle of nowhere in Lincolnshire, and no one will hear them. However, many were following the action in the skies very closely, as plotters and fighter-controllers: they knew the pilots whose planes were tiny symbols on their maps, and were only too personally aware of the casualty rate. Others were wrestling with monstrous barrage balloons bobbing above the airfields, splicing wire and learning to drive a winch, despite male misgivings about their physical ability to control these swaying 'Blimps'; newspapers were particularly partial to pictures of small female versus mighty balloon.

Given much less publicity were the 'Flying Nightingales', the WAAFs who volunteered for air ambulance duties. After initial training in a Dakota, this small group realised they were being got ready to go over to France just after the D-Day landings. It was no picnic: the first three – Lydia Alford, Edna Birbeck and Myra Roberts – found themselves flying over the beach wreckage, with action taking place just a mile or two inland. Often they flew without Red Cross markings, in ordinary aircraft ferrying food and ammunition, and they sat among bombs with their medical panniers. They followed the fighting, landing as near as possible on makeshift airstrips, and also landed at Arnhem after the disastrous airborne attack there. Every time they loaded up with wounded and high-tailed it back to Britain, and then were on call for the next flight. But the Nightingales were still regarded as 'extras' on the crew, and although quite a fuss was made officially after the first successful flight, the women themselves got the feeling that any instance where they were seen to be risking their lives was not quite what was wanted publicly. Women still had to be seen to be 'protected' where possible, regardless of the reality of their work.

Nevertheless, the first woman to be awarded the George Cross was WAAF Corporal Daphne Pearson. In May 1940 an aircraft crash-landed near her WAAF quarters, and Corporal Pearson ran out to it, even though it was still burning. The pilot was seriously injured, another officer had been killed outright and two airmen were slightly injured. She knew that the plane was loaded with bombs, but gave the pilot first aid next to the wreckage, released his parachute harness and got him clear. When he was on the ground about 30 yards away a 120lb bomb went off and Corporal Pearson threw herself on top of him to protect him from the blast and splinters.

Earning the first women's MBE (Military) a year later was Felicity Hanbury (later Dame Felicity Peake). Already widowed at twenty-six – her husband had been a fighter pilot – she was second-in-command at Biggin Hill airfield in Kent and gained a tremendous reputation for grace under fire during the Battle of Britain. After the war ended she was appointed Director of the WAAF at the age of thirty-two, with ninety thousand women under her command, guided by the principle that 'Women have to do much better than men or they don't get there.'

It would not have been a motto for everyone who served alongside Felicity during the war. Many women still had to be convinced that 'getting there' was either possible or desirable. The country had conscripted them, but most were not paid the same wages as men, and they were usually seen as substitutes or in support. The ferry pilots felt the inequality most keenly, but the majority of women just accepted 'being there' in their auxiliary role. Even with Felicity 'getting there' in charge of the WAAF, she was to have no female pilots under her command.

Members of the WAAF proving that women were perfectly capable of handling a heavy barrage balloon, in Coventry

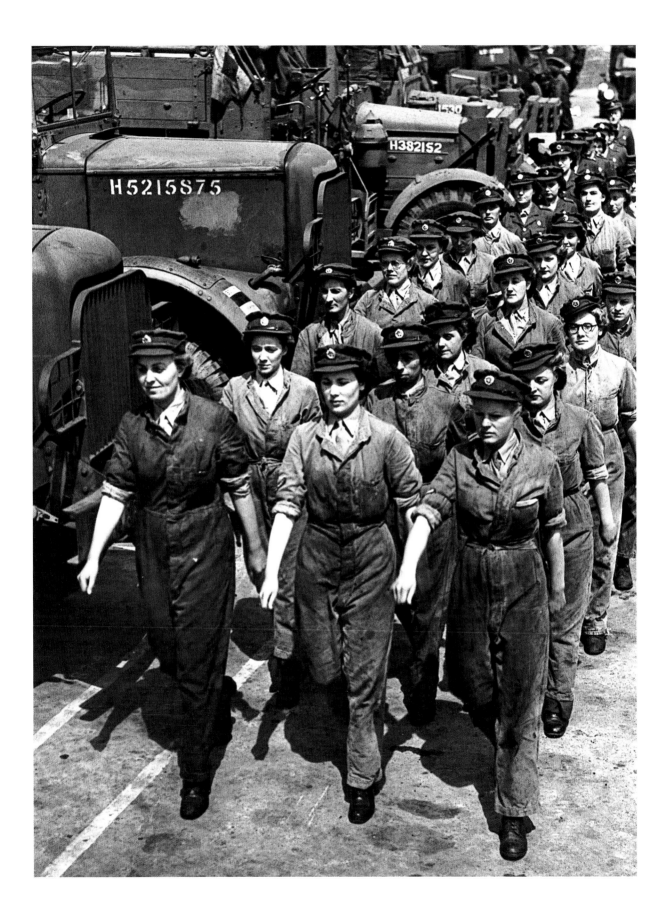

CHAPTER FOURTEEN

KETTLE AT THE READY

By far the largest number of women – over two hundred thousand of them – were in the Auxiliary Territorial Service. And in this war, unlike in World War I, they had equal status with the men in the forces, along with the WAAFs and women in the nursing and medical branches. For reasons known only to itself, the navy kept the Wrens at arm's length and they didn't come under the Naval Discipline Act; something rumoured to do with their 'ladylike nature'. Or whatever.

The ATS suffered from lack of glamour. Not that it didn't try hard, producing dramatic posters of svelte sirens wearing cute little caps which were then banned for overdoing it. The reality was a heap of kit, which Iris Bryce discovered included two uniforms, four pairs of lisle stockings, three pairs of khaki lock-knit knickers, two pairs of blue and white striped pyjamas (men's), eight starched collars and two studs, three pink bras and two pink boned corsets.

Opposite: The ATS after a hard day's work in REME (Royal Electrical and Mechanical Engineers) workshops

ATS image...

The greatcoat came down to my ankles and I lost one stud as I struggled to get it into the collar. I watched it roll under the bed and through a gap in the floorboards. The shirts, pyjama jacket and coats all did up the men's way. The shoes were so heavy I clonked along feeling like Frankenstein. I was luckier than some – I did have a complete kit. First day on parade the tall girl in front had a cotton flowered skirt and peep-toed sandals to go with her khaki jacket and shirt; nothing in the stores fitted her.

We'd been shown how to lay out the kit, everything folded in a certain way and placed strategically on top of your bed, and standing to attention by the side of the bed . . . I'd watched my neighbours and oh so carefully folded and placed everything in the right order. 'Where's the rest of it?' Sergeant's voice thundered the length of the hut. I looked at my kit and realised what she meant. I smiled and sighed in relief: 'Oh, you mean the bras and corsets. I couldn't wear those, all those bones. No, I've got my own roll-on. I've sent the others to my Gran for her jumble sale.'

The hapless Iris was marched out and put on a charge, when it was pointed out to her that every bit of kit, bras and all, belonged to the King's Uniform and could never be given away. Much later in the war the then Princess Elizabeth was put into ATS uniform, training as a driver and mechanic; in all the many photographs of this boost to the 'Cinderella' service her uniform is no different from anyone else's – except that it seems to fit.

Conscription, which was introduced in 1942, meant that war work of some kind was all but unavoidable. The volunteers from earlier, full of commitment and enthusiasm, were followed by hundreds of thousands who had little choice as to where they might serve or what they might do. In the ATS it was driving, typing, cooking, cleaning, admin – not a thrilling range of jobs, but the sheer numbers involved meant that life was changed out of all recognition for some, as they were shuttled around the country, directed into various trades and, like Iris, made to mix much more widely than before:

We were a real mixed lot in my hut. First there were the twins, who told me they'd volunteered as soon as they were old enough: 'Daddy's a major, we've always lived with the army – it's super.' Then there was Meg. She too 'lived with the army', but 'my old man's bin a regular for years, coo! You ought to see some of the places we lived in – this hut's a bloody palace; 'ere, give us yer shoes I'll show yer 'ow to bone 'em, give 'em a real polish.' But poor little Marion touched all our hearts. An only child from 'a nice part of Neasden', she'd worked as a filing clerk in a local printers 'only at the end of the

High Street – Mum was pleased as I could still go home for dinner'. After a life of gentle coddling she now found herself being shouted at, wearing uncomfortable, ill-fitting clothes, getting soaking wet doing PE on the barrack square and no mum waiting with nice warm dry vests, and then having to queue for a chance of a shower after. At the next medical she took one look as the needle went in and out of the girls' arms in front of her as we queued for our vac. jabs and she fainted straight away. By the end of the third week, as we groped our way out of the Gas Hut she just broke down and cried and cried and cried. No one could stop her. Corporal slapped her face, then we laid her on her bed, and finally she saw the MO and went into Sick Quarters. A week later her kit was collected and we never saw her again.

Iris then ran into a problem common to many armies: although there was a mass of forms to fill in to express preferences about training and work, they were probably regarded as an exercise in form-filling and nothing else:

When ability tests came along I decided not to let the army know I could type. I might as well try something completely different from office work, I thought. Oh, how little did I know the army's way of thinking. I wanted to be a driver, or even try catering, so I answered the questionnaire in that direction. That's how I found myself in Scotland on a course to turn me into a teleprinter/morse operator in the Royal Corps of Signals. Too late came the knowledge of the perverse logic of the army. If I'd told them I was a trained typist they would have sent me on a cookery or perhaps carpentry course.

. . . and ATS reality – female squaddies spud-bashing

For thousands, the gap between the glamour and responsibility offered in the official advertisements and the reality on the ground was exemplified by piles of potatoes to be peeled, and piles of forms to be shuffled. Girls thirsty for adventure and full of vim could find themselves shunted into dead-end jobs – and such was the nature of the military machine that it was often difficult to be in charge of your own life. Added to this, there was a pervasive sense of pressure because the country was perceived to be in danger – and 'you had to do it'. The sense of respect for authority was strong and women who had not been instilled with a streak of independence, or who felt socially insecure, had little opportunity for rebellion.

Others found that the sheer liberation from an existence bound by convention, lack of money and the confines of family gave them a platform from which they could view much greater possibilities for themselves. And eventually there was a substantial range of training available for jobs which hitherto had been a male preserve – electricians, draughtswomen, fitters, mechanics and radio operators. If some moaned about being posted hither and thither on a whim, others were gasping at being uprooted from a small village and plonked in the middle of London, or discovering that the countryside had few cinemas and a staggering lack of fish and chip shops. In 1939 it was not unusual for rural communities to be still waiting to acquire electricity, and a bus to market day in the nearest town represented 'an outing'.

Ceaselessly new vehicles roll off the production lines. Army units await them, the ATS deliver them

The economic slump in the thirties had made caution and worry about making ends meet automatic in the lives of millions. In the industrial towns there were huddles of stinking slums – my home town had won the doubtful distinction of being named the most overcrowded in the land in the 1931 census. Over a third of the population of Sunderland lived in 'undesirable conditions', with infant mortality at nearly one in ten – nearly twice the national average. An outside loo – the 'netty' – was the norm in the rows of Victorian terraces, and in 1935 the socialist Vera Brittan noted in her diary, while campaigning prior to a general election, that the north bank of the river, around the ancient monastery of Monkwearmouth, was especially foul:

Went round Monk Wearmouth housing – terrible slums, & crowded rooms with indescribably filthy bedding. In one house saw family of man & woman with nine children all living in two rooms – man an ex-serviceman who had never had a job since the War; woman looked very ill, shapeless & entirely overwhelmed by life. Children only semi-clothed. The couple had been there 20 years & obviously had not turned out the rooms all that time as there was nowhere but the street to put the furniture. Realised as so often what an expensive luxury cleanliness is. Have never seen such terrible housing before – not even in Glasgow.

Joining up was a way out for both men and women. And, not surprisingly, service life could appear startlingly luxurious to those who knew only slum conditions: it provided changes of clothes, insisted on soap and toothbrushes, and gave you your own bed. And you found yourself living with people who complained about draughty Nissen huts, lice inspections and not enough hot water. War might not break down social barriers, but it made people look over on to the other side.

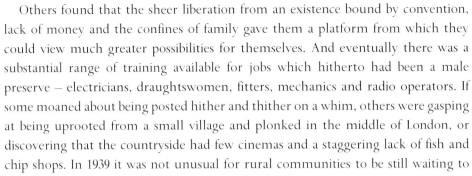

The very fact that the country needed you was at least recognition that the government was moving on from the time when women's unemployment was hardly registered as an official statistic. However, although the uniform gave a kind of equality in itself – and gave a status which hitherto many women had never experienced – unequal pay was a fact of life. So was the attitude that all cooking and cleaning is a uniquely feminine talent.

Norma Lodge joined the ATS determined to do anything but office work, and brandished her qualifications in maths and physics. To her delight she was trained as a radio location mechanic, in an experiment to see if women would be able to take on a job that had always been done by men. Posted to Charminster in Dorset, she

A junior ATS officer learning the technical aspects of a Sherman tank in 1944

learned to deal with technical maintenance and faults on the tracking equipment on anti-aircraft gun sites. It was complicated work and classified as highly secret, but it was a 'first' for women, reinforced by their being the first women taken into the newly formed REME – Royal Electrical and Mechanical Engineers. An energetic and confident team, they got their commanding officer to agree to give them rifle training 'so we could defend ourselves'; there were not many units in the army where this happened.

All in all, a success story, but. 'We worked a six-day week, three days from 8am to 6pm alternating with three days working 8am to 8pm. . . . This meant that we occupied the workshops until 8pm (or later if there was an emergency) so the cleaning took us until about 10pm.' The women had designated themselves the 'Charminster Chars' because somehow, along with the complex technical work, they had been handed all the mopping, dusting and polishing. Only an unintentional squawk of 'Charminster Chars' down the phone in response to their CO's complaint about a black-out infringement brought the matter into the open – and saw the men having to shoulder their share of the domestic rota.

But equality was by no means endorsed everywhere – Sybela Stiles was a head driver with a motor ambulance convoy in Egypt, and though she noted that the workshop fitters were 'very ready to impart their knowledge and show naïve surprise if we show signs of taking it in', she was ready to argue that women should not earn as much as men:

I think men should have more responsibilities. Either be married, or saving up for marriage; I prefer that a man takes me out and not have to share 50–50. If women are accustomed to earn a lot they are less ready to settle down and have children when they marry. They want to go on with their job, increase their joint income so they can have better clothes and a car instead of children. But I suppose I am old-fashioned.

Not only the workshop fitters would have been nodding in agreement.

And for Iris Bryce, there were some rueful reflections on her years in uniform:

I went into the ATS as a private and left some three years later, still a private. I enjoyed the life, but was never part of it. I always felt I was waiting for my real life to start again, where it had left off back home with my real friends, all those people I'd always known. I had thought that being called up was my big chance to escape, to leave that dreary cobbled street, the factories and barge yards. I soon missed the freedom of that life, oh the joy of going on leave and having a choice of what to wear each morning. I might only have a limited civvy wardrobe, but I could choose a pink blouse or a green one. I'll never forget the loathing on seeing my legs clad in khaki lisle stockings. I felt like my Gran.

NAAFI image . . .

The WRNS got sleek black stockings, again defining the invisible pecking order which operated throughout the services. However, even the ATS khaki was envied by another group, frequently obscured behind steaming tea urns and mounds of buns – the ubiquitous char and wads. 'You know how little the NAAFI girls were thought of . . . we always felt we were the poor relations of the services, as we did not come under orders of the armed forces . . . especially when I tell you that our hut was only a short distance from the danger area, where all the bombs were stored.' Nora Rivett was one of sixty thousand NAAFI girls, the providers of the essential cup of char, and served at RAF Sawston in Cambridgeshire and later at RAF Lords Bridge. 'There were four of us, manageress, cook, counter-hand and general dogs-body me. I was handed a recipe book geared to NAAFI regulations and had to get on with it. Five hundred cakes had to be ready by 10.15am break, there was staff dinner for seven to cook for, plus two airmen who lived out of camp and then about another five hundred cakes and suppers for the evening opening.' The girls worked from 6.30am to 9.30pm, often in bleak Nissen huts, scrubbing floors, serving cigarettes and sweet rations, peeling potatoes and washing up. They had fewer perks than others in uniform, and their own uniforms were referred to as 'something worn by Little Orphan Annie'. Off-duty, the girls were subject to a specific NAAFI rule: a soldier wishing to escort her had to give a receipt for the girl, and deliver her back to her base by a stipulated time.

. . . and NAAFI reality – in 1943 these four women produced fifty thousand pastries every week

The NAAFI at Catterick camp in Yorkshire demonstrated that, although it needed woman power, there were entrenched attitudes in the 1940s which put a brake on some recruiting. Lilian Bader (née Bailey) was twenty-two and had sent off her form for an interview. 'On seeing me, the interviewer said, "You did not say you were er, er. . . ." I looked her in the eye and retorted, "My form shows that my father was from Jamaica. It is our oldest Crown Colony."' After seven weeks she was dismissed on the rather doubtful grounds that her father had not been born in the UK. Undeterred, she eventually applied to the WAAF, becoming the first of its members to be trained as an instrument operator. Though she spoke with a broad Yorkshire accent, she was frequently referred to as 'foreign' and called 'Cherry Blossom' (as in shoe polish).

There were only a few dozen black faces in the WAAF and the ATS – no precise figures were kept. Prolonged argument had taken place in the civil service and political quarters about the 'colour question', with considerable resistance which was expressed officially in the phrase: 'Coloured women would find it difficult to adapt to British customs and climate.' In the end about a hundred women from the West Indies came to Britain – though the group was disproportionately white. The media welcomed them warmly, as reassurance that the colonies were standing shoulder to shoulder with the mother country. And there was also the cushion of wartime camaraderie, that 'we were all in it together', though the unspoken tolerance of a colour bar was always present. Despite this, Lilian Bader applied herself to her technical training and thrived, gaining the rank of acting corporal – a notable achievement, all things considered.

She had not been particularly enamoured of the life of tea-making in Catterick; however, those who stayed on in the NAAFI were renowned for their ability to conjure up gallons of the stuff, which, though of questionable blend and sometimes the colour of mud for very natural reasons involving the water supply, was forever welcome to tense, dog-tired people. They got no medals – but they ran the same risks as those stationed on bases and at camps. Many served abroad, and in the field the girls were given ATS uniforms. They ran shops and canteens, cooked and organised recreational activities, and produced ever more welcome, ever stranger tea.

The campaign against the Japanese in south-east Asia involved bitter fighting and great hardship – cloaked by the jungle and distant from the European theatre of war, the troops here often referred to themselves as the 'forgotten army'. Brewing tea out there fell to an intrepid band called the WAS(B). The Women's Auxiliary Service (Burma) had been working as encoders when the country was over-run by the Japanese. Rather than return to India or England, they reinvented themselves as a mobile canteen unit for front-line troops. Led by the redoubtable Ninian Taylor, who never lost the opportunity to tell generals that her girls were an official army unit, they popped up relentlessly in places which the army thought unsuitable – near

front lines, under bombardment, in the jungle. Frank Colenso, serving in the RAF, met them in central Burma: 'The unhealthy climate, heat, humidity, disease, the danger and the constant unsettling living conditions, with food and water in poor supply, in a war situation of killing and destruction was certainly no place for a woman. However, there they were – a dedicated small army of women in their various uniforms following the action over three and a half years . . . they brought a touch of normality back.'

Apart from tea the WAS(B) dispensed cigarettes, razor blades and all the other little comforts that boosted morale phenomenally, along with cheerful smiles. The men in the grim Burma campaign marvelled at them – Robert Sawyer, a private in the 2nd Battalion, Welsh Regiment, recalled: 'There was always a buzz when word spread that the girls would be coming into our company area – char and wads and those gorgeous tins of fruit, peaches and pears, hard to describe that taste after a diet of K-ration [US field rations, including the intriguing 'Defense Biscuits']. It was hard to imagine why these lovely ladies volunteered to serve in such a place as Burma.' In gum boots, khaki slacks and bush shirts they eventually served right across south-east Asia – in Sumatra, Java and even Japan. They offered tea to prisoners of war who'd survived forced labour on the infamous Burma Railway, the emaciated men often crying at the sight of the first women they'd seen for years.

Like others in this distant theatre of war, Elaine Cheverton found that coming home after years in the WAS(B) had its challenges:

On August Bank Holiday 1946 six of us arrived in Liverpool. It was very difficult to adjust to life in Britain, because we still had rationing. We were given a demob coat, skirt and two blouses, which we could get on coupons. We felt we had been privileged. Apart from the bombing in Akyab, we hadn't the experience of night after night of heavy bombing and all those years of rationing. People said, 'What on earth were you doing with mobile canteens in Burma?' Not in a nasty way, but they had no conception of what we were doing. It really was the forgotten army.

The cup of tea, associated as it was with the NAAFI, acquired iconic status back home. And not only were the NAAFI capable of a brew-up for a thousand men in appalling conditions, they'd also decided that the lads should be entertained; even before war broke out, plans were laid for the Entertainments National Service Association – ENSA. Unkindly known as Every Night Something Awful, this extraordinary outfit pulled off small miracles of show-business in the most unlikely places: conjuring in the desert, comedy in ruined towns, opera and musicals and film shows in tin huts and village halls and under canvas. From Vera Lynn to Sir Adrian Boult, Arthur Askey to Flanagan and Allen, ENSA provided Variety and variety. Crooners, dance troupes and novelty acts visited the farthest-flung outposts, and many ran the same risks as the troops.

Pianist Catherine Lovatt was touring the munitions factories in northern England with a cellist and violinist when she heard from the Drury Lane headquarters of ENSA that a tour abroad was being got up. Her sister Joan had just finished her musical training and been rejected by the WAAF because of a bout of pleurisy in childhood. Thinking that she'd soon be peeling potatoes, Joan followed her sister to an audition in London and both joined a Welsh concert party called Taffy's Twelve.

ENSA women organising costumes and props at their headquarters

It was extraordinary who got in. There were these men who didn't have any special talent – one played the bones, would you believe, but he had a lovely tenor voice. Then there was the manager, Maskell, and his brother Yanto – a lovely voice – both ex-miners and a proper tenor. And because we were Welsh there was this miners' scene in the concert, with proper Davy lamps and hard hats – it was supposed to be after an explosion and all dark. And all twelve of us were in the semi-darkness and we sang 'Jesus Lover of My Soul' to the tune of Aberystwyth.

We rehearsed for a fortnight, then after a

An Afternoon
Show by an ENSA
Company in a
NAAFI Canteen
Hut (detail),
*painting by
Frank Graves*

month round army camps near London we got our orders in October '43 and we were
all shipped out to a station somewhere, then travelled in a blacked out train – oh, it
seemed for hours.

Recognising the Liver Building, they boarded a Dutch liner, the *Marnix Van St
Aldegonde*, in Liverpool, along with three and a half thousand soldiers, QA nurses,
RAF airmen and ten other ENSA companies. The ship was still quite luxurious –
there was lots of mahogany everywhere, and Javanese stewards, and single cabins had
been converted to take four bunks each.

We had no idea where she was going. The rumour was that we were bound for India,
and the main thing that sticks in my memory is that we had fresh milk and white bread
on board – the first for a long time.

We were in a large convoy, and we had boat drill, twice, sometimes three times a day.
The klaxon would go off and you'd have to drop what you were doing and get your
lifejacket on with its little torch, but we thought it's never going to happen to us –
you're supremely confident at that age. We'd been at sea a fortnight, through the
Straits of Gibraltar, and we then saw Spain just beyond, with all the lights on – we'd
been so used to darkness in the war. Every day they used to give out orders on the
Tannoy – if there was going to be housey-housey – bingo today – and that sort of
thing, and then, when there was quite a sea-swell, they said that owing to a case of

acute appendicitis the *Marnix* was going to slow down while the operation was performed and she was going to the back of the convoy.

We were just in the cabin waiting to go down for the evening meal – it was 6 November – when all of a sudden off went the klaxon, and we all looked at each other and said, 'Not again', because we'd already had two drills that day. Anyway, on went our lifejackets, but then what never happened in ordinary boat drill, BANG . . . BANG – the guns of the ship started going off. And she shook, they were such huge guns, and then my recollection is what felt like an earthquake – the floor seemed to come up, there was an extra-loud WHUMP and every light in the ship went out. It was pitch-black and I remember grabbing Cathy's hand and saying, 'Oh God' and trying to feel for the zip bag where I kept my passport, but the boat was tilted and the other two girls' cigarettes were rolling all over the floor.

It couldn't have lasted for more than two and a half minutes when a voice came over the Tannoy saying, 'Keep calm. We have been hit. The emergency lights will be on shortly. Stay where you are until further orders, but keep calm.' So we stayed where we were – but we couldn't find anything in the dark, and I was still in my Palm Beach slacks and a linen blouse and my sister had on a dress for dinner. Then they called us, deck by deck, and told us to proceed slowly, with the crew in the corridors leading people. I remember an old lady – the character part – in the drama company muttering, 'God is with us, God is with us', producing the comment of 'Silly old woman' from the leading lady.

Once we got out on deck there was this sharp smell of cordite, and while we were queuing up for the boat we got a good idea what had happened. It was a radio-controlled aerial torpedo from a plane – they said it was one of the first used – and the guns had got the plane. It had crashed. It was also said that as we were going through the Straits of Gibraltar – and Spain had a lot of spies – they'd reported the huge convoy and alerted the planes.

We weren't the only ship in that convoy that went down, and I saw a fire at sea which I'll never forget. That was a whole ship burning – just a blaze of fire and flames – and she went down pretty quickly. On F Deck of the *Marnix* they'd been serving soup to the troops – hot soup in huge tureens – and when the torpedo hit the soup poured all over the men and there was panic and pandemonium, and the officers had revolvers and they shot into the air to calm everyone down. A lot of the Javanese stewards panicked and jumped – and they were taken in the first suction, and they were lost. Out of about three and a half thousand souls, they said we lost three hundred – it had been a direct hit on the engine room.

When we got to the boat station we were on the high-tilted side and the boat had had to be cut free of the davits and dropped. So they threw these nets over the side and down we went to the water – there was such a swell – and we got eighty of us girls into the boat with two stewards and guess who – the appendix man. We were squashed up tight against each other, and luckily the Javanese stewards had these tin hats and they kept saying, 'Likee hattee?' each time you were about to throw up.

Two ships came close, but then the worst thing we heard was planes coming overhead, and you'd read these awful things about being machine-gunned and so on – that was the only time I really felt frightened – but I'm not sure whose planes they were. We were in the boat for four and half hours and picked up by HMS *Croome* – a small Hunter-class destroyer. And then again there were nets over the side, and they were shouting 'Jump! Jump!' in very stern voices, and you got strong arms heaving you up. I can remember saying, 'I'm all right' and then falling over – we'd been so tightly packed our limbs were dead.

An older man took us to the wardroom and said to all of us girls, 'Take off all those wet clothes, and we'll see what we can find for you', and they found lovely warm woollies, men's things, and honestly, you were warm in two ticks. And we were given hot tea with, I think, rum in it, because it went straight to my head and as I lay down on the uncomfortable floor I said to my sister, 'Well, if this is being torpedoed I like it.'

Joan and Catherine were landed at Philippeville near Algiers the next day and, with other survivors, were stuck on the dock for hours, deemed to have made an 'unauthorised landing'. They met up with the other members of Taffy's Twelve – and realised they'd lost almost everything. But in true theatrical tradition they'd managed to rescue an accordion, a couple of miner's lamps – and the tenor was still clutching his bones. They all ended up in an empty villa with one grey blanket and a delivery of black bread, cooked beetroot and tinned peaches.

Within five days of having been torpedoed, they were on stage. Catherine was the only person who could remember all the party's music, and so, kitted out in battledress, the Twelve headed for the troops' camps and field hospitals – but not before being warned that they shouldn't go on if they couldn't take the sight of men who'd been burned in their tanks.

We did twelve weeks and we went through the desert – Tobruk, Tripoli, Benghazi as it turned out – but we still didn't know where we were setting off for every morning. I did enjoy it so much, and when we were singing in the desert – well, you could tell if an audience had been deprived of entertainment for a long time by looking out and seeing nothing but smiles. But the extraordinary thing was this thing with the Davy lamps – when I think of it now, I don't know how we dared put it on, with hats and lamps and hymns – but you could have heard a pin drop in the middle of the desert.

You just got on with things – whether you were in a bombed suburb of London or the North African desert. Joan was away for over a year on her first tour, then went to India and Italy and ended up in Germany and Austria just after Allied forces occupied them. Here was a war job which followed the battles – seeing the results of fighting, playing in all kinds of venues, living in a world of fighting men, wounded men and those whom the war had collected in its wake: 'We saw starving children in Vienna – but didn't dare give them chocolate, they'd fight so over it – so we just left our ration on the park benches. And women – we'd seen women in Hamburg moving the massive mounds of rubble with their bare hands, and in Vienna we saw Russian women marching in the streets. They had big square faces, they were bristling with guns – and they were built like tanks.'

From makeshift stages to makeshift wards: alongside all those who were in British uniform were nurses. Just as in World War I they crossed the Channel within days of war being declared, and army sisters set up a sophisticated network of hospitals, casualty clearing stations and ambulance trains. They then spent several months with relatively little to do, until Hitler's onslaught on northern France in May 1940. The next few weeks were a nightmare of confusion, as the Allied armies found themselves cut in two by the Germans and bombed relentlessly. Over a thousand nursing sisters were caught up in what became a huge evacuation culminating at Dunkirk. The staff of No. 3 Ambulance Train had a typical experience in the battle of Flanders, with the Germans only four miles away:

We picked up about fifty of the refugees and took them along to a safer place, the poor creatures being most grateful for the rest and food.

Early next morning we stopped at Verneuil, having heard that the convoy [of wounded] would meet us there. We were just finishing a meal when one of the batmen came racing down the train, shouting, 'Sisters, get your tin hats! Jerry's here!' We rushed to our bunks to get them. I glanced up and saw three planes, flying low and coming like the wind towards us. There were seven altogether, I believe. I reached No. 1 Coach, where our patients were, as the first bomb exploded. Two Sisters were seized by an Orderly, who made them lie on the floor and not move. . . .

At last the raid was over. Our beautiful ambulance was cut in two. No. 5 Coach was like a crumpled matchbox; broken glass and earth covered the train. The French troop-train was in ruins; the poor dead horses looked most pathetic; the station was devastated. Sadder still, one Orderly had been killed and nine or ten others more or less injured. Some of them had wonderful escapes, one being blown clear of the train as the middle coach collapsed.

The dead were taken to a convent near, poor little girls and women among them, also dead soldiers (French). In the evening we got away in the first three coaches of the train, feeling it dreadfully that we had to leave the body of our brave Orderly under the wreckage.

In this war, the sisters in Queen Alexandra's Imperial Military Nursing Service travelled the globe, serving in Europe, Africa, Asia and the Middle East. Merely reaching the theatres of war was a hazard, with convoys bombed and torpedoed, never mind setting up shop in such unlikely locations as a river steamer in Bengal. A striking aspect of the job was the number of nationalities they nursed. They dealt with troops from all corners of the British Empire, and with allies from Poland to China. They coped with patients who spoke no English and patients who were puzzled by bed-pans and pyjamas. Then there were the niceties of the Indian caste-system and the prohibitions of Islamic Ramadan, as well as wards to keep clean in the face of weird insects and no plumbing. Prisoners of war presented a particular challenge, with Italian and Japanese soldiers hard to convince that a sister approaching with a syringe was not intent on revenge. . . . Nursing highlighted the phenomenal reach of the war: so many nationalities, so many displaced and uprooted people. The colonies had responded with both money and personnel, and there were several women's services raised to help the war effort, such as the Women's Royal Indian Naval Service and the Women's Auxiliary Corps (Indian).

In North Africa, the scarlet and grey which looked so smart in the hospitals in Cairo had to be jettisoned, as General Montgomery and the 8th Army fought through the Western Desert. In slacks and battle blouses eight nursing sisters of No.1 Mobile Military Hospital slogged through sandstorms and battlefield debris as part of the expeditionary force, covering well over a thousand miles in seven weeks. Time and again it wasn't their nursing skills which impressed the patients – just the mere fact of being female and being there. No one expected women to submit to such conditions, and to be just on the heels of advancing troops.

For some young women it was a tough introduction to nursing. As the QAIMNS followed the troops into France after the D-Day landings in Normandy, they saw young men burned, maimed and disfigured – and then had to treat Germans brought in as prisoners. Many eventually moved on further into Europe and nursed survivors from the concentration camps. One sister's account of her time in Belsen after liberation is full of perceptive comments aside from her nursing duties. She noted that many of the young girls, emaciated and with their heads shorn, had not possessed a mirror for years, and when given one they did not recognise their own reflection.

Before the war began, the Voluntary Aid Detachment had been reorganised so that its members could supplement general medical services. They had civilian status, and were drawn from the Red Cross and the Order of St John and St Andrew's Ambulance Association. As well as working on the home front, VADs went to Burma, Malaya, Singapore, Thailand, Hong Kong, Sumatra and Java. Meg Minshull Fogg, who'd intended to join the navy because she liked the uniform, found herself lured into the Red Cross: 'I went to a concert raising funds for the Red Cross, and an officer got up and asked young ladies to join. I thought: this uniform looks pretty like a naval uniform, so I thought I'll join. The uniform was navy blue with white shirt and black tie, with gold shoulder tabs giving your unit – Red Cross Section No. 24 Buckinghamshire – rather smart, and hat to match.' After two years of handing out dressings and taking temperatures and passing round bed-pans, she heard that Red Cross nurses were needed in the Far East, so she volunteered:

> We thought it sounded great fun – to go on this jolly to India. We went to an interview in London with all these large ladies, large bosoms – the queen bees of the Red Cross and St John's, lovely old dears, Lady Reading, Lady Lithgow, Lady Louis Mountbatten – and they said to me: 'Why do you want to go to India, a little girl like you?' I can't remember what I said to them. We had no idea we were heading for Burma – we'd had contracts signed with the Indian government.

The Hadfield-Spears Hospital Unit in battledress in North Africa, with their CO, Lady Spears (far left)

After medicals we sailed, and in the Mediterranean the convoy was dispersed because of a submarine attack, and when we landed at Bombay one girl refused to disembark. We started nursing in Poona – dysentery and malaria and so on, and serious wounds on the surgical wards with the chaps on their way back to England from the fighting. After six weeks we were sent on to Calcutta, then Chittagong, Cox's Bazaar, and finally to Ramree Island in Burma. We were given the nickname the Blue Roses of the Arakan – the area. It sounds lovely but it was no picnic – it was hard work. Weeks on night duty, no days off – but there was nowhere to go. Although we were a very small number of women attached to the whole of the 14th Army – say no more. . . .

But there was so much work to be done, there was no time for histrionics – no room for that at all. I mean, when you saw how badly injured these men were – horribly shot up – and with awful liver diseases and dysentery . . . And the fighting was intense – at one stage there were so many casualties we never came off duty.

And oh, the mosquitoes! We were issued with boots, trousers and bush jackets – everything buttoned up – and mosquito beds and nets, and canvas beds and washbasins. Everything – the wards, the accommodations – all under canvas. We were nursing Indian troops as well – we had to pick up and speak BOR [British Other Ranks]

Urdu. They had their own wards and were fun if you liked curry, which used to arrive in buckets.

Once we had to be evacuated, all the patients got ready, because we were told that the Japanese were bearing down on the island in sampans. But the Royal Navy arrived and shooed them off.

We then had the first delivery of penicillin – it came in a huge box with dry ice, and we had to have theatre conditions to give the first injections, because we were dealing with pure gold. There was a surgeon and the theatre sister, and it was quite a performance that first injection. It made such a difference to the infections – usually all the wounds were covered in maggots, and we had to change dressings and tweezer out all those maggots every time.

I suppose you could have opted out. But I felt I was there for a purpose and I'd volunteered and there was duty to be done – and I'm very proud when I wear my Burma Star.

The VADs had to defer to the army sisters; nevertheless, at the beginning of the war even these experienced nurses were still not full members of the forces. In World War

I they'd been professional nurses who happened to be employed by the army, then in 1926 the sisters were given equivalent ranks to the army – though this only conferred a more or less honorary status. However, with the formation of the ATS sisters with years of military experience found themselves overtaken by teenage girls in battledress. Even though Regular Emergency Commissions were granted in 1941, the army nurses were left in a rather ambiguous position which might have been a mere quibble about shoulder pips had it not been for the treatment of prisoners of war by the Japanese. The military sisters were right up behind the front lines in many areas, and as much under fire as men on active service. And in the Far East, especially in Hong Kong and Singapore, many were captured by the Japanese. The sisters were refused the status of military POWs and their Australian colleagues had a truly terrible time, while continuing to nurse their fellow prisoners. Not until 1949 did the government sort out the anomaly of having nurses who were 'in' the army, but not 'of' it.

Married in uniform: Nursing Officer Mary Macdonald of the QAIMNS ties the knot with Captain William Spiers McKell, RAOC

One matter that was sorted out under pressure of circumstances was the right to wear practical clothing while knee-deep in mud, or facing a zillion enemy mosquitoes. Starched collars and cuffs disappeared, and after a lot of letter-writing and signal-sending useful khaki battledress was winkled out of the stores to replace grey dresses and white aprons. Even so, at the height of fighting in the desert in North Africa the sisters dug into their kit-bags on Christmas Day 1942 and distributed stockings filled with a piece of soap, tobacco, paper and pencil – while dressed in their frocks and starched white caps. Cigarettes and soap, tea and sticky buns, Davy lamps and hymns – little luxuries for the men which put them in touch with civilised life and stirred memories of home. The women who provided them were not dealing in trivia, but in the essentials to sustain morale.

CHAPTER FIFTEEN

WATCH THAT FIRE
AND KNIT FOR VICTORY

WAY FROM THE front lines, millions of women who hadn't had the slightest notion of participating in a war found themselves taking part willy-willy: in many ways the front line moved over Britain, with air-raids rendering the whole population vulnerable. Not only armaments works, factories and shipyards took a pounding – thousands of ordinary homes were destroyed. Bombs fell on shops and offices and schools, and as a small child I spent a holiday on a Cumbrian farm where a three-legged creature named Horace was still remembered for having been the only sheep on a remote hillside to be targeted personally by Herr Hitler. There were many households on the home front where the women and children saw a good deal more action than the man of the house away in the services. And wearing a uniform became ever more common, as women organised themselves to deal with the complete upheaval of normal life.

Opposite: 'Spotting duty': Staff Nurse Dorothy Sherlock on the roof of Great Ormond Street Hospital, 1940

The most organised outfit was the enormously flexible WVS, established by the formidable Dowager Marchioness of Reading, one of the long list of women in the first half of the twentieth century who used their upper-class confidence and contacts to establish and run a vast range of voluntary initiatives. These women took 'public service' very seriously, and often had more success than government departments when trying to anticipate the needs of a society under stress. The Women's Voluntary Service, dressed in green uniform – the only colour left to them by all the various military and nursing services – established canteens, set up knitting and sewing circles and ran feeding centres. The 'Women in Green' had no ranks, but boundless energy and common sense. Organised on a county basis, they basically melded communities together, providing over a million women to step into the breach when yet another emergency hit ordinary people. Their first test was evacuation – the huge movement of children out of the cities in response to fears that massive German air-power would reduce urban areas to rubble within a few days of war being declared.

Evacuation proved to be an earthquake, and not just geographically. Tales are legion of townies screaming in fear when faced with a thoughtful, albeit large cow. Of lice-ridden, scrofulous brats horrifying middle-class families. And of lonely, bewildered street-wise urchins being rebuffed and neglected by resentful country folk. Tales balanced with memories from children enchanted by the countryside, given love and affection – and toys for the first time. Trying to make sense of it all were the WVS, herding labelled youngsters to new homes. Miss G. Mackay Brown was the organiser for Bedfordshire's thirty-four rural parishes, and along with a local farmer who was the billeting officer she had to find accommodation for a London convent school, including seventy-two pupils, mainly boys, three nuns and a religious brother:

Lady Reading, Chairman of the WVS (Women's Voluntary Service), interviewing volunteers in 1939. Soon they would be organising the evacuation of city children to the country

The staff had cleaned up the children and issued new and clean clothes to them at the end of the July term, but the August holiday came and six weeks went by before the evacuation took place. The result was that most of the new clothes had been sold and nearly all the children arrived in a ragged and appallingly dirty condition. The sisters were very apologetic and distressed that this had happened.

The party arrived one afternoon about 5pm. The WI [Women's Institute] and other volunteers attended at the reception centre in the school and provided tea and biscuits whilst allocations were made. Some housewives came personally to (more or less) *choose* their children, so that ages and sex should suit their household. Other volunteers delivered the children to those who had stayed at home to receive them and every one was settled in their billets within an hour and a half of arrival. More girls than boys had been asked for, but only a few arrived, which created some household problems.

Then the trouble began. Many housewives undressed their visitors in an outhouse, gave them a scrub, put them to bed, *burnt* their clothes and sent SOS messages to the WVS representative for clean clothes. Luckily the centre of Bedford was prepared for this and a car-load arrived late that night and was sent to the cottages early next day, when another car-load arrived. . . . Nurse Eaton, the resident District Nurse, set up a clinic and it took three weeks to get every child free from 'creatures'.

There were a few problems, but most upsets were caused by visiting parents. Luckily they came by train to Bedford and the fifteen miles by road to Dean discouraged frequent visits. They had no compunction about demanding meals, and rations for a week disappeared in a day if the housewife was not prepared. Dean people are friendly and hospitable, but wartime curbed their natural instinct. One or two parents secretly took all their children's spare clothes back to London before the housewives realised this could happen. They no doubt sold them. So things likely to tempt them had to be hidden.

Many had never sat at a table for a meal – food had been thrust into their hands or they had been given a few pence to go out and spend it on what they liked. One small

Members of the Women's Institute busy in a kitchen 'somewhere on the east coast of England'. Even jam-making was subject to official secrecy

boy would only eat dry bread for the first few days and many had never tasted jam.

Jam was a major undertaking, never mind a treat for a small London boy. Miss Mackay Brown proudly records that thirty-one Bedfordshire WIs produced '25 tons of jam for sale on the public ration'. Then there was salvage – a mammoth task in which waste paper, old pots and pans, pigswill and wool were collected by the bin-load, and streets were shorn of their Victorian railings. The Government Knitting Scheme was another WVS responsibility, in which lumpy bales of wool were unravelled into skeins and parcelled out to be got up into infant vests and coatees and so on – many official wartime photographs show office workers, telephonists and factory girls on their tea-breaks wielding knitting needles, the suggestion being that Knitting for Britain was possible at any time. Listening to the all-important wireless was so bound up with the obligation to purl and plain that, long after the war, I recall some women being unable to hear a radio programme without reaching automatically for a pair of needles.

A picture of daily life for a WVS canteen worker – and determined knitter – comes from Mrs Rose Uttin, a housewife living at 41 Castleton Avenue, Wembley in north-west London with her husband Bill and teenage sister Dora. Rose's diary for 1942 records the relentless pattern of domestic routine interfered with by the madness of war.

Wednesday, 22 April

I am sitting writing this in the kitchen, wearing my tin hat – I wonder what people think about during a raid? Yesterday I met Mollie who worked with me – she lost everything in last Tuesday's raid and nowhere to sleep. All Clear just going 1.50 – thank God no damage done.

Thursday, 23 April

Warning went last night 9.20 – not long after we had got back from the hospital – only lasted till 9.55, and very little gunfire, and the flares were seen dropping over the City. Went to the knitting party – few there. The Conservative ladies dropped off when Mrs Barton, the Labour member's wife, was mayoress last year, and now the new Labour knitters have stopped coming since Mrs Plymen the Liberal member's wife took office. This political feeling should not be whilst we are trying to down a common enemy. How can we expect to make a universal peace if this political influence creeps in? Harold called last evening – just after he had left the Warning went, I wonder how far he got? I obtained 2 packets dried eggs today, and tripe as well.

24 April

Raid started tonight at 11.20 – such gunfire as to alarm me terribly. There must be a huge gun near, for the windows shook so much I thought they would fall in. After filling the kettle with fresh water and turning off the gas at the main, I sat down on the floor and knitted – like Madame Defarge in the Dickens' *Tale of Two Cities* – but instead of 'off came another head' it was off went another gun. I feel I must knit – I cannot sit without occupying my hands, and I won't smoke. Mother came back for a few hours today, she looks better and says she had not got up one night since she has been here. I called on Mabel and she gave me 3 eggs and then Marjorie gave me 3 more. Mother brought me nine oranges, I gave Mrs Cooper 2 of them. The All Clear has just gone – 1am, the longest raid we have had in some time.

But sometimes things were better; one entry reads:

We had 2 nights of quiet. Last night (my birthday) we, i.e. Daisy, Bill and self sat chatting till 12, decided it was time to go to bed, so went up and just falling asleep when we hear the trailer pumps rush through. Then a siren in the distance, so Daisy and I got up and dressed, as we heard slight gunfire. Stayed in bed dressed except for skirt and stockings – no raid here. Today has been lovely, we went to the Regal and enjoyed ourselves. Bill has gone to a fire guard meeting and we are on duty tonight. I do hope we have it peaceful.

Fund-raising, delivering ration books, providing a transport service, reuniting families after air-raids, giving instruction on how to make something from dried egg, a little unpleasant margarine and a very weird-looking fish: the WVS rose to each occasion and handed out comforting cups of tea to boot. They They also found the material for black-out curtains and liaised with the air-raid wardens.

Wardens were the guardians of the black-out; or the black-out busybody, depending on how well you got on with your neighbours. First in mackintoshes, later in navy battledress, equipped with gas-mask and torch and topped with a tin hat, the ARP were the butt of much wartime humour. Lurking to pounce on any tiny chink of light showing behind the curtains, they wielded a curious power – for contravening the black-out could land you in court with a hefty fine to pay; on the other hand, there was something in the warden's job which had echoes of the street snoop, and slightly upset the general feeling of 'all pulling together'.

A Mrs Hordahl of Seaburn in Sunderland found herself hauled before the beak and given a lecture: she'd banked up her grate before going out, and the warden spied a nice fire going before she'd returned to pull the black-out curtains. It cost her £3, a week's wages for many women, and the magistrate wagged a finger: 'It was a very foolish thing to leave a fire burning all day. Apart from the black-out the offence was a shocking waste of fuel.'

However, when the sirens went only the police, wardens and fire guards were on the streets – a lonely job, in which discovering an unexploded bomb, or coming upon a wrecked house where you knew the inhabitants, stretched already hard-pressed women; for many were also working, or looking after families. Civil Defence became compulsory in 1941, as an alternative to military service.

The strain on ordinary families is hard to convey – many preferred to talk in upbeat terms to keep spirits up. The sheer physical demands on those who were running a household, keeping down a job, and also committed to voluntary duties – all on uninspiring rations, which had to be queued for – is rarely mentioned. Mrs Uttin had to do her bit of fire-watching, as well as WVS work in a factory canteen, run a household – and knit. In June 1944 she was writing:

No raids to report up to date, but the invasion [D-Day] started last Tuesday 6th. Bill and I at midnight saw bright yellow flashes in the direction of Northolt Aerodrome. Audrey Coates married on Tuesday and the best man was Fred Taylor, Dora's RAF

Above: Mrs Edith Digby served as an air-raid warden in Bermondsey, London, while (opposite) other women of all ages found different but equally essential war work

friend. After weeks of dry weather we have rain at last. It must make it bad going for our boys in France. Will it all be over by next June?

16 June

We went to bed last night at 12.40 – partly dressed as the All Clear had not gone and slept till 5.50, not a sound so went off to sleep again till 7.20. Mrs Ireland called for me and we went to the canteen together. As we entered the All Clear from last night went, and the Home Guard workers came in having been on duty all night – 12 hours right off after a day's work, then duty. We served them with tea and buttered rolls and then we started work. Just as we were leaving the factory another warning, so we hurried along and called in at our WVS leader Mrs Haglear, who gave us a glass of wine. The gunfire was intense so we waited a little and after it had abated I went home. We have had warnings all day, some of short duration, for now the Germans are sending over pilotless planes. One rushed over the house last night – we thought our last moment had really come.

17 June

A day like the Battle of Britain again. So many warnings and All Clears we lost count of them. One went tonight at 11.20 and now at 1pm is still on. We saw the red light of the pilotless planes going over, then go out and the explosion followed. From Mother's window we could see eight following each other in a direct line. What a way to spend a June night, out on the lawn and waiting for what?

Civil Defence covered a number of organisations, but in general women could join all of them, though they might be restricted in one or two aspects of the job. And there was continuous fretting that women should not 'take' jobs from men, even though this was clothed in the language of gallantry:

It was agreed by Seaham Urban District Council [County Durham] last night, on the recommendation of the Civil Defence Committee, that consent to the employment of women as fire guards be withheld until this authority is satisfied that all available men are performing their full hours of duty. Mr T. McClaughlan said that the committee were determined that every available man who could possibly do fire-watching should do his share before women were called upon.

The police and fire services initiated auxiliary branches for women which concentrated on communications, manning switchboards and doing admin. in stations. However, as incendiaries rained down some AFS women graduated to pump crews, and when the National Fire Service was formed in 1941 women became full members, in a navy uniform with tapered trousers which fitted nicely into the necessary rubber boots.

Actual defence, the idea that women should take up arms should the enemy invade, was not an option. Winston Churchill himself disliked the idea intensely, and efforts to obtain weapons training were blocked at every turn. Dr Edith Summerskill MP was not to be thwarted, though. In 1941, after a meeting in London attended by a hundred women, she founded the Women's Home Defence League with the intention that it should assist the Home Guard – whose men were only just beginning to get proper weapons to replace an assortment of pitchforks and cricket bats and broom handles. The WHDL was to acquire the usual skills of communication, field catering and first aid – and also unarmed combat. But its members also intended to get rifle training – though they wouldn't be issued with weapons. Not surprisingly, they'd already tried to join the Home Guard and become armed – but had been rebuffed. Even so, the issue was not one of the burning topics of wartime conversation; it was generally accepted that men did the fighting – not

Evacuees at Ealing Broadway Station, London, supervised by a policewoman, 1 September 1939

only was there no need for women to have weapons, the thinking went, it was something which should be avoided if at all possible. Beneath this ran the argument that women should be protected, and that it would be seen as a shortcoming on the part of men if women had to be called upon to act like men.

Nevertheless, there was a hefty argument that invasion would be better countered if most of the active population could be involved. The government, after all, had already announced that invasion conditions would differ from Blitz conditions in that military labour would not be available for civil purposes. The *Kent Messenger* reported: 'Dr Summerskill was of the opinion that if invasion did come, it was stupid for more than half the adult population of the country not to know how to use a rifle.' In a year, the League had twenty thousand women in 250 units learning how to use rifles and grenades, and though they didn't wear uniform they had a brooch badge, a yellow-bordered maroon shield on which appeared gold crossed rifles with the letters WHD and an automatic pistol below – just to make a point.

Just over a year later, the Secretary of State for War announced in the House of Commons that a limited number of women might be nominated for service with the

Home Guard Auxiliary to perform such non-combatant duties as cooking, driving and clerical work. Most were older women and already involved in WVS work; no official uniform was issued, and their badge was HG with a laurel wreath – no crossed rifles and pistol, certainly not. However, stories abound of various units deciding that facing Jerry on the beaches with a broom handle was futile, if not demeaning, and a number of women are known to have received weapons training.

Added to jobs, voluntary work and Civil Defence, women kept their families going. Queuing, cooking and 'making-do' took up much of the time they weren't on some kind of war work. Many saw a great deal more action than the men who were in the services – with bombing, fire and destruction all around on the home front. They were as much at war as the military.

The Watford Women's Home Defence Unit 'get their eye in' on the shooting range

CHAPTER SIXTEEN

TURNIPS, BULLETS AND ANGELS

ERNEST BEVIN WAS Minister for Labour: 'Women's part in the war effort would be a very limited one,' he informed his parliamentary colleague Irene Ward very emphatically. The sight of a male political ostrich confronting a female MP, with his head firmly buried in a box of sand marked 'War: Men Only, Keep Out', was a common one. In 1914, women had been told to go home and sit still. This time the patronising tone was muted – but still present. Even when pressure began to mount on the labour market, with more men in the services, Bevin and Prime Minister Churchill still hoped that volunteers would fill the gaps, thus avoiding an official government summons which would render women part of the official war effort. There was a fear that domestic life would be under threat if men came home to find women still out at work, and no fire lit or meal on the table.

Eventually there was no avoiding it – women were going to have to be conscripted

Opposite: Women shipbuilders give the 'rightaway' for the lifting of steel girders, 1943

Above: The Royal Proclamation which made women liable for service being read at the Mansion House in the City of London, 19 December 1941

Below: Allies on the factory floor as well as on the battlefield

COVER YOUR HAIR FOR SAFETY

YOUR RUSSIAN SISTER DOES!

for the first time. In 1942, the local labour exchanges saw queues of women from eighteen to sixty, both married and single, registering under the National Service Act. There were exemptions, but not many, and although in theory there was a choice between joining the auxiliary services or going into the factories and selecting a job, in practice personal preferences had to give way to the steamrollers of Supply and Demand. Nor were the men at work waiting with open arms to greet their new colleagues. In Sunderland's shipyards, which were working flat out to produce over a quarter of the country's wartime merchant shipping, there was a rather sour comment about 'Unfortunate experiences' in World War I, when the effect of introducing women workers had been to 'positively retard production rather than to help it'. No reasons were given. Seven hundred women finally made their way into the yards, where they worked as welders, crane drivers, red-leaders, rivet heaters and catchers. Most, though, were occupied in an assistant capacity, and the majority were unskilled. The National Society of Painters, for example, managed to insist that women only do undercoating.

Work was just one of the changes which the war imposed on women. Most found themselves juggling the demands of the government with the demands of a hungry family and at the same time trying to follow the progress of a worldwide conflict that kept sweeping over their own houses. For much of the war Maude Seeley kept a diary which is a sharp-eyed record of the frustrations of daily life, interspersed with the conflict's faraway but significant events:

28 June 1941: I have at last got a war job, rivet making, starting at 9s ¾d per hour, 47 hour week – Previous to this I worked as a cook in a canteen at one of Vickers works, but I was so disgusted at the methods they used I gave it up. Half milk, half water for puddings. Gravy made only with greens and potato water. Greens and potato water left over from the day before served up. A disgusting way to feed men and women doing hard work. Dog meat is now 1s 6d lb and labelled 'fit for human consumption'. I must admit that sometimes it does look and smell good enough to eat (I haven't chanced it yet). – We hear nothing of Rudolf Hess now. It was stated in Parliament that he has not been photographed since he has been in England. I suppose we are afraid of hurting his feelings. We sunk the *Bismarck* a short time ago after she had sunk the *Hood*. The meat ration is now 1s 2d a head, a slight improvement.

A year later Maude was still at the factory, though lamenting the lack of clothing

WOMEN OF BRITAIN
COME INTO
THE FACTORIES
ASK AT ANY EMPLOYMENT EXCHANGE FOR ADVICE AND FULL DETAILS

coupons and speculating that 'some of us will be pretty near naked by this time next year'.

My job is not going at all badly . . . I wish now I had taken the job of salt bath operator when it was offered to me. . . . The temperature is 95 to 100° to work in, so perhaps it's just as well I didn't take it. We have added a parrot to our household, Audrey paid £5 for it. Russia is giving Germany a damn good hiding. I wrote in November that the general feeling was one of boredom. I must say now that people have really awakened to war. We are all realising that it is a struggle for existence and are putting our best into it. Only food shops are allowed to use wrapping paper. Everything else has to be carried home 'naked'. I have to take and fetch our laundry, and it's a funny sight to see people walking home with a pair of new shoes in their hands.

September 1942
We have now been at war for three years and I find myself at a new job in the Parachute Co. Have been there for 4 weeks working an electric sewing machine. It's funny to think how this war has altered my life. I anticipated (years ago) on being settled at my age, just turned 49. Instead I have learned a new job. . . . We have had a real treat today. Son sent us a food parcel through the Red Cross and I have opened the tin of butter. We can for a few days have butter on each slice of bread for sandwiches instead of on one slice.

On offer at the labour exchange was everything from timber-felling to aircraft manufacture, but a large number of women found themselves 'directed' into munitions. 'When I first saw it – well, I couldn't see it – it was covered in mist. That's why it was built there.' Alice Raine was seventeen and had been called up, though at the labour exchanges in Aycliffe and Darlington there seemed to be a choice of munitions, munitions or munitions. Twenty thousand people were wanted to work on a site which sprawled out among the fields of southern County Durham. Due to one of those quirks of the land, the area attracted mist, perfect for hiding scores of single-storey huts connected by a series of 'cleanways' – raised walkways which were kept scrubbed clean to minimise the chance of any particle of dirt causing an explosion. The two Royal Ordance Factories at Aycliffe covered such an area that few of the workers were aware of the size of the operation. They were taken in by lorry to the Shift House, plonked down in front of it, and taken back to the railway station eight hours later.

Once in the Shift House, they went from 'Dirty' to 'Clean', a daily ritual remembered by Ivy Davy from Darlington, up at four to catch the bus for the 5am train:

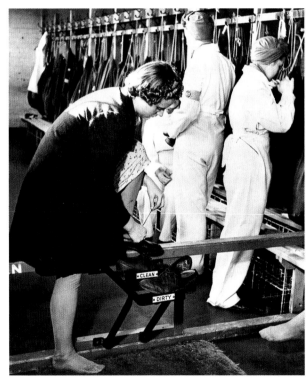

We went in on the Dirty side – there was a barrier across. You took all your clothes off, and your jewellery – you weren't allowed any jewellery, or hairgrips – and put them in your kitbag. Then you stepped over the barrier and you were on what they called the Clean side. And there were your Magazine clothes: trousers and jacket and a turban; they were a creamy colour, like flannel, and dipped in alum or something to sort of fire-proof them. Of course the buttons were rubber, and our shoes had no nails. The soles were attached to the uppers with wooden studs – no metal at all was allowed. If you had a wedding ring, it had to be covered with tape. Then you walked through on a sort of pier, what they called the Cleanways.

Ivy worked in Group One – the Danger Group, which involved TNT and various other explosives; the huts were spartan and windowless, scrupulously clean and scrubbed every day with sawdust and oil; they were also freezing cold, as no heating was allowed even in the depths of winter. As the mist swirled around in that first November, Alice Raine, who had been made a supervisor, was glad she'd left her pyjamas on underneath her overalls: 'I was so cold, frozen to the marrow. I didn't have a period for three months.'

Joan Talbot from Norton was in Group Five, having wanted to go into the navy at eighteen – 'lovely uniform' – but having had to defer to her parents who didn't want her to leave home. At her medical she saw 'some of the most ghastly women' also lined up for interviews, and recognised them as local prostitutes, but there was nothing for it but to sign on and 'take the King's shilling'. At least she liked her munitions uniform: she was fitted out with white wool overalls, which she thought 'absolutely beautiful', and black leather flat shoes:

I worked filling shells – 20 millimetre naval shells. And on piece-work bonus – can you imagine, with such dangerous stuff? But the shells came along, you used your treadle, filled your eight shells, and then one day one of mine blew up. I got up and ran and someone grabbed me and said: 'Where do you think you're going?' And I said, 'The ablutions' – we never said 'Toilet' – and she said: 'Yes, you can go – when you've finished these shells.' It was so I didn't lose my nerve. You never really thought of the danger, and you had to go with the detonators when they were moved on a cart from one shop to another, with one of you walking in front with a red flag and one behind. You must never do it when there was thunder and lightning. Someone was going into a shop one day, and there was a spark, and there were eight killed.

At least some of the problems with toxic materials had been solved since World War I, and working with TNT didn't cause poisoning fatalities any more. However, orange

A World War II line-
up of various
women's services at
a recruiting centre
at Harrods
department store in
London

hair and yellow hands were still common, and there were a number of incidents in which girls were gassed, such was the mix of gun-grease, chemicals and explosives. Ivy Davy didn't think about the danger at first:

It didn't really register until there were one or two explosions or 'blows'. I hadn't wanted to go into the factories – I wanted to be a WAAF, but my father wouldn't hear of it, so off I went. And I couldn't do anything about going into the Danger Group – you got no choice – but we did get danger money – a little, mind. You worked behind very heavy glass screens, with these leather gauntlets which had wooden pincers on the end of them. You put your arms round the screen and picked up the caps to fill them. See, things could go up – the powder was so liable to go up one grain would blow your finger off.

There was a friend of mine from Hunwick – I was bridesmaid for her when we left – and we were the two youngest. And there was all these lovely lasses from the pit districts all round Durham, and of course, when there was a blow, their first reaction was 'Where's the bairns?' and we always got a lovely cuddle from them.

I don't think we realised at the time about the danger. It was the magazines that used to go up – friction used to send the powder up, and if you were little bit lax – we were on piece-work . . . there were some nasty injuries. You've heard of hair standing on end? Well, there was one girl and I did actually see her hair – she was just like a golliwog.

The money wasn't bad, and in many cases it was considerably more than girls could expect to earn in peacetime. However, there was a degree of envy of those in the services, who were paid much less but at least had bed and board. Hours of queuing for buses and trains, then standing in the ration queue, and getting Saturday and Sunday off every third week – all added up to a rigorous routine with little fun. There was also the suspicion that the servicewomen – particularly the ATS – were having a *very* good time.

Gossip abounded about swarms of girls in uniform, rather the worse for drink, hanging around town centres and ending up pregnant. The old moral panic campaign reasserted itself, with allegations that VD was spreading like wildfire and that women in uniform were the sole cause of it. 'Up with the lark and to bed with a Wren' – the sort of remark that the Reithian BBC spent all its time trying to keep out of comedy shows – had an undertone which reinforced the prejudice against the very idea of young women on the loose and associating with men in uniform. Central London was seen by some as a uniformed flesh-pot, bolstering the worries of provincial fathers whose daughters were now being 'directed' by the government.

However, in County Durham Ivy Davy was determined to make the most of her time off – even if she wouldn't be wearing official woolly overalls in the streets: 'I used to go dancing. There were Americans at the base at Topcliffe, and they were so – different. We were all ready to do the waltz and foxtrot, and they knew about jiving. I'll never forget one coming up to me and saying "Come on, snake, let's wiggle."'

At work, if you wanted to smoke during your break you had to go through the entire palaver of changing from the Clean to the Dirty side, then collecting your cigarettes from the Contraband Office, going to a designated area for a quick puff, then going through the entire process in reverse. It took up the whole break. There were regular searches for 'contraband' – anything which could cause a spark, or something taken from the work areas. With great ingenuity, Ivy Davy saved the little punched-out rounds of paper from the detonator cap process and smuggled them out in her bra. These were saved up for weddings and substituted for yet another unavailable luxury – confetti.

It was hard work and there wasn't much time for reflection, as rows of girls concentrated on fiddling with volatile material in bleak conditions – and on piece-work, as well. They were aware that the men earned more than they did, but as their own money was better than they'd expected they rarely raised the subject. What did annoy them was to be valued less as workers: 'There was a fire one night, up a line of shells,' records Joan Talbot, 'and one of the girls managed to put it out – it could have been everything going up; but the man in charge was decorated for it – how do you like that?'

But most incidents and 'blows' were not mentioned at all – and the girls never spoke of their work outside the factory: 'Careless talk costs lives.' They got up before dawn if they were on the early shift, fell over all kinds of things in the black-out, bumped into shift-workers stumbling back from other factories, waited for crowded buses and then disappeared into this weird, fog-shrouded plant. However, even if their families or neighbours didn't know much about their work, these girls believed they were famous on the radio. It was rumoured that the propaganda spokesman William Joyce – Lord Haw-Haw – regularly threatened in his broadcasts that German bombers would find Aycliffe one day, and that the girls would all become Aycliffe Angels. Though they had good times when they could, the war brought down a cloud of seriousness on to young women like Ivy Davy who felt an obligation in what they were doing:

The only thing we thought of was that one of our lads' lives might depend on this; and there were women getting messages every day, that their husbands had been killed, or their brothers were missing, or in a POW camp. And I think it used to give you a reason

HUNDREDS OF OUR GIRLS ARE IN JAP HANDS

Hate is not enough WORK TO AVENGE THESE CRIMES

Poster propaganda: lathe workers exhorted to increase production

for what you were doing. They reckon this was where Hitler failed. He put all those slave labour camps to do all their munitions – and you can still see their bombs going off – they're still finding them today. Ours all went off, I hope.

One of the asides from Joan Talbot contained the view that she and her munitions colleagues thought that Land Army girls had a 'cushy time': 'I know a farmer who had to employ quite a few . . . they certainly never worked . . . and they had a jolly good time. I mean, they were finished every night when it was dark, except in the summer when it was hay-making.' The grass is always greener . . . and the sound of clashing pitchforks might be heard throughout the land!

The Women's Land Army might have been a cushy number for a fortunate few, but the rest were too busy rat-catching, baling, ploughing, weeding and ditching to have pondered the term 'cushy'. And as in World War I, the recruitment posters which presented a sun-kissed lansdcape gently tended by glowing maidens didn't quite match the reality of a Welsh hillside in November with a teenage factory-packer from Manchester trying to summon a herd of recalcitrant cows standing mutinously in the boggiest corner of the field. Nevertheless, thousands of girls decided to opt for a life on the land, and many equated the countryside with freedom – from a close family, from nosy neighbours, from a strict upbringing. Some were billeted on farms, but a great number were in hostels – with varying standards. Dorothy Wheeler (née Carson) found herself with forty-eight other girls in a 'mansion, taken over for the war, overlooking Lake Bala in North Wales. When I first went, I was on field work, and we used to go up this little hill, and they used to open the clamps of potatoes. Oh, it was horrible sometimes, like custard. And we had to separate them – one heap for the pigs and one for the humans. I felt all faint at first. "Oh, I'm going home in the morning," I said.'

In Buckinghamshire, Helen Collett was sharing eight to a room in a hostel that accommodated eighty girls, and up to her hocks in acres of parsnips and Brussels sprouts – but she did have one little moan: 'As you realise, coming off the fields etc. you were sweaty and dirty, and it would be great for a nice bath. But the Matron lined up six girls in turn, she ran our bath water – only 4 inches was what she measured, and she stood outside to make sure you did not turn the tap for extra water. The water never even covered your legs.'

Uniforms were smart or quaint, rather depending on how you wore them. Brown corduroy breeches, fawn knee-length woollen socks, fawn shirt and green pullover, and felt headgear in a style which I can only describe as Universal School Hat. If you were better off, you could have your breeches cut dashingly by a tailor – the *Land Girl* magazine, published to keep the girls in touch and combat loneliness on distant farms, carried lots of adverts: 'Look Smart in Hebden's Breeches. The Hebden Cord Co., famous throughout the land for their postal bargains in Ladies' Breeches, make this Special Offer to members of the Women's Land Army. For the remarkably low figure of only 12/6 post free we will tailor you a pair of hard-wearing breeches strictly to your measurements.' This was the smart 'walking out' uniform; for actual work there was a baggy set of brown dungarees with matching jacket, supplemented unofficially in horrible weather by a layer or two of sacking attached with string or binder twine. The scarcity of rubber made gumboots almost impossible to come by, and the muck-raking, greasy sheep and vegetable-picking wrecked even the neatest uniform.

There weren't a great deal of young men around on the farms – and some of the older ones were sceptical at the sight of office workers like Audrey Manning turning up in their new uniforms for training on a farm near Staplehurst in Kent: 'Some of the old hands doubted whether we'd stick it. I heard such scathing comments as "What have they sent *you* for?" and "This ain't no work for you young gals, you won't be able to 'ave no babies."' Sheila Kyffin was luckier, being sent to Agricultural College at Cannington in Somerset and getting eight weeks' instruction in dairy farming and arable work. However, despite being armed with such knowledge she arrived in Gloucestershire to be met by a farmer who much resented having a girl sent to him, and who instructed her to begin by beheading the cockerel, then watering the bull.

Nora Wright was desperate to join the Land Army – she'd been milking her father's cows since the age of eight; however, you had to be seventeen to enlist, and she was only just turned fourteen. Nevertheless she was taken on in one of the hostels, and spent the next three years cooking and cleaning and freezing during Cheshire winters. At Cholmondeley Hostel near Malpas she was up at six to clean and fill oil lamps, rake out and light the office fire, and call Matron with a cup of tea. At seven she started on the washing up from the night before, set Matron's breakfast tray and filled the coke and coal buckets – ten of them. The rest of the day was a procession of vegetable peeling and teacloth washing, and then there were all the bathrooms, toilets, dormitories and attic rooms to be cleaned. Two and a half hours 'off' in the afternoon – if she was lucky – was followed by washing up the pots and

Never mind the advertising – 'This ain't no work for you young gals,' insisted the locals when the Land Army turned up in their corduroy breeches

pans after the thirty Land Girls had had dinner. At nine Nora made supper drinks for the girls, then helped the cook make packed lunches for the next day. Oh, and there was the petrol generator to check and fill every morning and night. Just fourteen, but 'Happy days – and it was an education. Looking back over those years one remembers the feeling of true companionship, working very hard away from home and loved ones, but happy too in our lives.'

About a third of the girls came from towns, and tales abounded of bulls being approached with the milking pail and attempts to lead sheep in an orderly manner by speaking to them firmly. Mrs Hilda Billings (nee Tyass) was packing Rennies indigestion tablets in a factory in Salford when one day a bit of talk at the work-bench led nine girls to volunteer for the Land Army.

Mainly to get away from home, I suppose. I was sent to Shropshire – Stanton, near Shawbury. The first day I went in to tie the cows up, the cow came round and hit me in the forehead with her horn – and I came running out and thought: I'm going home. But you had to work – so I set to, getting up to bring in the cows at six, washing their udders with icy-cold water, drying and then milking them. Then breakfast and lots of other work until six. Haymaking time, you'd go back after tea and work till it went really dark.

As an eleven-year-old in 1939, Peggy Reed had no idea how the war was going to take over her life. A happy schoolgirl from Bromley in south-east London, she was evacuated with her sister to Biddenden in Kent:

Our cousins had already been evacuated from London and now lived in a large house with servants. We had hoped for the same! My sister Helen and I were very shy and hung back as the villagers came to take their children. Eventually we were the only ones left in the village hall. We were piled into a car with our gas-masks in boxes tied with string, holding our rucksacks and with name labels tied to our blazers.

We were very excited. We had never been in a car before. The WVS lady sounded very posh and we thought we were going to live with her down the winding country lanes. In fact we were being delivered to an old hop-picker's hut and were handed over to an old man with stubble and yellow teeth, who grinned broadly, and his wife had a wart and hairs on her chin. The Voluntary lady handed them a large bar of

Top of page: First day with the Land Army, and then (above) down to work with a barrowload of manure

chocolate for us and the man placed it on a high wooden beam above his head.

It was dark by now and we were shown into our bedroom by dim torchlight. Three heads popped up from a mattress on the floor. 'You can have our bed,' they choroused. I was secretly disappointed – I'd rather have slept on the floor. We were soon asleep after our day of adventure – but not for long, for the fleas began to bite. We awoke scratching and tearing at our limbs as we were eaten alive until morning.

Our clothes were taken away, we were told they were too good. The lady handed us two of her old floral dresses. They reached the ground, and we were ashamed. We now saw our surroundings for the first time. A large bare room with wooden floorboards, broken windows blocked with cardboard, and pictures with dead flies behind the cracked glass. A wooden table was laid with a newspaper, a half-filled jar of jam stood in the centre with the flies buzzing around inside. We were given a chunk of dry bread and shared a cracked mug of tea. It was the unhappiest day of my life.

That night at bedtime, Helen felt sick. 'Be sick on the floor,' 'Mum' called up. And Helen was promptly sick on the floor. I was thankful we had not been sent down the garden in the pitch blackness among all the stinging nettles to that grim dirty hut with newspapers and spiders amongst the trees.

'Dad' came home drunk that night. We cowered and shrank as he shouted abuse and swore at the woman as he chased her around the hut. We were frightened and prayed to God to keep us safe while the woman screamed. . . .

When our misery and flea bites were noted at school on Monday morning we were taken away. We were scrubbed in a tin bath until we shone. We were given our own clothes and were happy. The day we returned home was at that time the happiest day of my life.

It is slightly surprising that after her first taste of 'country life' Peggy ever ventured out of a town again, never mind became a Land Girl. She avoided another evacuation excursion and later left school at fourteen to work in the office of Hawker Aircraft, living through the Blitz and the V1 and V2 flying bombs. Her job was classified as essential war work, so again her life was entirely run by government directive. But she was bored, and knew that the only way out was to join the services or go into munitions. She wanted to join the WAAF but was too young by six months, so went into the Land Army. This time the countryside in Surrey held no terrors, even though the work was hard and back-breaking:

In summer we went haymaking, stacking up the hay stooks throughout the fields in long golden lines. . . . Threshing was hot, hard, dirty work – our eyes were sore and noses streamed from the husks of corn. . . . On cold frosty mornings we picked sprouts and we froze. But lunchtime in the barn with our sandwiches and flasks and chatter and gossip was a pleasure. We did hedging and ditching, and the farmer would burn debris on a huge bonfire and I can still smell the woodsmoke now. A waft of woodsmoke brings back the nostalgia for a time when I was young and carefree and happy.

There were other specialisations which were essential, but not the most obvious work for those who'd been in nice clean offices. Seventeen when sent to North Wales, Dorothy Wheeler was the sort of girl who was frightened of a mouse:

I was friendly with this girl – she was already on pest destruction – and that set me thinking. I was a bit apprehensive at first – I didn't think I could do it. But I did. I did rats, rabbits and moles. For moles we used to dig up worms the day before, and put them in a can, put strychnine on them, and then next day armed with this wooden trowel put them in the traps for the moles, and covered them up. You never saw the mole, but when you saw grass come over the mounds you'd know they'd gone. Rats? Well, you had to do it – trap – if the farmer didn't want poisons, and if they were just caught by the leg they were quite alive, and we'd have to hit them with a stick. Same with the rabbits – a shame really. We'd put the gas down the hole and wait for them. I did the work for three years – but, mind you, I couldn't give a pint of blood . . . anyway, I enjoyed those days. The Marines stationed in Barmouth used to come for us to take us to dances in the big wagons, and some nights they used to ring up the wardens to say they'd broken down so we could stay longer. In our generation we were brought up strict, so that we enjoyed the freedom.

There were few young men on the land except for the 'village idiots and odd farm-hands' noted by Peggy Reed; and the Italian and German prisoners of war who were often working in the fields were out of bounds, in every way. But there were servicemen stationed all over the country, and the Land Girls valued transport above any other perk in order to find a social life. Bicycles were sometimes supplied, and Hilda Billings hurtled off through Shropshire:

I used to go to the RAF camp dances on my bike. One night my back light had stopped working and I got pulled up by the village policeman and fined 5 shillings – a good part of the wages. We also had to be back in the hostel by half past ten, and if you weren't, you had to stay in and chop firewood for the week. I was eighteen and it was just a job, and everybody had to have jobs in those days, didn't they? I enjoyed it very much – and I'd probably do it all again. Even when I see a herd of cows these days, I feel like having a go.

Experiences varied, and those who recalled the camaraderie and subsequent friendships and reunions look back with affection. At their final reunion in Birmingham in 2001, several hundred women clearly relished the companionship and shared experience, regardless of the tough wartime conditions. Their jollity was contagious, their long-term friendships impressive. Nevertheless they, more than many groups, have felt unappreciated, as if their years of labour among the potato clamps and muck-heaps were actually 'something of a country holiday', away from the bombed towns. It rankles still, and in their memories there's no place for sentimentality: a commemorative figurine marketed with the words 'relive the spirit of the 1940s with the Land Girl' elicited a sharp response in 2001 in a letter to the *Daily Telegraph* from Mrs Jo Pearce of Epping in Essex:

I am an ex-Land Girl, and feel incensed by the statue. . . . It is all so wrong. We did not have 'designer' shirts, but awful Aertex fawn shirts and green pullovers. We did not work in 'cords'. They were 'best' wear. We wore slacks and smocks in a heavy grey-black material. We had hobnail boots, which the locals scraped for us when we were picking up rotted potatoes, because we could hardly put one foot in front of the other for the depth of the mud. Wellies, yes, for hedging and ditching. I never saw a 'trug' basket. We

were a hard-done-by band, never getting credit for what we did. One farmer said, 'You're here to do a man's job – get on and do it.'

Also out in the fresh air – and the rain and mud – were the Women's Timber Corps. Again, for many the outdoor life was second choice to the services. Ruth Sjoblom wanted to be a Wren, but found there were no vacancies for at least a year and applied to the Land Army. She was rebuffed, as she was a 'city girl and not used to winter conditions', and told she would be sent for in the spring. So she and a friend tried to harden up by walking in Hyde Park and rowing on the Serpentine, muscle exercise which proved useful as they were called up to the Timber Corps. An energetic life, bedevilled by damp clothes in damp woods despite the extra pair of breeches issued with the green berets. They felled, lopped, sawed and shaved. They measured for pit props and army telegraph poles. They split wood for fencing which was made for rolling out in front of tanks on beach landings so they wouldn't sink into the sand.

> Being stationed in Kent, which was near the coast, it was called Bomb Alley. The Germans would dive-bomb and drop incendiary bombs in the woods to try and burn all the piles of wood. We had one bad forest fire and had to fight it with brushes as no fire engines could get to us. Before the D-Day invasion most women and children were evacuated from the area, but not us. Round us, all camouflaged, were so many British, American and Allied servicemen in convoys. Then the news that the invasion had started – and it was reckoned that about 50 per cent of the soldiers we had waved on their way had been killed – and we'd thought they had just been on manoeuvres.

There were numerous songs which often had ironic lyrics highlighting the reality of work on the land; and the Timber Corps produced its own Poetry Book, lyrically suggesting that work in the woods 'encourages a harvest of genial versification':

Lament:

Sure there'll be fun again.
Satin and silk again,
Chairs by the fireside,
And places to go.
Breakfast in bed again,
Dances to tread again.
So whispered Renie,
Feller of trees.

Up before dayspring,
Walking till bedtime,
Waking to do it
All over again.
Carting and stacking,
Till muscles are racking,
So muttered Renie,
Soaked with the rain.

Oh for a manicure,
Bath salts and lavender.
Oh for a foxtrot
With Jimmy or Bill.
But miners are waiting
For props and for timber,
So said you Renie,
And worked with a will.

Ivy Verdon and Violet Platt, members of the Women's Timber Corps, clearing land and burning brushwood

98272.

Carte d'Identité

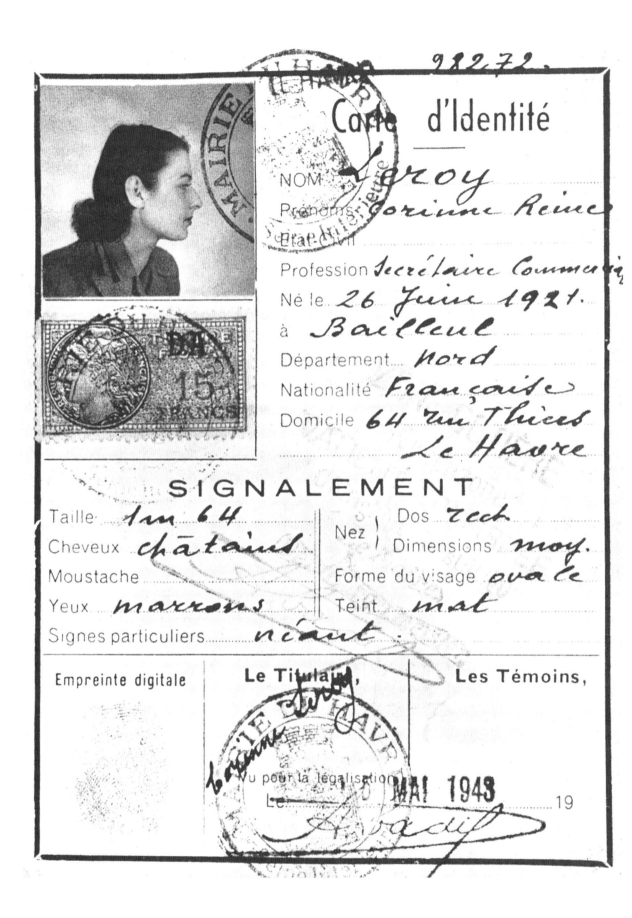

NOM _Leroy_

Prénoms _Corinne Reine_

État-Civil

Profession _Secrétaire Commerciale_

Né le _26 Juin 1921._

à _Bailleul_

Département _Nord_

Nationalité _Française_

Domicile _64 rue Thiers_

Le Havre

SIGNALEMENT

Taille _1m 64_

Cheveux _châtains_

Moustache

Yeux _marrons_

Signes particuliers _néant._

Dos _rect_

Nez

Dimensions _moy._

Forme du visage _ovale_

Teint _mat_

Empreinte digitale	Le Titulaire,	Les Témoins,

Vu pour la légalisation
Le **MAI 1943**

19

CHAPTER SEVENTEEN

UNSUNG STORIES

THE OFFICIAL ATTITUDE that women should be protected, wherever possible, from the actual violence of war was entrenched, and there is no doubt that a number of public figures had a great deal of difficulty acknowledging what women could achieve in the worst circumstances. Parachuting into enemy territory, organising resistance groups, committing sabotage and then facing torture and death – one might have thought that such acts would be celebrated and saluted. In March 1945, a brief statement in the House of Commons hinted that 'young WAAF officers' had played some sort of part in organised resistance in occupied territories. Admittedly, those involved in secret operations are, and have to be, reticent about their work, though there's a long tradition in Britain of obsessive secrecy regarding national security. Part of this has to devolve from the faintly gentleman-amateur image of the secret agent: a well-connected, well-

Opposite: Violette Szabo's fake identity card, brought back from her first mission to France in 1944

educated, capable sort of chap, who engages with a few chums in feats of derring-do. And indeed, the World War II operations carry more than a whiff of the country house set-up, with recruitment happening on a very ad hoc basis, mainly on knowing someone who'd be 'just the ticket'.

However, the exploits of the women who made the ultimate sacrifice only emerged slowly, and not until the fifties were their adventures chronicled by Dame Irene Ward MP, who well understood the behaviour of officialdom regarding women:

> There was always the fear – generally expressed by men – that there would be a public outcry against women being employed on dangerous missions. Yet all the time, secure from public comment, women were volunteering for, and serving, in the most dangerous and hazardous of operations, and where physical as well as moral courage was a paramount necessity. To those who understand women their successes come as no surprise, but it is right for future generations to know that women themselves desired no protection when national survival was at stake.

The work of SOE – Special Operations Executive – ranged over many countries, and involved gathering intelligence, coordinating drops of supplies in enemy territory, organising resistance units and blowing up key facilities. In order to run the administration securely and staff the houses where agents were trained, SOE called on the FANY. They were 'nice gels', and all through Dame Irene's excellent account of their work there is a discreet avoidance of the fact that the FANY were a class apart – in terms of class distinction. Recruitment, ethos, contacts and behaviour were those of the upper- and upper-middle-class girls – in the words of one casual remark by a Norwegian agent: 'The Fannies had their own cars, and very fine ones.' In 1942, a car was a dream to most girls.

They ran the domestic side of the 'training schools' – usually on country estates – where agents practised parachute drops and the use of codes and ciphers, along with weapons and security training and the arcane world of sabotage. The atmosphere was kept determinedly light, described by one agent as a first-class hotel with lots of free shootin' and fishin'. A Polish paratrooper had very fond memories of his time prior to going on a mission:

> The last few days before the flight were spent at waiting stations known by the code names 'Eighteen' and 'Twenty'. Our most likeable hostesses here were the members of the FANY. You couldn't have found a finer type of Englishwoman anywhere. Cultured and friendly, hard-working and smiling, they created the relaxed happy atmosphere so

necessary before the coming adventure. Though many of them came from the best families in the land, they carried out their hard tasks cheerfully and uncomplainingly. In the daytime they cooked, swept, kept the place in order, or drove cars. In the evening, exquisite in their long gowns, they danced with us, tangos, fox-trots, waltzes and *obereks* and *kujawiaks* as well. Though they were young and attractive, not to say beautiful, we had no heart pangs over them. They remained in our memories as the pleasant and unaffected companions of our last days before the flight.

Some of the women acting as 'escorts' to agents took their duties to include parachute jumping alongside them. Others prepared forged papers and packed sabotage equipment, while the BBC oversaw those dealing with transmissions to France of 'messages personelles' – the coded signals about arms drops and rendezvous locations embedded in various announcements.

By 1942 the decision had been taken by the War Cabinet to recruit women as operational agents. It was convenient to have them placed in the FANY, which would give them an official status, background and a uniform – should they be captured, a death sentence might be prevented if they could say they were officers of His Majesty's armed forces. The ATS could not provide cover for the women agents because they had a clause in their constitution forbidding members to take part in active military operations. At the same time, because of their expertise with communications, WAAFs were also taken on: they came from a service that had a better record of employing the best person for the job, irrespective of sex.

Again, with reluctance, the government had had to bow to necessity. In occupied countries women were less suspect and could move about more freely; therefore women were given the rare opportunity not only to work together with men, but to work as their equals.

So while some of the FANY were socialising, acting as friends and mentors to agents, others nominally in the service were undergoing training alongside the male agents. Inducted into a world of secret armies and false identities, they studied code and cipher techniques, used secret inks, and learned to became at ease with deception and bluff. They received weapons training, and became familiar with the fuses and detonators and explosives used in sabotage operations; and they were toughened up on exercises in the Western Highlands of Scotland before learning how to parachute. They had to be resourceful, unflappable and smart – and speak the language of the country they were dropped into. The course instructors looked for endurance and steadiness – and, not surprisingly, the drop-out rate was high. Whether at the time any of the War Cabinet knew what would happen to some of them isn't clear.

The first to be sent to France was Yvonne Rudellat, and it soon became obvious

that female agents were going to have to run precisely the same risks as the men. She shuttled between various resistance groups, carrying messages and information about aircraft due to drop weapons and supplies, and was known to whirr along the French roads with explosives in her bicycle basket. Adept at sabotage, she could lay claim to having personally blown up two railway engines at Le Mans. One night, as she was waiting for an aircraft drop, the Gestapo got her – though not before she had defended herself with her revolver. She was wounded and eventually sent to the concentration camp at Belsen, where she died.

Skill, presence of mind and luck – it was impossible to calculate what the odds might be for someone arriving in France to carry out work which was both secret and spectacular at the same time. The first WAAF officer to volunteer was M.K. Herbert, who landed by small boat off the south coast of France in 1942 and made her way to Bordeaux to act as a courier. Another agent from a very different background was Virginia Hall, an American based in Lyons who used her cover as a journalist for the *New York Post*, accredited to the pro-German Vichy regime, to put other agents in touch with resistance groups and find safe accommodation and transport. She stayed until 1942, when she fled two hours ahead of German troops arriving to occupy the city. Virginia seemed an unlikely person to be involved in secrets – a tall, red-haired reporter with an artificial foot which she called Cuthbert.

Language was one of the main stumbling blocks, as the women had to pass for French if apprehended by German forces, so those from Anglo-French families or French-speaking overseas territories were in great demand, along with a small number of women who had escaped from France. Lise de Baissac and her brother Claude came from Mauritius, and both volunteered. Denise Borrel and Lise were the first two women to be parachuted into France, where very different fates awaited them.

Lise – with her brother working not far away – was organising the pick-up of arms drops; though the work sounds simple, the odds were very quickly stacked against the agents as the Germans grew more aggressive, believing that spies were in every nook and cranny. Betrayal and treachery bedevilled the operations as pressure grew to uncover secret networks, and the Gestapo treated prisoners with extreme brutality.

Having completed her first tour, Lise was flown back to Britain but returned in 1944 to plan local operations in advance of D-Day, training French resistance fighters in the use of Sten guns and revolvers. A cool customer, she found herself sharing a house which served as the local resistance HQ – with a German officer. While he plotted the demise of the resistance from the front room, she planned sabotage in the back. When the Americans arrived after the D-Day invasion, Lise was waiting for them dressed as smartly as possible in her FANY uniform.

Denise Borrel, with whom she'd arrived, had undertaken sabotage including raiding a power station, as well as supervising weapons drops. Her fate was to be arrested by the Germans, sent to a concentration camp and murdered by injection in the prison crematorium.

Odette Sansom, the young French widow of an Englishman, was living in Essex with her three children when she responded to a BBC appeal for photographs of the French coast by taking some to the War Office. In the time-honoured manner of SOE, she was then contacted rather casually and, after training, parachuted into southern France to work for another agent, Peter Churchill. They worked together, organising attacks and sabotage – and later, after the war, they married. When they were both arrested, she was sent to Paris to be interrogated and tortured; they'd made out to the Germans that they were already married – making the Germans suspect, wrongly, that Odette was related to the Prime Minister. She endured hellish treatment and ended up in Ravensbruck concentration camp, where she was subjected to further appalling cruelty. Her survival is a testament to the strength of the human spirit, for which she was awarded the George Cross.

One of the thirty-nine women who worked as agents in the French section of SOE

Odette Sansom with her SOE boss Captain Peter Churchill, whom she later married

was Nancy Wake, an Australian who'd been a journalist in Sydney before marrying a Marseilles businessman. After war broke out she drove an ambulance and helped a number of British prisoners of war to escape. Arrested and questioned by French police, she talked her way out of trouble and eventually, at the fifth attempt, got away over the border to Spain. After SOE training in Britain she parachuted back into the Auvergne in 1944, apparently carrying two revolvers and a pair of high-heeled shoes. An energetic and exuberant twenty-six-year-old, she coordinated resistance groups in an area where German troops outnumbered the Maquis, as the resistance were known, by three to one. There was no doubting her bravery under fire: she led attacks on German installations, including grenading a Gestapo headquarters, and was known to have killed a German sentry with her bare hands to keep him from alerting the guard during an attack on a factory. Her fellow resistance fighters had to swallow their discomfort at having to work with a woman, finally accepting her as one of their own officers.

Nancy was an adventurous and extrovert character, very different from Violette Bushell, an English taxi driver's daughter. When very young she had lived in Paris, where her father was working, but then moved back to England and went to school in Brixton, South London, until she was fourteen. At the outbreak of war, she was working behind the perfumery counter of the Bon Marché store there. She met and married an officer in the Free French forces called Etienne Szabo, and their daughter was born in 1942, just before Etienne was killed fighting. An unlikely agent, perhaps, but one with an exceptional skill demonstrated in various London shooting galleries where she'd walked off with all the prizes.

Violette's first sortie into France was successful, even though she was arrested by the French police. Returning in 1944 to organise sabotage operations to coincide with the D-Day landings, she and a colleague ran into a party of German infantry. While giving cover for the other agent to escape, Violette, with a bullet wound in the arm, was reported to have fired her Sten gun until the ammunition ran out, shooting several Germans. She too was tortured in prison in Paris 'but never by word or deed gave away any of her acquaintances, or told the enemy anything of value'. Shipped off to Ravensbruck concentration camp, she was described by a survivor as 'outstanding' among the thousands of inmates. At the age of twenty-three she was shot in the back by the crematorium supervisor.

The citation for her George Cross states: 'Madame Szabo gave a magnificent example of courage and steadfastness.' Her escorting officer described her boarding the plane for France on her last mission: 'In a group of heavily armed and equipped men waiting to take off from the same airfield, Violette was slim, debonair. She wore a flowered frock, white sandals, and ear-rings which she had bought in Paris during her first mission. She zipped up her flying suit, adjusted her parachute, shook her hair loose and climbed, laughing, into the aircraft. . . .'

None of this was known to the British public during the war, and what happened to some of the agents could only be pieced together well after it was over. The women came from different backgrounds, and their reasons for volunteering are not fully known. However, one of the phrases quoted was that 'they could see, perhaps more clearly than men, what defeat would have meant. They have greater imagination.'

Women such as Violette Szabo, Christina Granville, Noor Inayat Khan, Pearl Witherington and many others lived lives of danger and deception, though their motivation seems to have been overwhelmingly that of serious commitment to a practical goal. They were not romantics engaged in a 'thrilling adventure'. To be sure, they were strong on ideals, but they were also realistic about what faced them. Nor was the organisation they worked for a smooth-running machine: SOE was at times chaotic, with all the hallmarks of stylish amateurism nurtured in the British establishment, and it had an unenviable record of betrayal. Its achievements can still be a matter of debate, but its agents' determination was unquestioned.

CHAPTER EIGHTEEN

WE DID IT –
NOW WHAT?

WHAT NAGGED AT the munitions workers, and the Land Army and several other groups after the war, was the lack of *any* recognition whatsoever. Having spent years working hard in a job which you'd been told to do – and knew to be essential – there was no ceremony, no certificate, no medal. And in many places, there was quite a to-do when it came to the right to march past a war memorial or take part in a commemorative ceremony. And there's no doubt that the extraordinary deeds of the members of SOE, as well as the exploits of the ferry pilots and the nurses who experienced as much danger as any soldier, were perhaps given less prominence because of the prevailing feeling that women ought not to have been exposed to such rigours in the first place. Taken together with the quiet indifference to the millions of women who undertook war work and voluntary service, it all adds up to a great unsung story.

Opposite: What a demobbed girl can buy – a utility rayon suit for £2 11s 3d and eighteen ration coupons

THEY ARE PLANNING THEIR FUTURE. ARE YOU?

SAVE WITH A PLAN

POST OFFICE SAVINGS BANK
NATIONAL SAVINGS CERTIFICATES

FOR WAYS OF SAVING - ASK THE OFFICER WHO PAYS YOU

Having spent a post-war childhood in Sunderland with bits of bomb embedded in the dining-room sideboard, and interesting bits of metal turning up under the fruit bushes at the bottom of the garden, the home front seemed to me a much more active place than many of the remote locations from which the men had returned. My home town was littered with bomb-sites sprouting irrepressible buddleia; over a thousand houses had been destroyed and another three thousand were described as 'useless', with a further thirty-two thousand damaged. There were smelly concrete 'pill-boxes' – look-out posts – on the cliffs, and there was an obsession with 'going down to the beach' in the teeth of a bracing north-east wind, which I much later realised was a reaction to the seashore having been a forbidden area of barbed wire and anti-tank traps for over five years. One of the weirdest reminders of the war came when the air-raid siren was tested; the swooping wail turned a lot of people rigid with fear.

War has its traditional mementoes, and the warriors are decorated accordingly. However, when the women left at home were coping with air-raids and the threat of invasion, while channelling most of their energies into the war effort, and others were taking the same risks as front-line soldiers, they were in some way taking part in the war as much as anyone on the fighting front. It's not a case of 'medals for everyone', but a case of credit where it's due. Former munitions worker Ivy Davy, now in her late seventies, put it simply: 'I think that I did as much as what the girls in the forces did. I would have loved to have got a medal to give to our granddaughter – because Grandad has his for our grandson.'

Medals were thin on the ground for the majority of women, who were instead encouraged to be aware of the difficulties that their returning husbands, brothers or fathers might be facing. The evacuees reappeared and, like many other children, were quite bewildered as to who this man in the house might be. From being relatively independent and digging out neighbours from underneath rubble, women were meant to revert to normal family life – and be, well, womanly.

'Once again individually, adequately and gracefully dressed' – this was the future for women in the words of the Secretary of State for War, Sir James Grigg, as he put forward proposals in the House of Commons for demobilisation after World War II. Men were to get a 'demob suit' but the servicewomen would get cash, with the underlying hint that they should return to how men remembered them – or at least imagined them. However, clothes rationing remained in force for several years, coupled with restrictions in the manufacturing industry, so although the famous

'New Look' shown by the Paris designer Dior in 1947 took the fashion world by storm, it took time for its nipped-in waist and yards of skirt material to reach the British high street. But nylon, at least, was on its way – so women could stop painting a line down the back of their bare legs to simulate the seamed stockings that had been such a rarity for so long. Nylon also led eventually to 'elasticated' and more flexible underwear – but the corset made a bid for fashion prominence once again, resulting in the mind-boggling, or perhaps eye-boggling, phenomenon of National Corset Week in 1952. The hour-glass figures of the models, with much more accentuated bosoms leading the way, were in direct contrast to the flattened, baggy shape in which many women had spent the war.

However, the prominence of the bosom – literally – in stitched and padded and conical bras was ascribed by some to the need to emphasise the 'nourishing' role of post-war women. Whether this was a profound observation or a desperate attempt to understand just why breasts appeared to have acquired a life of their own, unconnected to the chest, is not clear. However, women were having to adjust to a different life – and there is still debate as to what precisely was happening as they were sent home from their war work or got out of uniform. Many servicewomen undoubtedly missed the camaraderie and responsibility of service life. They'd left the confines of family behind and felt they'd 'grown up'. Uniform had given them a status – and they'd been associated with a certain ethos and style, despite their auxiliary role.

Other women couldn't wait for the war to end – they'd endured rationing, bombing, separation from their husbands, and years of coping – and then the government had put them in a factory full of noise and dirt. Some longed to get back to what they'd had and 'settle down' – and wanted to re-create the memory of pre-war peace.

And yet others had noticed that the war had put women in uniform, though mainly to perform traditional cooking, cleaning and clerical tasks – nothing actually on the front line. And when they undertook training in traditional 'men's' work they were never paid as much, nor were they put in supervisory positions. In particular, those who'd directly replaced men in heavy industry, in skilled engineering, on the land and ferrying planes found there was little recognition of their achievements, and no great desire by the authorities to build on them. And even the women who had performed outstanding acts in the SOE were only slowly acknowledged – it was as if there was a brief round of applause, before everyone had to get on with business as usual, the men were coming home, and they'd been fighting for a comforting – welcoming – domestic scene.

The immediate post-war increase in divorces and marital upsets takes some of the glitter from this picture of twinkling reunited families, but regardless of this there was a general sense — encouraged officially — that women should take up the role of home-maker with fervour. Marriage was still the teenage girl's dream, and it would take a decade for many to acquire further education and to begin to broaden their horizons. Even so, part-time work for women was now much more common, and women were no longer automatically excluded on marriage from certain areas of employment such as teaching and the civil service. Also, the war had produced a huge list of firsts. True, the circumstances were judged unusual; nevertheless, there was no denying that barriers had been momentarily broken down in many countries.

Britain was not the only place where women had been flying. In America, Nancy Harkness Love had been ferrying every conceivable kind of military plane: she was the first woman to fly a B-25 and a B-17. Her WASPs (Women's Airforce Service Pilots) delivered over twelve thousand aircraft of seventy-seven different types. Other women became instructors — 'A woman taught me to walk, why shouldn't a woman teach me to fly?' All manner of phrases and advertisements were employed to counter traditional attitudes voiced in Congress: 'Take women into the armed services in any appreciable number, who then will manage the home fires, do the cooking, washing and other humble tasks?' And to attract women there was for the first time the lure of designer uniforms: for a girl joining the WAVES (Women Accepted for Voluntary Emergency Service) in 1942 to be able to say she was dressed by the Duchess of Windsor's couturier, Mainbocher, was to be in fashion heaven.

In 1943, the *Saturday Evening Post* ran the ad: 'She's 5 feet 1 from her 4A slippers to her spun-gold hair. She loves flower-hats, veils, smooth orchestras — and being kissed by a boy who's in North Africa. But man, oh man, how she can handle her huge and heavy drill press.' The iconic figure of Rosie the Riveter had taken hold. There were firsts in both skilled and unskilled employment, opportunities to gain academic and trade union posts hitherto male-only, and even inroads into the very macho area of American baseball. But it was no push-over. Rosie's appearance on the scene was officially regarded as less than a 24-carat first: 'A woman is a substitute', said a War Department brochure, 'like plastic instead of metal.'

In Canada there was a parallel obsession with cooking and washing, and the majority of women who had joined up were directed into domestic and clerical jobs. On average, they were paid two-thirds of men's wages; but at least military nurses achieved a first in 1942, being the first in any Allied country to get official officer status with equivalent power of command.

The only woman who held combat command in World War II was an

Home from the front. With their men back, most women were supposed to return to their traditional role of home-maker, wife and mother

anthropologist with expertise in the hill tribes of Nagaland in north-east India. Ursula Graham Bowers had gone to India in 1937, when she was twenty-three, and had been welcomed in the territory of these former head-hunters – not without some embarrassment to herself – as the reincarnation of a Naga chieftainess. As war swept through Burma she found herself on the front line in Assam, organising the villagers into reconnaissance units to spy on the Japanese. Carrying a kukri (Gurkha knife), a Sten gun and a pistol, she led over 150 tribesmen to gather information, round up Japanese deserters and ambush enemy patrols. Ursula was made a captain in the Indian army, though the British press liked to call her 'the Naga Queen'. She was an impressive operator, causing General Slim, commander of the 14th Army, to remark that she was not a 'missionary in creaking stays'; and she knew what she would have done if the Japanese had caught her:

There was no hope I could conceal myself in the Naga village. First of all I am too tall, and light skinned, my hair was sunbleached, I was blonde, obviously a European. In Burma when British officers had occasionally hidden, the Japs tortured the villagers until the officer gave himself up. I fixed it up with Namkia [her chief bodyguard] that I wasn't going to be taken alive. So I would shoot myself, and he would take my head in if the pressure on the villagers got unendurable. But it never came to it, for which I was devoutly thankful.

A different kind of first had been dubiously bestowed on women in Nazi Germany. Under a regime which had steadily pushed them out of political positions, the civil service and the law, motherhood became the new ideal. Women were to be baby-bearers for the Third Reich. The Nazi ideology had placed them firmly in the domestic sphere, a move partly founded on the notion that educated women represented a 'Jewish-intellectual ideal'. A declining birth rate fuelled the argument, coupled with the desire to produce a 'racially pure' nation. Mothers became sanctified – and rewarded. Four or more children gained their bearer the Mother's Honour Cross, which came in three grades: bronze for four children and silver for six,

while eight or more offspring warranted a gold. Meanwhile all women should be wholesome, pretty, Aryan and housewifely.

Unlike their sisters in the Allied countries they weren't conscripted on a large scale for factory work, partly because of the use of foreign slave-labour by the Nazis. However, as the war went on even Hitler – who disliked the idea of the 'militarisation' of women – had to agree to some kind of force to relieve men for front-line duties. Female Wehrmacht auxiliaries appeared, though at first without uniform: the Nazis were adamant that women soldiers did not suit their view of the female sex. Meanwhile they were being bombed by witches.

As if on swishing broomsticks, the pilots of 588th Night Bomber Regiment used to swoop low out of the sky in their elderly PO-2 biplanes. When they spotted the enemy they cut their engines and, almost hedge-hopping, the wind whistling in their wing-wires, they dropped their bombs before restarting their engines and nipping away. A thousand Soviet women had volunteered to join the 588th – and their Motherland had accepted them partly out of communist ideological reasons, but mainly because they were terrific pilots. Including bomb-loaders and mechanics, the regiment was entirely female. There were growls from the male regiments, especially when the men learned that the women were expert at handling the 'flying desk', as the PO-2 was known – *and* they didn't have parachutes. They trained in spartan surroundings to the north of Stalingrad, where they were given men's uniforms which were nearly always too large. Belts hitched up folds of cloth, and newspaper got stuffed into boots. Breakfast, after a night's flying, consisted of a 3oz 'front-line allowance' of vodka, followed by a long snooze and another night's flying.

Their fame was considerable, their exploits renowned. Katya Ryabova and Nadya Popova one night raided the German lines eighteen times, and towards the end of the war those who had survived had flown over a thousand raids each. Lilya Litvak, the 'White Rose of Stalingrad', was an outstanding fighter ace in the mixed 586th

Regiment. There was grumpiness when she and her equally skilled colleague Ekaterina Budanova arrived to join mixed crews. It evaporated as they engaged in dog-fights with the Luftwaffe, Ekaterina scoring eleven victories and Lilya racking up twelve before she was shot down in 1943.

The Germans on the Eastern Front were shocked to learn that their opponents were sometimes female; and the Allies weren't too keen on lauding the role which they denied their own air force women. However, the Soviet male pilots found the Night Witches' determination impressive, if uncomfortable. One major declared that it shamed Soviet manhood to see women engaged in the unwomanly business of war. It can't have helped when the women decided that they would never be taken prisoner – they would rather shoot themselves. It was not an idle boast. Alina Smirnovna lost her bearings and crashed. As local villagers ran towards her she mistook them for Germans, and killed herself.

One of the Russian Night Witch pilots, who committed suicide rather than be taken prisoner

Although the Russian Death Battalion had had brief fame in World War I, it was the product of enthusiasm and the need to encourage men to fight. A quarter of a century later communism preached equality, and though it never got to grips with shared domestic responsibilities it steered women into heavy labouring work and eventually into uniform. Fascism had an opposing view, confining women to children and kitchen. So in two nations women had little choice as to their roles, for both home and family were subject to heavy ideological interference. While people in Britain were 'muddling through' the unusual circumstances of war, in both the Russian Motherland and the Nazi Fatherland men and women had to adjust their views of the opposite sex in order to conform with the state's vision.

But all this was now over. The extraordinary times were receding, and though the 'firsts' were acknowledged, albeit sometimes rather grudgingly, 'seconds' were not expected. The fifties were approaching and, in the West, conventional roles such as had prevailed before the thirties and forties were reasserting themselves.

CHAPTER NINETEEN

WIMMIN AND WAR

HALFWAY ACROSS THE world, one woman was still determined to reject a post-war domestic role and pursue her interests, even if it meant crawling through sodden undergrowth for days. Brigitte Friang, dressed in a parachute regiment blouson and khaki trousers topped with an American helmet, was one of a dedicated team of mostly French war correspondents in Indo-China (now Vietnam) during France's bitter and long-running colonial war there. South-east Asia had a new conflict flare up again immediately after the Japanese surrender in 1945, with the Vietnamese communist leader Ho Chi Minh aiming to win independence from the former colonial power, France, and stirring the cauldron that was to bubble for another quarter of a century. Martha Gellhorn had seen that the area was not likely to be peaceful, reporting in 1946 from Java as the Indonesians engaged in throwing out their former rulers, the Dutch. Of Vietnam, she observed

Opposite: Anti-war protest during the Vietnam conflict, Washington DC, 1971

Clockwise from top left: Brigitte Friang in Indo-China, Martha Gellhorn in Italy, Edie Lederer in Vietnam, and Marguerite Higgins in Korea

that 'The tall white man had been conquered and debased by short yellow men; why should anyone accept the white man as master again?' She was to report from Vietnam twenty years later as the Americans slid into the cauldron.

Meanwhile, Brigitte Friang had the particular distinction of parachuting regularly into front-line positions, and accompanying the BPC – the Colonial Parachutists Battalion – on their uncomfortable and risky forays against Vietminh troops. Teased greatly, she ran up against the standard anti-women, anti-journalist traditionalists in the army's upper echelons. However, she was accepted as courageous and professional company and sent off despatches efficiently to her newspapers.

Brigitte's credentials were formidable. Frequently she was recognised by Para veterans who, a decade earlier, had been her fellows in the French resistance. They knew her story: she was Galilee II, an agent hoping to go to Britain for parachute training, and meanwhile organising drops and supplies, scurrying about delivering information to dodgy rendezvous in the French countryside. In 1944, aged twenty, she was betrayed, shot while trying to escape arrest, interrogated and tortured, then deported to a concentration camp. But Brigitte survived and, doggedly clinging to her dream of parachuting, eventually headed for Hanoi and Saigon as a journalist. She was a product of exceptional times – who else would have scrutinised the more German-sounding members of the French Foreign Legion near Dien Bien Phu, on the look-out for 'some familiar SS face' from the concentration camp. She was an intrepid reporter in a profession which had brought a small number of women to the fore in most conflicts – the BBC's elegant Audrey Russell, the intrepid Clare Hollingworth, and the doyenne, Gellhorn.

While Indo-China's jungle fighting ground on, United Nations forces were heading for war in Korea – and an American reporter, Marguerite Higgins, had gone ashore with the assault troops during the Inchon landings. Again, hers is a tale of grit and perseverance in the face of rival pressmen and a sceptical military, but she never wavered from repeating: 'I'm here as a correspondent, not as a woman.'

The Korean War saw nurses following the troops as Britain sent a contingent with a multinational force in 1950, to work alongside the American MASH (Mobile Army Surgical Hospital) units. It's claimed that about two hundred thousand women, mainly American, were on 'active duty' – some nursing in theatre or med-evac flights, and the majority in neighbouring countries such as Japan in support units – but they tend not to get much of a mention in the official accounts. However, there are notable accounts of 'uncompromising women commandos' on the Korean side.

There were no such female warriors coming out of Britain, where matters were handled rather differently. After World War I the government could hardly wait to disband the various women's military outfits; in 1945 there had been no such haste, even though thousands were demobbed within weeks of VE-Day. Nevertheless, in 1946 the House of Commons heard a speech from the Secretary of State for War which didn't sound like a particularly thundering endorsement of the ATS: Mr J.J. Lawson merely said he *hoped* the ATS would remain, in one form or another, a permanent part of His Majesty's services. Undeterred, the ATS, the WAAF and the WRNS all manoeuvred with the top brass about rank, discipline and new names. The ATS had a close call with Royal Army Territorial Service. By 1948 legislation was enacted to bring into being the Women's Royal Army Corps, the Women's Royal Air Force and the Queen Alexandra's Nursing Corps; there was separate legislation for the WRNS. These services could now regard themselves as permanent, though with very specific roles, all of which excluded any participation in combat front-line duties. Most progressive was the RAF, with more shared work than the other services, but despite the role of the wartime ferry pilots the nearest women got to flying was as stewardesses. Another decade passed before they were allowed to be quartermasters – later loadmasters – in aircrew. However, during the war there had been debate among the senior officers in all three services on the fundamental dividing line between killing 'directly' and 'indirectly', and the Director of the WAAF made a precise case in 1941 about her position vis à vis the ATS and the WRNS:

These Directors [of the ATS and WRNS] are of the opinion . . . that psychologically there is to their service a great difference between women having immediate responsibility for the killing of men and being indirectly responsible. . . . The[y] . . . believe it would be detrimental to the 'womanliness of women' to be actually responsible. . . . Our service has been doing the equivalent of 'indirect killing' since the outbreak of war. . . . It was suggested by the other services . . . that the other ranks would think there was a great difference between the handling of lethal weapons and indirectly handling them. I think our airwomen must be of a higher mentality. It is perfectly clear to them that they are indirectly responsible for the destruction of human beings and that there is so little difference between this and being directly responsible that it is not worth considering. It should be realised that there is little hypocrisy in our service.

Curiously, those perhaps nearest to 'indirect killing' had been the women on the anti-aircraft batteries – in the ATS – targeting a plane, and in some instances, training the gun-sights on the enemy. However, such thoughts were very much the stuff of internal discussion, and did not figure largely in the setting up of the permanent women's services eight years later.

If the WAAFs weren't in the air they couldn't grumble, because the Wrens were definitely not at sea, and their new organisation stuck firmly to the traditional roles – admiral's social secretary being a particular speciality; but at least they still had very cute hats, and somehow managed to avoid the clomping shoes worn by WRACs. And pity the WAAF ladies who finally made it as loadmasters in the seventies, wearing a flared Crimplene dress – with a pair of slightly flared matching trousers underneath for scrambling up the ramps of transport planes. . . .

Designing a uniform is a nightmare – one style to fit all shapes; make it too fashionable and in a few years this expensive kit will be a badge fit for derision – frozen fashion, and a formidable bar to recruiting. Add to this the inevitable involvement of a raft of men from the Ministry and senior male officers, all dreaming gently about what they think a woman should look like (a dream rooted firmly thirty years in the past), and it's a small miracle that something wearable appears. I remember spying formal evening wear – 'Mess Dress' – at a military dinner in the early nineties. It was gorgeous and flattering on the men – peacocks preening – and then I saw a huddle of variously shaped women in identical faded gold lamé, some bulging, some stick-like, trailing a weedy shoulder sash in green and looking for all the world like a harvest of corn on the cob, wilting. It probably looked terrific when it was introduced to the army ladies in the seventies, but two decades on. . . .

However, when it was first formed the Women's Royal Army Corps was a confident outfit, for the first time an all-woman corps in the Regular Army. Its role followed very much the pattern set out in World War II, when the Secretary of State for War had stated that 'Women will, of course, be employed only on work for which they have a special aptitude.' So *Suaviter in modo, fortiter in re* – 'gentle in action, resolute in deed' – the WRAC embarked on forty-three years as part of the British army, directed by women, but only in the last few years actually given weapons training.

The fraught issue of being armed surfaced in an innocuous report into employment in 1976, when the WRAC discovered that they weren't legally non-combatants, as had always been assumed, and were therefore now liable to be deployed in any role except those involving direct fire. After a lot of legal undergrowth had been hacked through it became clear that there was no going back, especially if they wanted to be used efficiently in the future, working alongside men. Having male escorts with guns seemed a waste of manpower. There was much shilly-shallying about public opinion, even though the US military had made weapons training compulsory for all its servicewomen the previous year. It took several years for the British government to bite the bullet, as it were, announcing plans for small arms training in 1981. The WRAF went ahead straightaway; the WRAC took a little longer, seven years to be precise, and began training their recruits in 1988.

The WRAC was a genteel outfit, reinforcing the ladylike aspect of women's soldiering – though frequently with more than a whisper of gay orientation. Dressed in a wholly high street-tailored suit in lovat green, which emphasised the feminine and was absolutely useless for marching in, they constituted a support service with a very definite sense of *esprit de corps*, but which offered a strictly limited range of career opportunities to officers and the usual crafts for ordinary servicewomen.

The FANY survived – to become an all-woman volunteer organisation, specialising in communications work with the army. However, with their penchant for galloping across battlefields or joining sabotage units they still exuded a military *je ne sais quoi*.

When in the late fifties I first encountered the two formidable service ladies who came to my school, clomp clomp clomp, in huge shoes surmounted by neatly pressed shapelessness, I could not conceive of wanting to spend adult life looking like that. Nor did I ever hear anything subsequently during my teenage years which might have suggested an exciting career in the military. It appeared to be the usual round of typing and filing, while being subject to rules which were the reason for leaving school behind. True, there were posters and adverts suggesting that these activities sometimes went on in exotic climes, where no one mentioned mosquitoes, but this wasn't enough to lure anyone I knew; and at a dance with the eligible locals in the Territorial Army I once ventured that it would be fun to fly a helicopter, which drew the reply: 'Girls don't. Girls can't.' And that was that.

Paperwork, typing, communications, administration, lots of sport and good opportunities for travel – the women's services were consolidating their roles in the fifties. For some it seemed liberating, with postings in Libya, Cyprus and the Far East; for others it seemed a restricted career, with most army jobs barred to women. However, in the Middle East there'd been a significant development which has lingered to this day in myth and legend about front-line women. The guerrilla war which led to the formation of the state of Israel saw many volunteer women trained to fight aggressively. Integrated into underground units, they engaged in sabotage and attacks on the occupying British military, which had had a mandate over Palestine since shortly after World War I. The subsequent War of Independence in 1948 saw many of these women absorbed into the newly formed Israeli Defence Forces, and several thousand trained and fought alongside men. However, pressure was very soon exerted, particularly by the Orthodox Jewish community, to segregate the troops: women began to be sidelined into support functions and were finally ordered out of the front lines by 1950. Subsequently, well into the sixties, there were reports of women still being allowed into combat. However, much of this misconception may stem from the fact that the IDF were organised on a militia basis with conscription for both sexes, so that girls with rifles slung over their shoulders were a common sight at the bus stop and in the market place. However, they have mainly served in the clerical and secretarial sections and in the technical and mechanical trades – despite that Uzi on the shoulder.

The first Israeli female fighter pilot graduated in 2001 – this is one of the combat areas which many countries have found relatively easy to integrate. However, just as in other Western states, lack of resources has forced the Israeli army to change its rules. With some reservists refusing to serve during the Palestinian uprising as the twenty-first century dawned, women were sent to mixed front-line defence units, mainly as field engineers and technicians. Then, as some of the religious settlements came under increased threat, women were sent to guard them, provoking the very people they were sent to protect. But religious arguments about modesty, blended at times with chauvinism, have had little impact, particularly as many of the women have been openly critical of the limited role traditionally available to them. The IDF have taken the decision to encourage women to volunteer to serve in combat support positions.

This is ironic, considering that for half a century the rest of the world has entertained an image of the young 'Israeli woman–soldier' – a striking figure, especially in the Middle East – apparently ready to go into combat. Time and again, the arguments about attitudes to women in the front line – and the reaction of men

to them – centre round a piece of folklore involving an unspecified Middle East conflict, a wounded Israeli woman soldier, and the subsequent chaos as the men throw down their weapons to rush to her aid, thus buggering up the battle. This scene has the strength of an urban myth, and I've heard it repeatedly, always presented as a concrete example of what happens when women go into combat.

What hasn't lingered so much is the image of Russian women who were in front-line combat – though it has to be said that news of their full participation in World War II only began to emerge in the 1980s. Joan Lovatt, touring in Austria in 1945 with ENSA, had seen female Russian troops in Vienna: they seemed to be absolutely part and parcel of the Red Army, and formidable. They were also just a handful from among perhaps eight hundred thousand who had either volunteered or been conscripted during the war. And now that more is emerging from the files of post-Soviet Russia, it's clear that large numbers of women were engaged in desperate fighting, as well as operating as snipers and medical orderlies, and, of course, flying bombers as the Night Witches. Perhaps the dour and unfeminine aspect of communist womanhood militated against their becoming mythologised – nor, for all their trumpeting of equality, were the Soviet authorities particularly attentive to female liberation.

An Israeli Defence Forces soldier guarding a Jewish settlement

As the sixties rolled on, the women's movement emerged as a potent force in a decade of colourful and noisy change. And in a time of protest and demonstration, one of the strongest images was that of a pretty girl in a mini-skirt planting a flower in the rifle held by a grim-helmeted military man. Demonstrations against the Vietnam War ranged across continents – and an anti-war stance seemed natural to many women caught up in questioning the status quo. Anyway, one look at the military told you it wasn't somewhere the women's movement would find a sympathetic ear. In 1967 John Laffin wrote in *Women in Battle*: 'Woman's place should be in bed and not the battlefield, in crinoline or terylene rather than battledress, wheeling a pram rather than driving a tank.' They should 'stop men from fighting' rather than joining the fray.

And indeed, for different reasons, this was happening. In the USA, the tradition of waving off the lads to war went into reverse, with many young women encouraging guys to dodge the draft. The military was associated with all that was male and authoritarian, traditional, hierarchical and anti-women, so what better than to turn up and protest in secondhand camouflage fatigues – the trousers, of course – and

Cambodian women
soldiers trekking to
the front near
Kompong Trabek,
1972

mock the military? The very notion that going off to serve your country was honourable took a lot of knocks. Smart young men didn't go: 'student deferment' rendered conscription a tool which dug out the poor and the 'country boys' in disproportionate numbers.

Not that there weren't women serving in Vietnam; indeed, hanging on the coat-tails of the bitter complaints of Vietnam veterans that indifference and embarrassment have been their reward for serving in a grisly and eventually pointless conflict have been the complaints of women who claim that no one ever noticed that they too were in 'Nam. They resent the image that they always served in 'safe' places and saw little of the violence, when the reality was a war which crept through the streets and wriggled round military bases with effective terrorist tactics. 'The military, which prided itself on the records it kept in Vietnam – counting the number of enemy weapons captured, for example – cannot to this day say with certainty how many women served. The army that sent them never bothered to count them. The *estimate* most frequently given is that a total of 7,500 served in the military in Vietnam,' wrote Laura Palmer in *Shrapnel in the Heart*. On the memorial in Washington, DC are the names of eight military nurses who died in Vietnam, and there were others from the Women's Army Corps (WAC) who provided administrative and logistic services, along with aid agency workers, journalists and missionaries – though to be sure, it was a tiny minority when put alongside the massive American presence over a decade, and the huge number demonstrating against the war.

Also in the battle zone were female Vietnamese guerrillas, typical of the way insurgencies or revolutionary movements welcome women more easily than standing armies; the Tamil Tigers, the Palestinian Liberation Organisation, the Sandinistas in Nicaragua, and many more – the last decades of the twentieth century saw a stream of pictures of female fighters across the globe: it's almost axiomatic that Western press coverage of a guerrilla group uses a photograph of a woman in fetching fatigues clutching a gun, particularly when realistic footage or pictures are hard to come by. There's also the underlying message that the guerrillas are supported by *everyone* – that is, even the women are prepared to risk their lives in the cause. A message delivered happily by the revolutionaries, keen to convey determination and solidarity, and received ambiguously in the West: yes, they're keen – but aren't these groups a little bit unreasonable, rather 'flaky', wanting women involved in guerrilla combat? Generally, there's ambiguity in just how images of women with weapons are used, for when it comes to standing armies, such as in Iraq or Libya, there's been a definite public relations confusion about the impact of pictures of a battalion of women cradling Kalashnikov rifles. The Arab world intends to convey determination and resolve, regardless of the fact that their women have less equality. The Western world views the marching female columns as rather wacky, regardless of their own laws advocating equality.

Against a background of increasing recognition of women's rights, one small band of campaigners took heart and redoubled their efforts to gain recognition after more than four decades of battle with the US government. Merle Egan-Anderson and her 'Hello Girls' were not going to give up. Their story goes right back to World War I. . . .

The Middle East conflict: a pro-PLO wall painting

In 1917, the French telephone system had all but defeated the commander of the American Expeditionary Forces in France, General John Pershing. Fed up with the tangle of wires that rendered communication a tragedy of errors in the trenches, coupled with enlisted men who couldn't use a switchboard, he asked Washington to send him modern equipment and French-speaking female operators. The response was swift, for not only were the women assumed to be better at the job, according to the Chief Signal Corps Officer, 'if it is true that the hand that rocks the cradle rules the world, it is also true that the soft answer which turneth away wrath – the voice with a smile – is exceedingly effective in expediting the all-important telephone connections under the stress of combat, when tempers are apt to ruffle and cuss words to impede the channels of swift intercourse'.

Over two hundred girls sailed for France, having been sworn in as members of the US Army Signal Corps Telephone Units. They were subject to all army regulations, and to an additional ten rules designed 'to assure their moral character'. Some served just behind the front lines and under German shelling, where thunderous artillery competed with their shouted messages. They learned about tactics and weaponry, and were very conscious of the need for precision – garbled orders could have terrible consequences. One girl wrote home to Oregon about '250 girls who plug from morning until night, who scream their lungs out to trenches over lines that are tied to trees, to fence-posts, and along the ground. Not that we care. We came over here to do our work and to give quick service and to help the boys a few miles ahead of us.' When the war was over, they returned to the USA and applied for their honourable discharges, only to be told that they could not have been sworn into the army because the regulations stated that 'males' were sworn in and said nothing about 'persons'.

From 1930 onwards they tried to get bills through Congress, but not until 1979 did they finally win their battle, being given veterans' status and finally getting their discharge papers and victory medals. As Louise Le Brenton wrote: 'We were 225

Back our girls over there

Y.W.C.A.

United War Work Campaign

A 'Hello Girl' in France in World War I. But it took sixty years before the US government finally backed 'our girls'

altogether, going to France in 6 different units. Half of us have died, the others in their seventies, some in their eighties. It was kind of bitter to find out that the Yeomanettes, who never left these shores, were enlisted members of the Navy receiving bonuses, veterans' benefits, hospitalization, etc., whereas nothing was ever done for us. *C'est la vie* or *C'est la querre?*'

One consequence of Vietnam in the USA was the end of conscription in 1973 and the advent of an all-volunteer force – which showed that joining up was not seen as the most attractive career option open to young men. Thus, out of necessity, the Americans looked at a section of the population which was much less likely to get drunk and fight each other, had better educational qualifications and was more obedient in training – women. Necessity began to drive the recruitment machine – large numbers of young people were required to service the military machine in the Cold War and to be trained in increasingly technological warfare. More jobs – 'specialisations' – began to be opened up for women, and living conditions were improved in an effort to repel the image of concrete-floored barracks where hairy-bummed males eschewed normal living and tore open ration tins with their teeth.

At the same time, the women's movement was bringing joy to the hearts of America's battalions of lawyers: equality was being defined and legislated on. But there was also the discovery that the military was a hugely complex animal in terms of 'rights'. Not surprisingly, the first problem that increased numbers of women caused was further increased numbers – due to pregnancy. This natural problem had always been treated very easily by the military – a woman got the option of termination or ending her military career. But this solution was now thrown into disarray by the lawyers, who argued that, if a serviceman and a servicewoman had conceived a child, there was no equality if the woman lost her job while the man merely became a proud parent (regardless of which party had forgotten about contraception). The forces wrestled with this – and the net result was the US forces becoming the only major military outfit in the world to issue maternity uniforms.

In Britain, as there wasn't such a uniform, you just left, and there wasn't quite so much agitation about equality to match the American experience. (Added to that, those women who were in the forces seemed to be the only people who were passionate about skirts. In an era of ubiquitous jeans and the arrival of the trouser suit, servicewomen were conspicuous by their demure hemlines.) Moreover, the British had fought the Falklands War in the early 1980s and had a large number of troops on active service in Northern Ireland. The forces' image was of males engaged in a tough and often dirty business, one that brooked no softness. Military nurses were somewhere in the background, but the actual task of getting stuck-in was a grim and violent reality – and furthermore Hollywood, with its sanitised violence and simplistic heroics, does not shape European attitudes to warfare.

However, television does shape some attitudes, and the image of women at the time of the Falklands War – other than in the centre-stage presence of Prime Minister Margaret Thatcher – was almost solely one of waiting relatives. In interviews with service families, brothers, fathers and sons hardly appeared at all – they did not seem to meet the convention that it was men who were away and in danger: it was the exclusive job of women to wait and worry. And an analysis of the interviews *about* the war shows that the 'man in the street' was always asked: 'What do you *think* about the war?' while women were asked: 'How do you *feel* about it?' Even though the TV pictures took an age to reach Britain, entirely because of political obstruction, the Falklands conflict had a gritty profile of sweat and endurance. It also reinforced an unpalatable fact to those who believed high-tech soldiering was becoming the norm, for at the battle of Tumbledown the order had been given 'advance to contact', which is the moment when bayonet-led fighting becomes a bloody reality.

Meanwhile, the Americans were engaged in legal hostilities with the equal rights lobby, as the military came under increasing scrutiny as a wayward beast which had so far evaded close inspection. Close-up and cornered, the military was displaying its most powerful weapon, the CEL – the Combat Exclusion Law, formulated in 1948 to keep women off combat naval vessels and combat air squadrons: 'Women may be assigned to all units except those with a high probability of engaging in ground combat, direct exposure to enemy fire, or direct physical combat with the enemy.' One of the trickier points for lawyers and military alike was what actually constituted 'combat', and 'engaging in it'. Was it being in a battle zone – which could perhaps mean an entire country? What if you were in a ship or an aircraft and fired at an enemy 'over the horizon' – one you couldn't see? Or they fired at you. Did you 'engage' an enemy by pressing a missile button? Did you actually have to *see* the enemy – eyeball-to-eyeball stuff – or just on the radar or through a telescopic sight? Perhaps it meant only physical contact – fighting man-to-man (language was the least of the problems to be addressed).

The service top brass were unhappy and passed the problem to the politicians – who looked to the lawyers, who were then assailed on all sides by interested parties. One of the contemporary difficulties was that fewer politicians had much military experience themselves, and the women activists had almost none at all. With the Gulf War in sight, women constituted over one-tenth of the American military machine. They were by now dressed in camouflage 'combats' just like the men – but were still unable to serve in front-line positions in the infantry, artillery, armour and combat jets.

CHAPTER TWENTY

THE RIGHT
TO FIGHT

NOTHING PREENS QUITE like a journalist when putting on a military uniform. And having swallowed my schoolgirl objections in a trice, hoping that desert-coloured 'combats' might – just *might* – make me feel more like Goldie Hawn in *Private Benjamin* than a middle-aged stray Brownie, I headed for the Gulf.

As the Allied forces poured into the desert of Saudi Arabia, the press were already engaged in full-scale hostilities with the military. For several months hundreds of journalists – television crews, radio reporters, photographers and print scribes – had been penned up in the dusty east coast town of Dharan, a scruffy dump of toiling Asian 'guest workers' and other foreign traders. Frequently insulted by 'our Saudi hosts', who greatly resented the very idea of journalists poking around their primitive society, and fed up with evenings spent gazing at limp curries accompanied by orange

Opposite: Female US marine training in a trench

juice, the press resorted to baiting the various military press officers, most of whom had not been expecting the journalists to field a battalion-sized force.

Having filed stories, day after day, about the preparations, the build-up and the expectations, there was frustration all round. The Americans had a particularly irritating time, interviewing hundreds of GIs all of whom appeared to be programmed to answer every question by staring into the distance and barking, 'Goin' to do my dooty ma'am.' Many then resolutely refused to give their names and say where they hailed from: 'See, Saddam could send his sneaky spies to find their families and kill 'em,' explained the goofy US public affairs officers dogging the journalists' footsteps. The prospect of Iraqis setting off to lurk in the smaller towns of Idaho and Kentucky was beyond contemplation.

The British army laid on various exercises, which involved a lot of very satisfying explosions for people carrying microphones, and the French forces – as usual – spoke only to the French press, treating everyone else's soldiers and journalists as uninvited guests at a private do. And so much of the press interest centred on the future prospects for the journalists themselves: who was going to accompany the troops into the action?

Newsdesks in London manoeuvred for precedence, there being limited spaces on offer ('Now look – this is the Ministry of Defence you're dealing with, sir, not Thomson Holidays'). Tabloids claimed huge readerships, all ready to cheer on 'our boys'. The broadsheets complained that they wouldn't yield a place to a popular rag's reporter who couldn't spell Iraq. Those of us in TV blackened each other's reputations, then ganged up to disqualify stations which couldn't produce a cameraman bearing bodily scars acquired during wars in Beirut and Afghanistan. Hacks who had spent their lives wearing rude T-shirts and torn jeans suddenly announced their desire to wear uniform.

The British army thought that a good way to sort out the battle-ready sheep from the lard-carrying goats might be a spot of PT. Bit of a mistake there – we were all a disaster, shambling past a horrified Royal Marine who viewed us as a kind of slow-moving suicide squad. Eventually, a couple of dozen British press representatives were told they would be accredited as official war correspondents, and told to report to a tent near the airbase.

It was then that I learned a very old military lesson: uniforms are measured by the time-honoured method of some bloke giving you a half-second once-over, before burrowing in a heap of clothing and chucking various items at you. All my female antennae waving, I reckoned I had about fifteen seconds to discover if the bundle of sandy camouflage material was going to make me look like a medieval jousting steed trailing yards of flapping material, or merely flatten my boobs and delineate my rear end too precisely. The tent was full of men wrestling with multi-coloured material, and pawing floppy desert hats to see if they had any discernible shape. I shifted to the back of the melee, aware that no other female was involved in this operation, and pulled on the trousers: far too big; jacket, ditto. I arrived back at the trestle table, which now had a much smaller selection available, and with a ruthlessness born of years of practice at Harvey Nichols' sales grabbed the lot and embarked on a feverish try-on session.

After a few frantic minutes I found something suitable, and took a breather to observe my colleagues. Some seemed to have no instinct whatsoever for matching clothing with body size; twig legs were suspended from gorilla-wide jackets. On the other hand, there was a regular fashion parade in progress in one group. Sleeves were being rolled up neatly to regulation above-elbow level. Floppy hats were being adjusted – 'This side, do you think? Brim up or down?' And bits of cotton scarf were being fashioned into cravats, for heaven's sake. My BBC colleague Martin Bell was already adjusting his helmet straps and sorting out a flak-jacket, as was his cameraman Nigel Bateson, a giant cuddly bear of a man for whom the British army took some time to find a flak-jacket that didn't look like a bra on his manly chest. My own crew had transformed from denim jeans and 'Don't Shoot I'm a Journalist' T-shirts, and now paraded in front of me as if army uniform were their second skin. One small protest about individuality was maintained by our video editor, Duncan, who insisted on going to war in a pair of purple sneakers, rather than desert boots.

It was curious to see the press kitted out with gas-masks and water-bottles, bed-rolls slung across bergens, Swiss army knives, plastic mug and torch dangling from bits of string attached to webbing belts. Misshapen yellowy-fawn Christmas trees trudging off across the sand, media in uniform, unrecognisable under helmets. With me in the rear, desperately trying to remember if I'd got all the pieces of kit I was supposed to have, because if I had to turn round, bend over and get it I would surely end up as a new species of desert turtle, destined to remain forever flat on my back until one of Saddam Hussein's tanks ran over me.

That I was there at all was a small miracle. The British army had no women in combat units, and no women who were intended to serve in the front line. During the months of preparation I'd come across lots of women in uniform, but all in the traditional roles in supply units, transport groups and, of course, the extensive medical facilities which were being set up in the base areas. True, they all wore the same outfit as the men – 'combats', consisting of loose jacket and trousers in camouflage pattern, and army boots. But there was no doubting the division which was about to take place: the men moved forward, the women remained behind. Occasionally, a personable girl would be seen during an exercise – an assistant adjutant from the Women's Royal Army Corps attached to the Royal Artillery, perhaps; but even then, it was made clear that when 'Go' came, she would not be going with her colleagues.

There were vastly more American servicewomen to be seen. By 1990, 11 per cent of the US military was female, as was 13 per cent of the reserve forces, and of over four hundred thousand American personnel eventually deployed to Saudi Arabia 6 per cent were women. They were indistinguishable from their male counterparts in their 'chocolate chip' camouflage – fawn and brown with odd 'pebble' blotches – carrying large back-packs, and dragging M-16 rifles around; but it was noticeable that they tended to drag their rifles around, rather than carry them. Such were their numbers that it appeared as if they would automatically be part of any major assault; however, they were still subject to the US army and Marine Corp policy of keeping women out of combat units.

They sorted stores, stood guard, did admin, repaired and fuelled vehicles, issued kit, cooked, nursed and drove trucks – much to the apoplexy of the medieval Saudis, whose zealous religious police, the *mutawa*, occasionally attempted to interfere with what they judged to be lewdly dressed trollops: women soldiers in trousers and T-shirts. The *mutawa* tend to be getting on in years, though this didn't stop them trying to whack the foreign floozies in uniform with their sticks. 'Real weird,' was how a six-foot black infantry sergeant described it to me. 'I mean, does this guy know what's coming?' She gestured, and I gathered that the *mutawa* had been given a lesson in flying.

Nor were women to be found on the combat ships in the Gulf waters – though there were plenty in support vessels, and on the ground crews of the air force. But they were in close proximity to the men in the huge holding areas and camps that were spreading across eastern Saudi. And that's when we started to hear about the impact of their presence, for there was little 'real' news for weeks on end, other than logistics, as the huge C-5 aircraft and the hulking supply ships kept up round-the-clock deliveries of tanks and armoured vehicles, trucks and helicopters.

We reporters had almost given up counting and measuring, particularly as there appeared to be only one adjective to describe the flow of American war machinery – inexhaustible. We amused ourselves by noting the home comforts that seemed absolutely necessary to support US boys and girls abroad: several tons of chewing gum, portable showers and dental floss. Even so, we passed by the press desks set up by the military, just to see if anything other than fatuous public relations hand-outs and leaflets in child-friendly language were being doled out by the press officers. And gradually we began to take notice of the list of 'incidents' reported on an American daily bulletin board.

Most were RTAs – road traffic accidents – usually involving sturdy military vehicles encountering squashy Saudi saloons. But there were other 'incidents', reported in truncated army-speak but – unsurprisingly – indicating that not everyone was a shining example of discipline. Buried in the obscure language was a steady current of fights and brawls, a number of suicides, and other fatalities involving weapons. After a couple of months the sum total of deaths – including RTAs – had climbed over the hundred mark. And, although the press officers denied it publicly, rape was also a factor in the incident list. Considering the hundreds of thousands of young people herded together in a foreign land, combined with the atmosphere of tension and impending war, there were no grounds for shock horror reporting. But it was a development. Women were no longer the baggage-train or the 'odd bird of passage' – whole flocks of them were part of the US forces' migration to the war zone. Many of the women were single mothers, for the US military was – and is – one of the few places where a young person who has dropped out of school with few or no qualifications can get an education, a training, a pension – and child-care benefits. Indeed, there were difficulties deploying some of them immediately because they hadn't arranged for their child to be looked after. 'I never expected to go to *war*,' was one of the phrases uttered to me regularly by wide-eyed GI ladies, somewhat incensed that the army had had the temerity to suggest they go and do their bit. Other women didn't make it right through the war – they were shipped home pregnant. Clearly, the military were now dealing with welfare problems that were as old as the hills, but new to a deployed fighting force.

The British merely had me to deal with. In true British fashion, the officers in charge of our unit were courteous, laid back, and clearly thought that women should deal with women's things. That I was the only woman in the front line, and in a unit of two thousand men, they addressed with the all-purpose army phrase: 'Not a problem.' So I slept with thirteen fellow hacks in the same tent, and evolved survival techniques. Dressing and undressing proved less of a problem than I'd thought – we journalists were so incompetent at putting up our tent that we invariably failed to get more than one feeble light-bulb to function, not having much clue where a desert electricity supply might be. Anyway, you can do a lot of wriggling in a sleeping-bag. The morning wash was something of a poser. Outside in the glaring sun the blokes stripped down, and I looked thoughtfully at my plastic bowl. Soon, the novelty wore off and I merely turned my back to my own unit, squatting on the hard gravelly ground, sloshing on our limited supply of water and staring into the distance – at the next unit all in their full glory less than a hundred yards away. Deserts may be most people's idea of an infinite empty expanse. Plonk half a million soldiers into one in orderly formations, and life becomes very un-private indeed.

Still, the army was infinitely patient. And never patronising. However, we never quite solved the Loo Problem. Later, just after we'd entered Kuwait, I met up with the first British women in uniform I'd seen for months. Three of them, transport WRACs, were attempting to crawl under a truck in a crowded area, with huge tracked artillery pieces thundering past.

'Hi – what are you doing?' I shouted.

An agonised face squinted out. 'Where the hell do you pee in this sodding desert?' she squeaked.

'Ah, there you have me,' I said. 'I've been looking for the right spot for over four months and I don't seem to have found it yet.' Then added: 'Mind the truck doesn't drive off – that can be a bit awkward. Believe me, I've tried everything.'

And I had.

The Americans hadn't had these problems. Included in the home comforts shipped halfway across the world were a phenomenal number of strange plywood constructions, like four old-fashioned telephone boxes stuck together. There was a door at one end, and three window spaces at the front, but no glass. Inside was a bench with three, sometimes four ovals cut into it. It was very narrow and cramped, and thus a very social loo, involving a lot of 'Excuse Me's' and much staring out of the window spaces. But at least American women could appropriate their own and write 'Latrines, Female' in letters large enough for the most desperate creature, male or female, to identify. Some British units acquired these loos – the Americans were incredibly relaxed about acquisition or just didn't notice when things went walkies. But as there were never enough to go round, I decided that a formal request involving me versus two thousand men with equal needs was something to be avoided.

To my rescue came a gallant officer, one of our escorts, who put the whole problem on a military footing. Whenever the need came about, I was to give a signal. We would head out into the far distance in his Land Rover and I would discreetly disappear round the back, while he remained at the front, gazing in the opposite direction and thinking of England.

In all other aspects, I was treated equally. No concessions, no exclusion. No one behaved in a sexist manner – no one questioned my being there. However, I was merely a reporter, not a soldier – though, had things got critical, all of us in the press group were expected to put our intensive first aid training into use and deal with the wounded. Interestingly, the issue only surfaced in a number of tabloid newspapers in

London, with a woman MP writing abusively about my presence in the Gulf. She it was who invented the nonsense about my losing my pearl ear-rings and having soldiers look for them. Another tabloid got very excited about 'a girl' on the front line, suggesting that there'd be protests, and asking their man in Saudi to 'get a few pix' which would prove that I 'couldn't hack it'. It was the usual sexist stuff, supposedly reflecting the views of 'the lads' in the army, but much more the product of a resolutely old-fashioned — and middle-aged — newspaper editorial view which cannot reconcile the changed position of women in society with the need to maximise profits from a 'boobs and girlies' approach. Interestingly, the most laddish of the tabloid newspapers got a frosty reception amongst the ordinary soldiers. They objected to being portrayed as dumb patriots, only interested in nudes and nuking Saddam. They were nineteen-year-olds, with feisty girlfriends and wives back home, who readily volunteered that the way the Saudis treated women would get their own women mad as hell, and, as one corporal put it, 'up for coming here and sorting out those blokes in frocks'.

I found it interesting that the usual old stuff was being trotted out at home, with no serious thought as to what changes might really be on the way. The presence of so many American women in uniform alongside the men in the camps was a constant reminder that the last few years had seen a major development in the arguments about women and war. Even though they weren't combat troops they *looked* like them: identical to the infantry soldiers from heavy boots to cropped hair under bulletproof kevlar helmets. They didn't live in separate units, and they lugged about heavy fuel hoses and ammunition boxes, the sweat staining their T-shirts on which clanked their identification dog-tags. They hooted and whooped and yelled, and lounged around wearing shades; from a distance, there was nothing to say they were women. They were observed by thoughtful British officers, many of whom had a shrewd idea that they were looking at the future.

The question of women in combat came home to me as we went off to an exercise in infantry trench-clearing. Screaming young men tore up and down walls of sand, howling like banshees, their faces contorted with emotion, every sense of their bodies alert as live ammunition was fired by them and over them, and the sand erupted with grenade explosions. They'd been psyched up to this state, and were reacting to a carefully controlled series of orders which rendered them frighteningly fierce. In fact, ready to kill. Their lean and cool officers stared at them in the manner of trainers watching thoroughbreds on the gallops at

US soldier in Saudi Arabia during the Gulf War, 1991

Newmarket, occasionally snapping an order. I'd never seen anything quite like it, for it was light years removed from the heat of a brawl or even a full-scale riot. It was animal behaviour let rip on the end of a taut leash. The actual noises made were way beyond the shouts and grunts and snarls of a fight; it made football fan trouble look like a tea-party, and it was nothing like any training course or official film I'd ever seen.

Apart from having to break off observation of this scene in order to join in and be thrown down into the trenches and pushed up the other side, hugely conscious of not being a nineteen-year-old and terrified of getting a bullet in the bum, or worse, I realised that the sharp end of the infantry was not pretty. Everyone around me, as I flopped on to the sand amazed not to find myself a human colander, considering that I'd been hauled bodily the last 30 yards of the course, was mildly surprised at *my* surprise about the exercise.

'Bog standard stuff,' was the view. 'Not all assaults are sneaky-beaky.'

'Bit more enthusiasm needed over there, ma'am,' said one NCO, heading off to shout a lot at a red-faced bunch of lads shuddering with adrenaline.

I immediately counted myself out of any assessment of how women might fit into this scene. Journalists of a certain age with a tendency to burrow to Australia at the sound of detonating grenades are not part of the argument. However, I wondered long and hard about the number of women who would or could participate utterly competently and automatically in such behaviour.

Some weeks later, I saw the same controlled, maddened state during the artillery raids. Scores and scores of huge artillery pieces were ranged in line for a massive bombardment of the distant Iraqi forces. After a fearful silence as we counted down, the guns started a continuous thunder that flattened the senses. But in amongst the massive explosions were the screams and shrieks of the young gunners as they hurtled around their metal beasts, feeding shells into them and yelling obscenities to Saddam Hussein at each detonation. It was physical war, every ounce of their energy thrust into making sure the guns spoke regularly and with death to the enemy.

And next to our guns were those of the Americans. Again, no women in the gun crews – no women on the front line at all, except for this one middle-aged reporter. But behind us were thousands of women – and many of them were in the forces because there aren't enough men who want to don uniform. How long before they move into the combat area? What might the 'feminisation of the forces', as it was termed, mean?

For the Gulf – almost by default – pushed the Americans further down the road towards full integration in the services, even though there was rarely, if ever, any discussion in the field about women taking part in combat. And even from the women who had made the army their career there seemed to be no loud demands to join their colleagues 'with fixed bayonets'. ('Fixed bayonets' are a conventional fixture of the discussion about integrating women into the services – conjuring up an image of screaming Amazons skewering men and eviscerating them at close range.)

Even though, as we pushed onwards through Iraq into Kuwait, there were no American women to be seen among the blazing vehicles and charred bodies of a crushed army, it became the norm after the war to report that 'several US women were killed in combat'. Admittedly, a dozen women had died, but not as the result of fighting. Some were involved in accidents with helicopters or mines, others died as the result of a Scud missile hitting their barracks, but most were killed in traffic accidents. Two women had been captured and one of them sexually assaulted by the Iraqis, but the nightmare of their being tortured in front of male colleagues did not arise, perhaps because an Arab culture which is mainly embarrassed by encountering foreign women in public life has not yet resolved quite how to deal with them, even as prisoners of war. I recall an Afghan warlord, years ago, solemnly informing me – through a third party, I being too unspeakable to be addressed directly – that he did not believe that women were any part of war. 'What if a woman threatened to shoot you?' I enquired. 'A fighter could not be killed by a woman,' he replied. 'Bullets would not obey her.'

However, so much popular publicity was attached to the idea of women in the front line – becoming casualties, no less – and, of course, the war saw thousands of women return home unscathed but victorious, that the push for women to be allowed to participate in actual fighting units grew stronger. I came home with no burning thoughts on the subject except for the knotty question of personal privacy. I even found myself lecturing the senior officers of the Women's Royal Army Corps shortly afterwards, only to realise that loos figured rather higher on my agenda than the debate about women's role in the conflict. Added to which, I realised that as a mere journalist I'd seen more of combat than any of the professionals in front of me, even though they'd spent their lives in a military environment. And they, too, were aware that they weren't quite across the changes that were happening to women's employment.

The WRAC, along with the WRNS and the WRAF, seemed to have had an uneventful life being useful and supportive. I thought back to that day in school in the late fifties, those huge legs, clompy shoes and lisle stockings, and realised that in all my years knocking around military establishments and operations I'd never even noticed the WRAC. The moment things became 'interesting', the women were left behind. I'd met the occasional Wren officer in Hong Kong and Cyprus, but they confirmed my prejudice that smart admirals' daughters got nice jobs organising gin and tonics on the quarter-deck. I had noticed that they had a better cut of uniform, cute hats, and seemed to have wangled decent shoes with high heels, rather than horrible lace-up flatties. I hadn't a clue what WRAF did, but obviously they didn't fly anything remotely warry.

Joining these women's services didn't seem remotely glamorous. Assuredly, they performed an array of technical and mechanical and technological work which kept pace with any civilian opportunities, but they hadn't been seen in the Falklands in the 1980s. They had also been very low-key through three decades in Northern Ireland, with endless arguments as to whether they would be allowed to carry a weapon while on patrol with their male counterparts.

A year after the Gulf War, the axe fell.

The 'policy for greater integration in the Army' was resulting in the abolition of all-women units, with the WRAC being permanently posted with specialised corps such as Transport or Signallers, and the majority moving to the new Adjutant General's Corps. As the women prepared for their final parade in Guildford, and a service attended by their first – and only – Commandant in Chief, the Queen Mother, there were very mixed feelings. They had had great pride in their Corps and had cultivated a careful line when justifying their support role: within the Corps there was no great agitation for taking on a fighting role. Indeed, the kind of woman who was happy and fulfilled in the WRAC was probably not the sort who desired to be side by side with men in the front line. And they demonstrated this by their very ability to justify their non-combatant status so strongly. They were also not a little worried that once absorbed amongst the men, ostensibly with much more opportunity for promotion, they would find themselves in an unfair competition, because there's no doubt that having combat experience counts for a great deal when push comes to shove up the career ladder.

However, they were not in tune with the times; the argument of 'separate and distinct', used by many women over the century to define what they saw as an ultimately stronger role for women, was seen as, at best, a protectionist strategy. If women wanted equality, they had to come out of their 'special place' and rough it with the rest. But even if they were 'integrated', what about the bar on participating in combat units? Strange equality.

At least they would at last look the same – more or less, for skirts were still part of the uniform issue. But for much of time, and always on operations, they would be in camouflage, virtually indistinguishable from the men. Indeed, the first time I saw women deployed to Bosnia in the mid-nineties I didn't recognise the figures who clambered down from the driving seat of 10-ton trucks, helmets jammed on, rifles slung over shoulders, as they wielded shovels to dig out their lumbering transport from the mud, to the chatter of machine-gun fire in the distance. And after a short time, you ceased to notice them. Girls with their hair pinned awkwardly under berets or screwed into odd little buns became commonplace in all the camps and posts throughout a broken jigsaw of front lines. Fighting took place up to the very barbed wire of one British camp in Vitez, and any journey through the Balkans was a nightmare negotiation of roadblocks and factional division. Peace-keeping it might be, but front-line work, bringing considerable numbers of women into battle areas and nearer to the arguments about combat-capability. And, after all, the army needed the numbers: with recruitment getting tougher women filled the bill very well, adding to their virtues by not having so many days off sick due to booze and brawls.

And in the States, the manpower – personpower – question was also pressing. Added to which, the Gulf War had acted as an incentive to the equal rights lobby, who were now pressing hard for access to more posts. Women had been all over the TV screens in 'chocolate chip combats' and high-laced boots and helmets – and had frequently been described as having been 'in combat': hadn't they earned the *right* to be in combat – officially? And wasn't the military to be subject to the same test of rights as any other workplace? If you can die for your country when a Scud missile hits your camp, why can't you kill for it or at least die fighting for it?

Other consequences of the Gulf were more difficult to accommodate. We'd heard of those instances of rape in the camps in Saudi, and significant numbers of women had had to be shipped home due to pregnancy, with some conceptions clearly having occurred in that country.

As the President and the politicians and the top brass pondered, the whole issue was given a massive kick in the rear by an event which became known as Tailhook, a naval aviators' weekend convention, which got out of hand and resulted in an immense scandal. Lurid headlines and a story which eventually engulfed the entire navy emanated from three incidents of 'sexual assault' (not rape) which mushroomed into an image of mass Bacchanalian aggression. Whatever the rights and wrongs – and the entire affair reeks of a number of unpleasant or unseemly incidents which took on a monstrous life of their own once in the full glare of the media – sexual harassment in uniform became a national issue and the military found itself with its defences down. The full force of gender-led thinking marched into the barracks and on to the airfields and ships; the result has not been any sort of victory, just a low-key running battle.

In 1994 the media were in a happy frenzy as a huge aircraft carrier left Norfolk, Virginia. The USS *Eisenhower*, one of the world's largest warships, off to war? A gunboat going to settle a distant dispute? No, the journalists were gathered to watch what they called the first 'Co-ed Cruise'; there were four hundred women aboard.

Back in the seventies I had discovered that trying to find the ladies' loo on any aircraft carrier was one of the trickier tasks in life. Such places did not exist. The arrival of the occasional female on board led to much fussing and a nifty conversion of very definitely male conveniences, to which one was conducted with rather too much ceremony.

A sister ship to the *Eisenhower*, the USS *Nimitz* is a vast vessel with a fearsome set of statistics which the American navy is only too pleased to trot out. When I was on board in the mid-nineties, a kindly supply officer reeled off his favourite figures: eighteen thousand meals served daily, four tons of laundry washed daily, thirteen thousand rolls of loo paper issued each month. A floating city, complex and densely populated, with a crew of five and half thousand. Finding the ladies' loo, though, had become a little easier. There were 452 women embarked at the time.

I confess that it was a novel sight for me on the deck of the *Nimitz*: every single specialisation had women working there. As a score of fighter planes were prepared for take-off, the team checking the instruments, crawling over the air-frame and making the final safety adjustments was led by nineteen-year-old Kelly Green. 'Didn't fancy being a housewife,' she screamed into my ear-defenders. Signalling to the refuelling unit, she stood aside as a minuscule creature labelled Mary-Jo lugged a thick squirming hose towards an F-18 plane.

The din on the deck was truly deafening: the ear-splitting roar of take-off, the sudden blasts as the jets pirouetted into place, the hiss of the catapult take-off systems. It was also quite intimidating. The F-14s strained on the catapult for up to eight seconds before release, their pink after-burners like twin flame-throwers. The planes jinked around the deck, with a dozen on the move at once, folding up their wings as they passed with inches between them. A metal ballet, with no room for error. All fully bombed-up – Harm missiles and Sidewinders being given a final tweak into position by two young women from Colorado.

I felt somewhat old-fashioned as I asked if the truly nasty job of crawling under the powering-up planes to supervise the catapult release was also done by women. 'Why not?' came the withering reply. 'Just getting the facts,' I said.

It goes without saying that Lieutenant Sarah Joyner flew her F-18 fighter as if she were born to it. The pilots are the elite, and the four women fliers in their twenties were a very prominent demonstration of ability at the sharp end of warfare, and a successful extension of specialisations recently opened to women. Lieutenant Joyner was raring to have a go over southern Iraq. She was also, according to one of her male colleagues, pretty cute.

CORSETS TO CAMOUFLAGE

This last remark was a very rare statement. Made by a pilot, it drew forth sighs of exasperation from those not on the flying wing. 'Pilots are so darn contrary,' I was told, 'they think they can get away with anything.'

'Rats', said the pilots, 'sjust clear as day you caint sleep your way to flyin' an F-18.'

For in operation was a rigid and detailed code of behaviour to control and regulate the relationship between the sexes on board – a code which covered clothing, language and relationships. The No Touching rule was observed to the letter. Bodies shrank against walls, hands were twitched back from a friendly pat,

Aircrew on the USS Eisenhower, 1994

hugging was not in evidence. Men complained privately of being reported for swearing mildly. Women confided privately that they were bullied or isolated in a male-dominated team. Officers dreaded handling lurid disciplinary offences. And the American obsession with politically correct language ensured that problems frequently cannot be dealt with honestly. The fluctuating number of women assigned to the carrier caused an accommodation nightmare. One petty officer mused that Congress should be asked if it wanted an efficient war-fighting vessel or a politically correct floating hotel.

'Teething troubles,' commented a senior officer tolerantly. 'This is progress, and we've got to make it work.' The same view came from the most senior medical assistant – with years of sea-going behind her. She welcomed the influx of women. 'Just wait till they get like me,' she said, as she stood by during the dangerous task of refuelling the carrier at night. She loved her job, earned more than her husband, and talked frankly about missing her three children, all under ten.

The youngest women, especially the unskilled, exuded confidence. They found their place on board natural, and were willing to tolerate the discomfort and relentless ordering of daily life. It beat stacking shelves in a supermarket any day. And the No Touching rules just made it all a bit like high school, they said, only tougher.

As for clothing – a sea of shapeless overalls, shirts and rather badly tailored trousers, lots of bulky 'float-coats' with reflective strips, odd headgear like babies' caps sprouting ear-defenders and microphones, topped with goggles – the entire ship's company was an amorphous mass, with names plastered on the front and jobs emblazoned on the back. Almost no one is immediately identifiable by sex; ear-rings are your best bet, if you can see them under the paraphernalia.

On board the USS *Ulysses S. Grant* in the late nineties – same class of ship, same warren below decks, but higher percentage of women on board – I headed off one evening to find the loo. As I searched I became aware of quite a lot of quiet scuffling and giggling at the end of dimly red-lit passages.

The Captain's Orders – a list of misdemeanours dealt with on a daily basis – covered the usual disciplinary problems such as people being late for duty, instances of poor work and complaints about attitude; it also contained a number of strikingly blunt descriptions of sexual behaviour, including a couple found at it like rabbits in the air-intake of an F-14 fighter plane. The phrase 'love will find a way' might apply to some liaisons on board, but much of the problem stems from the fact that ship-life is often monotonous and the crew are young, healthy and cheek-by-jowl with each other. So despite the rules, despite the public relations image, despite the high-minded intentions of the equality lobby, they have sex. And to call it a 'problem' is something of a problem in itself. 'Pregnancy is akin to appendicitis,' is one of the frequently used phrases of the PR staff: something natural, it just occurs, and it's dealt with according to the regulations. Women are flown off the ship at a specific point in pregnancy, not because they are deemed unfit for work but because the law protects the foetus being harmed by any of the chemicals or radiation which might be encountered on board.

Pregnancy is dealt with in the US services in mind-boggling detail: there are pages of regulations, orders and advice on the subject, and lots of variations to uniforms as the months progress. One of the military handbooks, written by a female officer, begins with the clear statement that 'pregnancy is not a disease or affliction. With proper management and education, a female soldier can be a productive member of your unit up until the date of delivery.' Hmm. There follows a lengthy list of occasions and reasons which seem to invalidate that statement:

Soldier should not be reassigned to/from overseas assignments during pregnancy.

Soldier is exempt from physical training programme/ fitness testing, wearing of load-bearing equipment, all immunisations, and NBC [nuclear, biological and chemical] training.

After 20 weeks:

Soldier is exempt from standing at parade rest or attention for longer than 15 minutes, and weapons training.

After 28 weeks:

Soldier must be provided a 15-minute rest period every two hours.

All highly commendable for sensible pregnancy, but not the sort of thing that fits comfortably into anything other than clerical duties. And in time of war – what then? Undaunted, the handbook insists: 'The maximum utilization of a pregnant soldier may require some creative thinking . . . within a unit. While this may be mildly disruptive . . . it can be a positive step. Remember, it is not her brain that is changing, only the shape of her body.' In response to this, the anti-female lobby in the US military tartly observed: 'When the going gets tough, the tough get pregnant.'

Obviously, better treatment and facilities in any group within an organisation should lead to an overall increase in performance. However, as was demonstrated by the Gulf War, pregnancy – however healthy the woman – leaves the forces less able to react instantaneously to a crisis, and the military must now factor in considerable extra resources to ensure children are looked after. They cannot merely rely on 'the wife at home'.

Yet in the last decade of the twentieth century, as the armed services across the Western world faced ever-greater shortages in manpower – literally – the focus had to shift *within* the forces to the actual physical power now available. Time and again women have proved capable of the technical and mechanical jobs being opened to them; but sheer body-strength is where the difference lies – and women are more prone than men to lower-limb injuries in training and exercises. And although a desire exists to paint future conflicts in terms of technological wizardry and virtual combat, no one in the last years of the twentieth century seemed to have got that message across to the Chechens or Serbs or Sudanese or Tamils. Or to anyone else, for that matter, engaged in bloody, messy conflict. Indeed, a good many of the 'peace-keeping' duties in which Western forces have been involved, particularly since the end of the Cold War, have seen brute force and blunt punching and pummelling become the norm, as crowd control, road blockades and rampaging mobs are dealt with. And military commanders are not going to be able to put two women in a confrontation line for every man, as is the unacknowledged habit of civilian police forces when planning to contain civil disorder. And in pure, gut-grabbing, close-contact fighting, bigger blokes, built differently from women, are more effective. Not a problem if you value equality of opportunity above everything. Bit of a problem when the enemy fields only bigger blokes.

Again, in the Gulf, in an empty desert, there was a multitude of grumbles about the basic jobs which needed to be done which involved heaving weighty loads about, carrying awkward equipment, erecting temporary buildings and tents, and digging vehicles out of soft sand. Women did them – but more slowly, less efficiently, and with more injuries. There wasn't the time to implement the complex mixed-rota patterns with which the individual task is solved on a 'gender-friendly' basis back in Kentucky.

The US military has engaged in years of study and discussion and experiment on 'gender differences', albeit against a background, not so much of producing an

effective fighting force, but of creating a force that is 'another arm of American society', to quote DACOWITS, the Defence Advisory Committee on Women in the Services. As a result levels of fitness, standards in training, competitions and targets have all been tampered with, the underlying philosophy coming from a civilian society which believes fervently in equality at all costs, coupled with a tendency to see men as the source of all aggression and violence. On training courses now, bolstering self-esteem and being satisfied that 'you've tried, you've done your best' is the only standard of excellence to be sought. Criticism, never mind abuse, is not part of the educational pattern. During training, instead of the traditional bullying and bellowing of NCOs, the stream of personal abuse and the ethos that no one will ever treat you this badly again, encouragement and understanding are now expected to achieve better results. Just 'going for it' now equates with 'having done it'.

The net result is a weaker, less fit and less 'militaristic' outfit, which has haemorrhaged experienced male personnel unwilling or unable to adapt to the new order. Admittedly, it has phenomenal resources and state-of-the-art weaponry. And it also has excellent understanding of the needs of its individuals, fitting into a society based on equality, encouragement and reaching one's own goals. Much of the rest of the world, though, is sexist, violent, muscular, unforgiving and, face-to-face, unimpressed by anyone unless they're bigger, nastier, tougher and stronger.

The American experience has been watched by a number of nations who are heading towards equal opportunities in the military with varying degrees of enthusiasm. In Britain there has been much less political activism; nevertheless, the face of the forces has changed. In the Royal Navy and the RAF, there are now very few areas where women do not work: submarines being the most obvious, with the interesting suggestion that the answer might well be an all-female sub. Loos and privacy are the biggest stumbling blocks, and when defence budgets are tight there's reluctance to spend on comforts rather than essential weapons. Apart from the usual fuss in the British tabloid press, eager to play up prejudice and lick lips at the thought of 'hanky-panky' (the language reveals all), there seems to be much less tension afloat and around airbases, at least when compared to the USA. Full-blooded political correctness is not a major issue, and so far there's been less fear of legal interference in the daily routine.

Touching someone's uniform to point out a fault in dress, putting an arm out to push a recruit over a training course obstacle, even yelling at a junior to reinforce discipline are all now 'out of bounds' in most US military establishments. Wanting to meet female crew members aboard US ships, I've had to wait while a male officer knocks at the door of their quarters and the inner curtain is pulled aside – mandatory, no sneaky peeps allowed. Then the male is left outside. There are absolute rules now which lay down the meaning of privacy, and if this means rigid and awkward behaviour, so be it.

The Royal Navy has learned to be more grown-up, and there is no doubt that in the years during which women have been on board there has been a 'civilising' effect, which is not the same as a 'weakening' of the ethos afloat. They've also discovered that there needs to be a 'critical mass' when it comes to integration. Being the only woman on board is not only lonely, it leads to evaluation of 'women' on the basis of one individual's personality.

Nor, in Britain; is there the politically correct threat which prevents many US service personnel from even raising complaints which involve 'gender'. Royal Navy ships feel like any other mixed environment, and seem to have avoided the outwardly sterile, floating American pressure-cooker model of equality.

In the British army there are more women than ever in uniform, no longer Auxiliary or camp-followers. They wear camouflage much of the time, or shirts and trousers – although there's still the option of a skirt. There are new rules about relationships, and the pressures of civilian society are changing many of the traditions not only with regard to women. They're deployed automatically to conflict areas, having seen service in Bosnia, Afghanistan and again in the Gulf in 2003. The Ministry has even grown circumspect about disclosing the percentage of women on operations, trying to give the impression that it's so routine that it's irrelevant. That the number is growing all the time is evident from the American statistics – one in seven of the personnel initially deployed to Kuwait in 2003 was a woman. Not surprising when women now make up 15 per cent of those on active service and 17 per cent of the reserves. Unlike the first Gulf War, there was a decrease in the number of official stories about how women were thriving in the military – the novelty's worn off according to the Pentagon; female soldiers are not an experiment any more.

But there is still a definite barrier across which women have not been allowed. Tanks, infantry, the Marines and the SAS are still male-only, with the government citing physical strength and the problems of 'group cohesion' as the main obstacles to integration. The sticking point is still high-intensity close combat – the military words for getting stuck-in, the primitive bit of warfare which a lot of people would like to think is not part of modern, laser-guided military operations. 'Fraid it is, despite all the high-tech. In 2002 a British government report reviewed the physical performance of women relevant to military duties and, reinforcing earlier studies, concluded that only 1 per cent of women can equal that of the average man. Psychologically there were few differences, except a perceived lower capacity for aggression, which the report's authors thought could be raised 'given sufficient social licence and provocation'.

However, it was 'group cohesion' which proved to be the problem. The army waffled carefully round this phrase in polite language, saying that 'the attitudes of group members, particularly positive and negative attitudes to gender and gender stereotypes, could affect group dynamics and ultimately group effectiveness'. After a century in which women have peeled away the layers of law, bans, restrictions and prejudice, they have arrived at a hard core which still demands that it remains single-sex – male – to retain its hardihood, which it argues is central to what the army is for.

A pack of male animals loaded with testosterone, thundering along in the red mist of controlled mad aggression, is not how modern strategists justify the defence budget. However, this behaviour may well be needed, and for this pack, the report politely suggests, 'it might be easier to achieve and maintain cohesion in a single-sex team'. The old arguments that women distract, disrupt and may in the end divert the pack from its job echo and resound.

It's a dilemma: how an organisation is run versus what the organisation is for. If you see life in the armed forces as just another job, one which has to adjust to social progress and alter its traditions to come into line with gender and diversity issues, then you may need a 'reconceptualisation of the very character of military organisations', as sociologists put it. In other words, change what the army's for. However, if you accept that the military are different because of what they're asked to do (who else trains to bayonet people?), then you may have to face compromise on absolute conditions of equality.

With some jobs off-limits, there's no doubt that promotion prospects for women are poorer. Service in the tough, up-front fighting units is regarded as a necessity for some command posts, and so the women will automatically lose out. As to competitive career behaviour, which many women in the WRAC feared would be much more common among men, the services are merely finding out what everyone else has experienced in civilian life.

Curiously, for all the dinosaur image which the military everywhere tends to acquire, having to grapple with the issue of women in uniform has forced them to confront issues which much of the rest of the population is coy or confused about, regardless of the progress which has been made in equality for women. Getting people to risk their lives – and kill others – is a complicated business, especially when it is sanctioned by a government and you get paid for it. The most fundamental of attitudes are stirred in all men and women; discussion harks back to images of cavemen and club-waving. The functions of giving life and taking life are in sharp relief. Tradition, culture and sexual relationships come into question; and whether our attitudes are learned or instinctive. Are the forces part of society, reflecting it? Or apart, and carrying the unique task of fighting for it?

To argue that women have no part in war is naïve – and mistaken. They have started wars – they may even be the cause of it at times. They have declared war and mobilised forces – and made outstanding leaders. They have made the instruments of war and ensured that the fabric of society has been altered to support the war effort. They have been on battlefields – to feed, nurse and supply. Arguments about bravery, heroism and resolve are borne out in history – women have proved they can rise to the occasion. And they are still taking part in war, and are increasingly on battlefields in uniform, controlling long-range weapons, indirect fire, missiles and electronic systems. Or in planes and in ships. They are armed, they drive vehicles to front lines, carry out communications and intelligence work, and organise supply lines in battle zones. And the battle zone can include their own home, far from the front, as bombs and rockets reach them.

But they rarely fight. Gut-gouging, face-to-face combat, where killing is expected. And this is where the decision lies for those who have to resolve equality with effectiveness, and at the same time take account of our need to feel at ease about who will protect and defend us – all of us.

Ultimately, the old soldier is honoured and sheltered by those he fought for. In Britain, the symbol is the splendid figure of the Chelsea Pensioner in his scarlet coat and tricorne hat, representing over three hundred years of military tradition. Since King Charles II laid the foundation of the elegant building in London in 1682, there have been only two women with an official connection to the Royal Hospital: Hannah Snell, the marine, and Mother Ross, the soldier. But in future, in proportion to the number of women now serving, there will be a new figure in uniform, the pensioner in *her* scarlet coat and tricorne hat.

Captain Samantha Shepherd of the Royal Artillery on patrol in Basra, Iraq, in 2003

SOURCE NOTES

Manuscript sources (e.g. from the Imperial War Museum and the Public Record Office) are given in full here. However, for published sources full details will be found in the Bibliography.

CHAPTER 1

p.3, 'I put the carcass…': Defoe, *The Life and Adventures of Mrs Christian Davies*
p.4, 'We spared nothing…': Defoe, *The Life and Adventures of Mrs Christian Davies*
p.5, 'Which I had scarcely done…': Defoe, *The Life and Adventures of Mrs Christian Davies*
p.8, 'The sun was just setting…': Carey (ed.), *The Faber Book of Reportage*
p.16, 'I became grimly aware…': Chandler, *The Art of Warfare in the Age of Marlborough*

CHAPTER 2

p.27, 'In the early days of…': Tucker, *Royal Ladies and Soldiers*

CHAPTER 4

p.38, 'Dirt is the distinctive feature…': Lyndon Dodds, *A History of Sunderland*

CHAPTER 5

p.43, 'The members wore khaki…': Gwynne Vaughan, *Service with the Army*
p.44, 'Now, it must be distinctly…': IWM DOCS: The Papers of Mrs M. Brunskill Reid (78/39/1 and 1A)
p.45, 'The Colonel asks me to tell you…': IWM DOCS: The Papers of Miss C.F. Shave (77/88/1)
p.45, 'The dump was completely…': IWM DOCS: The Papers of D. Odburn (Misc. 6188)

CHAPTER 6

p.52, 'Every sort of class…': IWM DOCS: The Papers of Miss K. Hodges (92/22/1)
p.53, 'The size of the Battalion…': Farnborough, *Nurse at the Russian Front*
p.53, 'What was important was…': Botchkareva, *My Life as a Peasant, Exile and Soldier*
p.55, 'I'll go anywhere and…': Sandes, *The Autobiography of a Woman Soldier*

CHAPTER 7

p.61, 'I was sent to Hastings…': IWM DOCS: The Papers of Mrs L. Downer (79/15/1)
p.62, 'When first called on…': IWM DOCS: The Papers of Miss O. Taylor (83/17/1)
p.63, 'Two very grandes-dames…': IWM DOCS: The Papers of Miss C. Smith (98/9/1)
p.64, 'I travelled on a tram…': IWM DOCS: The Papers of Miss A. Woodroffe (95/31/1)
p.67, 'Mountains of washing-up…': IWM DOCS: The

Papers of Miss O. Castle (Misc. 61 948)
p.69, 'Perfect ladies…': Furse, *Hearts and Pomegranates*
p.69, 'Wanted, female motor-cyclist…': IWM DOCS: The Papers of Mrs P.L. Stephens (P348)

CHAPTER 8

p.74, 'Some comforts and…': Bowling, *The First Eighty Years*
p.75, 'It would amuse you…:: IWM DOCS: The Papers of Miss S. Harry (84/41/1)
p.78, 'Monday 13th September…': IWM DOCS: The Papers of Miss M. Starr (81/12/1)
p.82, 'He had never heard anything…': Knocker, *Flanders and Other Fields*
p.84, 'That village was…': IWM DOCS: The Papers of Miss K. Hodges (92/22/1)
p.86, 'Colonel Vassovitch…': IWM DOCS: The Papers of I. Ross (84/43/1)
p.87, 'An awful blizzard…': IWM DOCS: The Papers of G. Holland (88/26/1)
p.91, 'Referring to what…': Garrett Fawcett, *What I Remember*

CHAPTER 9

p.96, 'The girls here are…': IWM DOCS: The Papers of Miss G. West (77/156/1)
p.101, 'Then there were the air-raids…': Parsons, *Women's Work in Engineering and Shipbuilding during the War*
p.102, 'They said there was…': IWM DOCS: The Papers of C. Rennles (DSR 000566/07)
p.102, 'At Woolwich I had…': IWM DOCS: The Papers of Mrs G. Kaye (P371)
p.108, 'Doctors were horrified…': Allinson, Sidney, *The Bantams*, quoted in Brett, *The Amazing World of Sunderland*
p.109, 'We were brought up…': Gibson, *The People's History of Southwick*

CHAPTER 10

p.116, 'Outdoor gown, house…': Laver, *Concise History of Costume*
p.128, 'I sailed from New York…': O'Reilly, *Health and Medicine 1987*

CHAPTER 12

p.137, 'Uniform is a tremendous…': *Daily Telegraph*, 16 August 2002

CHAPTER 13

p.140, 'This country has not…': Curtis, *The Forgotten Pilots*
p.143, 'To many people…': Stubbs, *The Navy at War*
p.144, 'We get up at…': IWM DOCS: The Papers of Lady R. Pierrepont (88/3/1)
p.145, 'Feeling very despondent…': IWM DOCS: The

Papers of Mrs P.M. Damonte (95/32/1)
p.147, 'If after a dance…': IWM DOCS: The Papers of Miss N. Mullet/Mrs N. Walton (88/2/1)

CHAPTER 14

p.152, 'The greatcoat came down…': IWM DOCS: The Papers of Mrs I. Bryce (96/4/1)
p.155, 'We worked a…': IWM DOCS: The Papers of Ms N. Lodge (97/34/1)
p.155, 'I think men should…': IWM DOCS: The Papers of Ms S. Stiles (89/4/1)
p.156, 'You know how little…': IWM DOCS: The Papers of Mrs N.G. Neale (97/34/1)
p.157, 'On seeing me…': Bousquet and Douglas, *West Indian Women at War*
p.158, 'The unhealthy climate…': Jaffé and Jaffé (eds), *Chinthe Women: WAS(B) 1942-1946, CHAR and WADS on the Frontline, 2002*
p.163, 'We picked up…': , Hay, *One Hundred Years of Army Nursing*

CHAPTER 15

p.170, 'The staff had cleaned…': IWM DOCS: The Papers of Miss G. Mackay Brown (78/4/1 and PP/MCR/168
p.173, 'I am sitting writing this…': IWM DOCS: The Papers of Mrs R. Uttin (88/50/1)

CHAPTER 16

p.180, '28th June 1941…': IWM DOCS: The Papers of M. Seeley (93/22/1)
p.191, 'I am an ex-Land Girl…': *Daily Telegraph*, 5 May 2001

CHAPTER 17

p.196, 'The last few days…': Ward, *FANY Invicta*

CHAPTER 18

p.207, 'There was no hope…': *Ursula Graham Bower, David Child 2001*

CHAPTER 19

p.214, 'These directors…': PRO Air 24/1645 appendix X, 1941
p.217, 'Woman's place should…': Laffin, *Women in Battle*
p.221, 'What do you *think*…': Marris and Thornham, *Media Studies: A Reader*

CHAPTER 20

p.240, 'Given sufficient social…': *Women in the Armed Forces, HMG May 2002*

BIBLIOGRAPHY AND SOURCES

BOOKS, NEWSPAPERS AND PERIODICALS

BAUDOT, François, *A Century of Fashion*, Thames & Hudson 1999

BINNEY, Marcus, *The Women Who Lived for Danger*, Hodder & Stoughton 2002

BLANTON, DeAnne and Lauren M. Cook, *They Fought Like Demons: Women Soldiers in the American Civil War*, Louisiana State University Press, 2002

BOLTON, Angela, *The Maturing Sun*, Imperial War Museum 1986

BOTCHKAREVA, Maria, *My Life as a Peasant, Exile and Soldier*, Constable 1919

BOUSQUET, Ben and Colin Douglas, *West Indian Women at War*, Lawrence & Wishart 1991

BOWLING, Helen G., *The First Eighty Years*, 1965

BRADSHAW FAY, Sidney, *After Sarajevo: The Origins of the World War*, Macmillan 1928

BRETT, Alan, *The Amazing World of Sunderland*, Black Cat Publications 1994

BRYANT, Louise, *Six Red Months in Russia*, George H. Doran Co., New York 1918

CAREY, John (ed.), *The Faber Book of Reportage*, Faber & Faber 1987

CHANDLER, D., *The Art of Warfare in the Age of Marlborough*, 1990, quoted in Newark, *Brassey's Book of Uniforms*, 1998

COOKRIDGE, E. H., *Inside SOE*, Arthur Baker 1966

CORDINGLY, David, *Heroines and Harlots*, Macmillan 2001

COWPER, Col. J. M., *A Short History of the QMAAC*, 1967

CURTIS, Lettice, *The Forgotten Pilots*, Eastern Press 1971

DEFOE, Daniel, *The Life and Adventures of Mrs Christian Davies, the British Amazon, Commonly call'd Mother Ross*, Richard Montague 1741

DUCHEN, C. and I. Bandhauer-Schoffman, *When the War Was Over*, Leicester University Press 2000

DURHAM, Edith, *High Albania*, Phoenix Press 2000

Edith Cavell 1865-1915, a Norfolk Heroine, Swardeston Parochial Church Council n.d.

EMERSON, Gloria (intro) et al, *War Torn: Stories of War from the Women Reporters Who Covered Vietnam*, Random House 2002

EWING, Elizabeth, *Women in Uniform Through the Centuries*, Batsford 1975

EWING, Elizabeth, *Dress and Undress*, Batsford 1978

FARMBOROUGH, Florence, *Nurse at the Russian Front*, Constable 1974

FRIANG, Brigitte (trans. J. Cadell), *Parachutes and Petticoats*, Jarrolds 1958

FURSE, Dame Katherine, *Hearts and Pomegranates*, Peter Davies 1940

GARRATT FAWCETT, Millicent, *What I Remember*, Fisher Unwin 1924

GELLHORN, Martha, *The Face of War*, Hart Davis 1959

GIBSON, Peter, *The People's History of Southwick*, 1999

GOLDSTEIN, Joshua S., *War and Gender*, Cambridge University Press

GUTMANN, Stephanie, *The Kinder, Gentler Military*, Scribner 2000

GWYNNE VAUGHAN, Dame Helen, *Service with the Army*, Hutchinson 1942

HASTE, Cate, *Nazi Women*, Channel 4 Books 2001

HAY, Ian, *One Hundred Years of Army Nursing*, Cassell 1953

HOLDEN, Wendy, *Shell Shock*, Channel 4 Books 1998

HOWARTH, Patrick, *Undercover*, Routledge & Kegan Paul 1980

JAFFÉ and JAFFÉ (eds), *Chinthe Women: WAS(B) 1942-1946, CHAR and WADS on the Frontline*, 2002

KNOCKER, Elsie (Baroness T'Serclaes), *Flanders and Other Fields*, Harrap 1964

The Lady magazine, 1914-19

LAFFIN, John, *Women in Battle*, Abelard-Schuman 1967

LAUGHTON MATHEWS, Vera, *Blue Tapestry*, Hollis & Carter 1948

LAVER, James, *Concise History of Costume*, Thames & Hudson 1979

LENEMAN, Leah, *Elsie Inglis*, NMS Publishing 1998

LYNDON DODDS, Glen, *A History of Sunderland*, Albion Press 1995

MARLOW, Joyce (ed.), *The Virago Book of Women and the Great War*, Virago 1998

MARRIS, p. and S. Thornham, *Media Studies: A Reader*, Edinburgh University Press 1997

MENDES, Valerie and Amy de la Haye, *20th Century Fashion*, Thames & Hudson 1999

MILBURN, G.E. and S.T. Miller (eds), *Sunderland: River, Town and People* Sunderland Borough Council 1988

MILLER, Harry, *Service to the Services, the story of NAAFI*, Newman Neame 1971

MUIR, Kate, *Arms and the Woman*, Sinclair Stevenson 1992

NEWARK, Tim, *Brassey's Book of Uniforms*, Brassey's, 1998

O'REILLY, Salaria Kea, in *Health and Medicine* 1987

PARSONS, Lady, *Women's Work in Engineering and Shipbuilding during the War*, NE Engineering Society, Newcastle 1919

ROBINSON, Alistair, *Sunderland Empire*, TUPS Books 2000

ROWBOTHAM, Sheila, *A Century of Women*, Penguin 1997

ST CLAIR STOBART, Muriel, *Miracles and Adventures*, Rider 1935

SANDES, Flora, *An English Woman-Sergeant in the Serbian Army*, Hodder & Stoughton 1916

SEBBA, Anne, *Battling for the News*, Hodder & Stoughton 1984

SMITH, Angela K., *The Second Battlefield*, Manchester University Press 1988

SOCKETT, E.W., 'A Concrete Acoustical Mirror at Fulwell', in *Durham Archaeological Journal* 1990

STUBBS, Bernard, *The Navy at War*, Faber & Faber 1940

The Sunderland Daily Echo, 1914-18 and 1939-45

TERRY, Roy, *Women in Khaki*, Columbus Books 1988

THOROGOOD In *War and Peace: the Life and Times of Daphne Pearson GC*, 2003

TUCKER, A.B., *Royal Ladies and Soldiers*, 1906

WARD, Dame Irene, *FANY Invicta*, Hutchinson 1955

WARD, Marjorie, *The Blessed Trade*, Michael Joseph 1971

WELLS, Maureen, *Entertaining Eric*, Imperial War Museum 1988

WENDEL, Else, *Hausfrau at War*, Pentland Press 1957

WHEELWRIGHT, Julie, *Amazons and Military Maids*, Pandora 1989

WILSON, Trevor, *The Myriad Faces of War*, Polity Press 1986

Women and Images of the Spanish Civil War, Royal Historical Society 1991

Women in the Armed Forces, HMG May 2002

WOODHAM-SMITH, Cecil, *Florence Nightingale*, Penguin 1951

WOOLLACOTT, Angela, *On Her Their Lives Depend*, University of California Press 1994

INTERVIEWS BY, AND LETTERS TO, THE AUTHOR 2001-2

Mrs Hilda Billings (née Tyass), Miss Helen Collett, Ms Lettice Curtis, Ms Doreen Davis, Mrs Ivy Davy (née Alderson), Ms Kathleen Duffy, Mrs Vera Greenhouse (née Bartholomew), Ms Julie Hutchings, Ms Eira Jones, Mrs Olive Kinghorn (née Helyer), Mrs Sheila Kyffin, Mrs Elizabeth Lapham (née Oldham), Ms Joan Lovatt, Ms Audrey Manning, Mrs Mavis Middleton, Ms Meg Minshull Fogg, Ms Emily Newbold, Mrs Joan Parkinson (née Talbot), Ms Alice Raine, Mrs Peggy Reed, Mrs Mary Rulton (née Costello), Mrs Ruth Sjoblom, Mrs Dana Stankovic, Mrs Edna Starr (née Smith), Mrs Joan Thompson (née Butler), Mrs Dorothy Wheeler (née Carson), Mrs Nora Wright (née Bate).

INDEX

PHOTO ACKNOWLEDGEMENTS

IMPERIAL WAR MUSEUM LONDON:

Photographic Archive: i (Q31028), iii (HU90888), 13
bottom (Q106986), 20 (Q107119), 23 (Q69131), 26
(Q81831), 32 (Q105767), 34 (Q4669), 35 (Q107297), 36
(Q6788), 42 (Q115182), 43 (Q108005), 44-45 (HU90882),
47 (Q30686), 48 left (Q30656), 48 right (Q30720), 54
(Q106250), 57 (Q32704), 58 (Q31083), 61 (Q68242), 62
(Q5746), 63 (Q8052), 65 (Q106181), 67 (Q7891), 69 left
(Q108051), 69 right (Q19766), 70 top (Q27255), 71
(Q72641), 74 (Q108193), 76 left (Q108174), 76 right
(Q2606), 77 left (HU90880), 77 right (Q68949), 78-79
(Q2520), 81 (Q8749), 82 (Q2966), 83 (Q2970), 84
(Q32347), 87 (Q69129), 88 (Q69144), 90 (Q32930), 96
(GSA Album 155 photo114), 97 (Q27880), 99 left
(HU90887), 99 right (Q101840), 100 (Q107128), 101
(HU90879), 102 (Q108454), 104 (Q27894), 107 (GSA
Album 155 photo 142), 109 (Q30859), 112 (Q103694),
117 (GSA Album 156 photo 38), 119 top (Q72625), 119
right (Q5739), 120 (Q8477), 124 (HU32986), 129
(HU33160), 132 (TR471), 136 (KY2773D), 140 (C380),
145 top (A9115), 145 bottom (A23966), 147 (CH13693),
148-149 (CH7346), 150 (HU90885), 153 (HU90884), 155
(HU90893), 157 (HU90886), 165 (E8308), 166 (IND3352),
167 (E29546), 168 (HU36256), 170 top (HU776), 171
(D4857), 172 bottom (HU687), 174 (D9724), 176
(HU55937), 177 (HU90887), 178 (HU36242), 180 top
(HU36279), 181 left (HU90889), 181 top right
(HU90897), 182 left (HU90890), 182 right (HU36287),
184-185 (HU90888), 186 (HU36288), 188 bottom (D8795),

188 bottom (HU63800), 191 (HU63799), 192 (D14124),
193 (TR907), 200 (HU57120), 202 (KY14885F), 206
(TR1643), 209 (HU90892), 212 top right (NA11895).
Department of Art: 72, 78, 110 top, 114, 160, 172 top. *Poster
Collection, Department of Art*: i, 40, 48, 68, 70, 92, 138, 143,
146, 152, 154, 156, 170, 175, 180, 181, 187, 204.

ADDITIONAL PICTURE SOURCES:

Courtesy Army Medical Services Museum,
Hampshire: 9. ©Corbis:12,13 top,14, 207 bottom.
© Corbis/Archivo Iconografico SA:127.
© Corbis/Bettmann: 207 top, 218. © Corbis/Anna
Clopet: 222. © Corbis/Hulton Deutsch
Collection:137,148,159,212 bottom left.
© Corbis/Wally McNamee: 210. © Corbis/Medford
Historical Society Collection: 6. © Corbis/Sygma: 235,
Gyori Antoine 217. © Corbis/David Turnley: 229.
© Corbis/Peter Turnley: 219. © Corbis/Patrick Ward:
238. © The Defence Picture Library/John Mills: 241.
Edith Durham *High Albania* published by Edward
Arnold, 1909: 52. Mary Evans Picture Library:18, 39,
50. *Everybody's Weekly* 1939: 131 artist unknown.
Florence Farmborough frontispiece from *Nurse at the
Russian Front, A Diary 1914-18* published by Constable
and Company Limited, 1974: 53 artist unknown.
Brigitte Friang *Parachutes and Petticoats* published by
Jarrolds Publishers (London) Limited, 1958 (translated
from the French *Les Fleurs du Ciel*): 212 top left

photographer unknown. © Chick Harrity: 212
bottom right. © Hulton Archive/Getty Images:10, 91,
110 left, 199. *The Lady*: 105 (1916), 115 (1915). © Ken
Lennox: 224. Courtesy of the Director, National Army
Museum, London: 5. Courtesy Navy Art Collection,
Naval Historical Center, Washington DC: 207 centre.
© Newcastle Chronicle and Journal Ltd: 98. North
Carolina Museum of Art, Raleigh. Purchased with
funds from the State of North Carolina and the
North Carolina Art Society (Robert F. Phifer
Bequest): opp. page 1. Courtesy The Orwell
Archive/UCL Library Services: 126. Private
Collections: 4, 8,158, 194, 208, 220. *Punch* January 31,
1917: ix. The Royal Archives © 2003, Her Majesty
Queen Elizabeth II: 28. The Royal Collection © 2003,
Her Majesty Queen Elizabeth II: 24. SOE Advisor to
the Foreign & Commonwealth Office: 198 top. Special
Forces Club: 198 bottom. Courtesy Summit County
Historical Society, Akron, Ohio: 128. Courtesy City of
Sunderland Libraries and Arts:111. Courtesy Lauren
Cook Wike:17.

Every reasonable effort has been made to contact the
copyright holders, but if there are any errors or
omissions, Hodder & Stoughton will be pleased to
insert the appropriate acknowledgement in any
subsequent printing of this publication.